TECHNIQUES OF NATIONAL
ECONOMIC PLANNING

INTERNATIONAL DEVELOPMENT
RESEARCH CENTER

William J. Siffin, Director

Studies in Development: No. 9

TECHNIQUES
OF NATIONAL
ECONOMIC
PLANNING

Abdul Qayum

INDIANA UNIVERSITY PRESS
BLOOMINGTON & LONDON

152090

Published in Canada by Fitzhenry & Whiteside Limited,
Don Mills, Ontario

Manufactured in the United States of America

Library of Congress Cataloging in Publication Data

Qayum, Abdul.
   Techniques of national economic planning.

   (Studies in development; no. 9)
   Includes bibliographical references.
   1. Economic policy. 2. Planning. I. Title. II. Series: Studies in development
(Bloomington); no. 9.
HD82.Q33 1975   330   73-16677
ISBN 0-253-35833-7   1 2 3 4 5 79 78 77 76 75

CONTENTS

FOREWORD

The literature on the theory of economic planning is so vast, recent, scattered and unorganized that systematization and evaluative analysis of main approaches are essential to forward movement in the field. The practitioner of planning, no less than the academic, should find much of value here. There is value in the sheer scope of the materials covered, including not only a major-scale review of mainstream English-language sources, but also the rich store of Dutch and Norwegian contributions developed by Tinbergen, Frisch and their co-workers. A sense of context is afforded by the successive examination of economic plans from a very few, but embracingly comprehensive, vantage points. Finally, there is the author's probing effort to join dispassionate description with undaunted assessment.

Professor Qayum has brought to this project a unique background. Trained in Indiana and Holland, he has been a long-time teacher in Egypt and the United States. He has worked with planning bodies in a broad range of situations. The wealth of the sources and examples he cites attests the breadth of his talent, his knowledge and his experience.

Planned economic development has yet to find its established place as a tool for progress. Failures of effort and abuse of technique have been unduly mingled with success. The present work goes a considerable distance toward documenting, in the high tradition of scholarship, why both political rhetoric and neutral observation so often come out on either side of a basic issue. And—hopefully—this study will help us move some modest distance beyond such ambiguity and indeterminacy.

The present volume is the ninth in a series, Studies in Development, book-length contributions sponsored by the International Development Research Center. Launched during my tenure as director, its appearance marks one of the most rewarding occasions of my many with that institution.

George J. Stolnitz
Director, 1967–1972

PREFACE

National economic planning is in vogue today in some form or other in almost all countries of the world, developed as well as underdeveloped. More books and articles have appeared in recent years in the field of development and planning than in any other field of economics. Most of the literature can be broadly divided into two categories: one descriptive, not infrequently containing ideological overtones, and the other theoretical, generally using mathematical techniques. In the first, planning experiences in various countries are discussed often with the purpose of establishing the case for or against planning on the basis of its success or failure as interpreted by the writers. In the second, abstract theoretical analysis of supposed planning problems are undertaken often by using plain mathematics. This book falls into a third category—that of a limited number of books which purport to bridge the gap between the two broad categories. It endeavors to present a systematic and logical organization of problems and considerations faced in national economic planning while at the same time discusses techniques and methods of handling them.

Planning, which is in the author's view nothing but a rational approach to achieving an objective, can only do some good to a country, socialist or mixed, developed or underdeveloped. Planning techniques and methods are neutral and are applicable to all countries subject to their particular circumstances. This basic fact characterizes the discussion throughout the following pages.

This book is intended to be useful for those involved in drawing up national economic plans as well as to serve as an introduction to planning for students, research workers, and practitioners in the field. As such, it is hardly the place for mathematical discussions and theoretical refinements. An earlier draft, more than double the size of this book, did contain these aspects. However, an attempt has been made to maintain a uniform level of discussion, and most of the mathematical discussions have been relegated to the chapter appendices.

Professor George J. Stolnitz, Director of the International Development Research Center, 1967–1972, has taken keen interest in this project from the very beginning. He has read, with great care, the final draft of this book. If the book has a "personality" of its own, and is readable, the credit should go wholly to him.

My friend Professor Leif Johansen of the Oslo Institute of Economics read the first draft and made very helpful comments and suggestions, all of which have been included in the text.

Professor George Minty of the Department of Mathematics, Indiana University, was always ready and willing to help me whenever I faced a mathematical problem. He read and checked all the mathematical sections of the first draft, of which a part appears in the appendices of this book.

Professors Franz Gehrels and Robert W. Campbell of the Department of Economics, Indiana University, read the first draft and made valuable comments. Parts of the first draft were also read by Professor Frederik Pryor of Swarthmore College, Professors Richard Stone and Richard M. Goodwin of Cambridge University, and Professor H. Bos of the Netherlands School of Economics.

I wish to express my appreciation of all the help and advice given to me by these friends and colleagues.

Finally, I would like to acknowledge with thanks the very objective and balanced reviews by Professors J. B. Clark and Alfred Zauberman, who were formally requested by the International Development Research Center to evaluate the manuscript.

TECHNIQUES OF NATIONAL
ECONOMIC PLANNING

CHAPTER ONE

National Economic Planning

I. A Short History

1. *The Beginning of Planning*

The term "economic plan" was introduced when the socialist government of the Soviet Union presented its First Five Year Plan in 1928. Since then until World War II the notion of economic planning was coupled with communism and discussed in a context of its admiration or disapproval. In both professional and popular discourse, it frequently carried unsavory connotations of centralization and regimentation.

Western experts long remained skeptical of the merits of economic planning. They looked with disbelief upon the early high rates of growth claimed for the planned Soviet economy. The lower growth rates of the Soviet and Eastern European economies in the 1950s and 1960s dispelled some of the misgivings. Further studies of these economies by Western economists have led to a better understanding of the problems and prospects of planned economies.

2. *World War II*

World War II necessitated mobilization of national resources in all the warring countries. This required various direct and indirect controls, including price controls and rationing. A number of these emergency measures had been in use in the planned Soviet economy even before the war.

In the mid-1940s, the war-ravaged countries of Western Europe had

1

to deal with the tremendous problems of economic reconstruction. Their governments found it necessary to organize allocation of resources. The Marshall Aid Plan, launched in 1948, also required them to prepare blueprints for their aid needs. These developments made the notion of planning more familiar and acceptable.

3.   *Expansion of the Public Sector*

Besides providing an impetus to economic planning, World War II brought about an unprecedented expansion in defense expenditures and in the public sectors generally. The war was followed by a growing demand for such public goods as health, education, transportation, and other items of infrastructure not readily allocable through the market economy. In some Western countries key industries like iron ore and coal could no longer be left to the vicissitudes of private entrepreneurship. With the expanding size of the public sector, the complementarities and inter-dependencies between private and public investments had become more pronounced and vital. Projections of the expansion of the private sector were needed for sound allocation of investment in the public sector, and a proper indication of the activities of the public sector was required for making investment decisions in the private sector. Thus it became necessary to undertake economic forecasts and projections in most Western European countries.

4.   *Emergence of Newly Independent Countries*

Another impetus to economic planning was the decline of colonialism. The newly independent countries had no aversion to socialist planning. Looking at the rapid, planned economic development of the Soviet Union and the great role played by governments in the reconstruction of Western Europe, the leaders of many newly independent countries concluded that only through conscious and determined governmental policy could speedy industrialization be achieved. The extent of consensus on this conclusion is shown by the fact that hardly any underdeveloped country has failed to develop a national plan since its independence.

5.   *International Agencies*

The UN and other international lending and aid-giving agencies have found national-plan documents to be a convenient means of assessing the economic prospects of a country. In particular, planning has served as a mechanism for expressing financial and technical requirements of developing countries. Thus planning in underdeveloped countries has been greatly encouraged by lending and aid-giving agencies.

6. *Discovery of Programming Techniques and Methods*

A factor instrumental in popularizing planning has been the discovery of techniques that are especially suited to planning purposes. These techniques include input-output and activity analysis techniques developed by Leontief,[1] Dantzig,[2] Koopmans,[3] and earlier by the Russian mathematician Kantorovich.[4] Great improvement has also taken place in data processing, making it possible to formulate computable models of national planning. It is interesting that economists and statisticians of the Western hemisphere have been ahead of those of the Eastern bloc in developing and improving programming techniques and applying them to actual national data.

7. *Recent Popularity*

The positive stress on reconstruction and development goals, the need for designing workable programs of action, the evolution of analytical devices to formulate policy, and the introduction of computable methods to solve plan-oriented problems have led to the acceptance of the basic ideas of planning. Even private enterprises and corporations freely use the term "planning" in making their decisions regarding production, investment, and sales.

Thus within the last decade the term "planning" has become so popular and has been applied to so many different kinds of activities that it can now refer to almost any kind of economic analysis or policy in almost any country of the world. It is, therefore, necessary that an attempt be made to define national economic planning and delineate its scope for the purposes of this book.

II. Definition of National Economic Planning

1. *Essential Elements*

Everyone, individually or collectively, makes preparations for future exigencies. If the preparations are designed to achieve certain well-defined goals in a definite period of time, they form a plan. If the preparations are to be realistic and workable, the individual must have adequate means at his disposal to achieve the goals. The adequacy of the means depends on how systematic his preparations are, how he has selected his approach, and the alternatives available.

A national economic plan relates to the country as a whole. The national government is the institution designated to represent national goals and to ensure action at the national and subnational levels. A national economic plan, therefore, is assumed to have the backing, sponsorship, or authority of the state.

An economic plan consists of a program of action for utilization of national resources to realize the national preferences. This may involve spatial, interindustrial, and intertemporal considerations. Economic management of the desired resource utilization may be accomplished either through direct action by the state and its agencies, by directives, by indirect fiscal and monetary measures, or simply by furnishing indications and forecasts of future economic trends.

An economic plan may envisage ownership by the state of almost all, a sizable part, or only a small fraction of the economic resources of the country. It may cover all economic activities of the country, or only some, but in the context of the economy as a whole. In principle, the interconnections and interdependencies of the planned part with the rest of the economy should be determined, all cross-effects and repercussions evaluated, and projections made for the whole economy.

A plan covers a definite number of years whose provisions may or may not be related to developments in the postplan period. We may now synthesize these points in a simple definition.

2. *The Definition*

A national economic plan is a systematic and integrated program of action covering a definite period of time, approved or sponsored by the state to bring about a rational utilization of resources to achieve certain national targets using direct and indirect means with or without substantial state ownership of resources.

The key words in the definition are "rational utilization" and "national targets." Rational utilization is a feasible, consistent, and optimal allocation of resources among sectors and regions, and over time. A set of national targets is an indispensable part of a national economic plan. There cannot be a plan without targets. But targets by themselves do not make a plan. A rational program to achieve the national targets by the utilization of national resources forms the backbone of national plans.

The inclusion of state approval and sponsorship in the definition stems from institutional considerations. No institution other than the state, both at the central and lower levels, has the power or the ability to execute a national program. Planning, however, does not necessarily involve an increase in state ownership or an expansion of the public sector. A variety of indirect measures, including encouragement of competition, may be used to achieve the targets.

A national plan must have a definite period for its execution. Without this, the national targets cannot be well defined, as is further discussed below.

3. *Planning Models and Techniques*

The preceding definition relates to national economic plans, which have to be distinguished from planning models. The former are mandatory in character and are approved by the state. They are drawn up by state departments with or without any consultations with private and semi-private institutions and individuals. Planning models have no mandatory sanction and have nothing to do with state approval or authority. They may be constructed by government departments and officials, as well as by semiprivate and private institutions and individuals.

There is only one national economic plan in a country for a specific period. But there is no limit to the number of planning models related to the same period, which vary in specifications and the use of techniques. They may be comprehensive or they may be concerned with a specific aspect or problem. A national economic plan covers a specific period of usually five to ten years. A planning model has generally a finite, but may have an infinite, time horizon.

Models involve different techniques and varying levels of sophistication. They provide the guidelines and tools for the formulation of national economic plans. The planning models, though they remain in the background, epitomize all the hard thinking and arduous intellectual efforts preparatory to the actual launching of the formulation of a national plan.

III. The Spectrum of Economic Plans

1. *A Broad Classification of Plan Types*

No two countries have identical systems of economic planning. Although any attempt at classification of planning practices will, to some extent, be arbitrary and may vary according to particular purposes, a broad scheme is useful to distinguish among the following:

(i) centralized physical planning;
(ii) socialist competitive planning;

(iii) democratic competitive planning;
(iv) indicative planning;
(v) forecast planning.

The reason for a summary discussion of each of these types is to show later that planning techniques are neutral to them, though some techniques may be more suited to one particular type than to others.

2. *Centralized Physical Planning*

Centralized physical planning has characterized economic planning in most Communist countries, namely, the Soviet Union, Mainland China, and the East European countries, but excluding Yugoslavia and, to a degree, Hungary. Under such planning all enterprises except small-scale industries like production cooperatives, household farming, and retail trading and services are owned by the state and operated by state functionaries. Allocation of almost all resources is undertaken by a state central planning body, after consultation with lower planning agencies. The output and input levels and supply sources of each enterprise are ultimately decided by a central planning agency. Prices of all major commodities are fixed by the state, including the price of labor, and interest and exchange rates. The worker is, by and large, free to seek jobs wherever he wants, and the consumer is free to spend his earnings in whatever manner he wishes. In other words, there is consumer choice but no sovereignty, and workers have choice of work but no freedom to strike. Economic efficiency is attained by setting input and output norms. The rate of capital formation is decided by the state. Plans of Soviet-type economies are approved by the Party and the highest central legislative bodies, and the governments are committed to execute them.

3. *Socialist Competitive Planning*

A good deal of theoretical literature exists on what is known as "democratic socialism," or what we prefer to call socialist competitive planning. The only country which can be regarded as practicing such planning is Yugoslavia, where competitive efficiency is to be achieved under state ownership of resources. As in centralized physical planning, resources are owned by the state, but it does not allocate them directly. Allocation is effected through provision of loans, foreign exchange, and other facilities to individuals and groups of individuals who can start an enterprise. No input or output targets are imposed on individual enterprises, which are free to sell their output and buy their inputs however they want. An enterprise is allowed to fix the price of its products, but has to give advance notice of price changes. Prices are generally formed in markets, but there are certain restrictions for some essential goods. Targets of the plan are achieved through indirect means by taxation, licensing, and especially allocation of foreign exchange and investment funds, and so on. Freedom of work and consumption are assured. The rate of capital formation is determined by the state and achieved through taxation.

The plan is approved by the Party and the central legislative body, and the government is responsible for its execution.

4. *Democratic Competitive Planning*

India and many other newly independent countries following her example have attempted what can be called democratic competitive planning. The basic distinguishing feature of these countries is their multiparty systems of government. Hence the plan reflects not only the preferences of the members of one party but also the influences exerted by other parties. The private sector of such planned economies is as private as in any planless, private-enterprise economy. Prices are formed in the market, and individuals have free choice of work and consumption. However, there are certain key sectors of the economy in which investment can be made only by the state, and other sectors in which investment can be made by private entrepreneurs only with permission of the state. The national plan contains detailed targets of investment and production in the public sectors and targets for the private sector which are partially based on forecasts. The government may control production, prices, supply, and distribution of "essential commodities" and important raw materials. Private enterprises are fostered through such institutions as industrial finance, credit and investment corporations, and through allocation of foreign-exchange quotas and subsidies. The rate of capital formation depends partly on public and partly on private investment. Public investment, which now accounts for sixty to seventy percent of planned investment in India, is financed from domestic revenues and borrowing, deficit financing, and foreign loans and aid. All Indian plans are approved by the Parliament, and the government is responsible for executing them and achieving the set targets.

5. *Indicative Planning*

In France what has been termed "indicative planning" was introduced first in 1946, and later plans still conform to the basic model worked out almost thirty years ago.

The course of the economy may be influenced by the plans in three ways. The first and most distinguishing feature of French indicative planning is the participation of many decision makers from various fields and industries in the Modernization Commissions,[5] through which the plans are formulated.[6]

The first principle of planning through participation, which aims at diffusion of information and reduction of risk, has been supplemented by a second—planning through public ownership. Among non-Communist countries,[7] France has probably the largest publicly owned sector of industries, including transport, electricity, coal mines, communications, and aviation, as well as important banks and enterprises. The public sector accounts for more than fifty percent of total annual investment. As the sole purchaser of electronic and mining equipment, building materials, and services, it necessarily influences the private sectors.

A third feature of indicative planning in France is the application of a suitable mixture of inducement and coercion to the private sector. Some main inducements to adhere to plan are tax concessions and favorable loan rates to on-plan firms, and occasionally preferential tariff protection for industries agreeing to some specific on-plan proposal.

French planning, being of a micro-type, rests on informed individual motivations and behavior of producers and other groups with no one-way central direction. This is in contrast with other classes of planning, which are largely of a macro-type, with aggregate national magnitudes controlled and established by the central authorities.

The French First Plan (1947–53) and Third Plan (1959–61) were published merely as governmental decrees, and Parliament, which had not asked to be consulted, supervised the application of the plans only through its annual vote on budget appropriations. The Second Plan (1954–57) was approved by Parliament, but only after the plan had been in effect for two years. The Fourth and Fifth plans marked a change in that they were put before Parliament before being implemented in 1962 and in 1966, respectively. Procedures similar to indicative planning in France have been followed in Belgium, Ireland, very roughly in some African countries, and, to an extent, in Japan.

6.   *Forecast Planning*

Closely related to indicative planning, but quite distinguishable from it, is forecast planning. Forecast planning does not contain any firm targets or governmental commitment to fulfill them, and these forecasts are related to macro- rather than to micro-variables. Such planning is practiced by the Scandinavian countries and by the Netherlands. The planning bodies in these countries were created immediately after World War II and are mainly advisory. They are either attached to a ministry like finance or may have independent directorates under the prime minister. The usual procedure is to prepare forecasts on an annual basis as well as over a longer term of four to five years or even of twenty to twenty-five years. Usually, the annual forecast plans are readied before the budget sessions so that the finance minister may use them in his budget presentation. The plans are reliable sources of information for the government as well as for the private sector in planning economic activities, but it is debatable whether they should be treated as plans proper, as they do not contain any definite targets or programs of action binding on the state. The forecasts, even when prepared by government divisions, are not placed before the legislative body of the country for approval, and the executive branches may or may not be influenced by them.

IV. The Plan Period

1. *Medium-Term Plans*

Though the period of plans has varied from one to twenty years or more, the five-year period has been most common, at least for mandatory national plans. The longer the plan period, the smaller will be the proportion of projects which overlap between two plans. The plan period should be long enough to allow a majority of the investment projects started in the early part of the plan to be completed before the end of the plan.[8] The plan period should also take into consideration preliminary preparations and other administrative arrangements that must precede the actual start of projects. Long-period plans may be more advisable from the political point of view, since these can contain proportionately more projects and thus accommodate larger numbers of regions and groups of people.

2. *Annual Plans*

A frequent practice is to break down a main plan of five or more years into annual subplans. The targets of an annual plan are set by subdividing the longer-run overall targets. Such an exercise has the advantage of focusing the attention of administrators on the need to take immediate measures, thus reducing procrastination and laxity. Although the annual plans may not be approved by the parliament of the country concerned, they may have concrete budgetary provisions, a crucial factor in the execution of the plans. The degree of success achieved in the implementation of annual plans brings into clear relief the extent of the overall plan that remains still unfulfilled. Annual plans may not be fulfilled exactly as planned, but by rescheduling annual targets in accordance with actual performance and in light of experience, it may be possible to fulfill the overall plan more closely than a yearly plan.

3.   *Moving or Revolving Plans*

Some writers have suggested the idea that a plan, though finalized, need not be strictly adhered to. Instead, the plan should be revised and modified each year in accordance with experience to allow for unforeseen developments. Thus a five-year plan would have to be prepared again each year, and only the first year of each five-year plan is really operative. In the words of Professor Frisch, who has been an advocate of moving plans for more than a decade:

> When we work out a medium-term plan, say a five-year plan, the meaning is of course not that we will, so to speak, put the whole economy in a procrustean bed defined by this five-year plan, and not make any departure from this plan in the next five years, regardless of what happens in the world around us and regardless of what new experiences we make. We must be prepared to accept changes and to introduce revisions in the plan.
>
> This leads to what I call *moving planning.* A five-year plan must be worked out on a moving basis. Every single year we must work out a new five-year plan. Each such new five-year plan must take account of the irrevocable decisions which have been made in the past. These irrevocable decisions represent the already-committed-to aspects of the new five-year plan.[9]

So far moving planning does not appear to have been tried in any country,[10] even though it makes for flexibility in the process of planning, enables constant revision in tune with new developments, and facilitates better understanding of the changing economic structure.

The main shortcomings of moving planning are as follows: (i) It is too costly to prepare a plan every year, even though the successive five-year plans may not be as difficult to prepare as the first one. (ii) A moving five-year plan prepared every year may become something of a regular phenomenon and may not create the same popular enthusiasm, interest, and incentive as a five-year plan prepared at an interval of five years. (iii) If a moving plan has to incorporate the experiences of the preceding year, it may not be completed before the middle or the end of its first year; hence it may become largely obsolete before it appears. Confusion may also occur between one moving five-year plan and another. (iv) Most five-year plans in several underdeveloped countries have been timed to enhance the electoral gains of the party in power or to strengthen the hold of ruling factions. A scheme of moving plans is unsuited to political exploitation, and, whereas this may be a merit rather than a demerit of the scheme, it reduces the chances of its being adopted.[11]

Some of the advantages of moving planning can be realized by not having the targets of the five-year plans fixed rigidly or unalterably. Targets should be arrived at after as careful and detailed analysis and programming as possible but should be subject to revision if later circumstances and developments make it necessary.

4. *Perspective Planning*

A perspective plan is intended to consider longer-run outcomes or time patterns. Whereas an actual or mandatory national plan may run from three to ten years, a perspective plan may cover a period of fifteen to twenty-five years or even longer.[12] Its chief purpose and advantage is to facilitate setting or evaluating the targets of the main national plan. Targets regarding capital structure, availability of skills, and construction of infrastructure must be related not only to requirements of the plan period but also to future trends beyond the plan. This aspect is important because of the indivisibility of items of capital and infrastructure and the consequent economies of scale over the life of these items of twenty to thirty years or even longer. Hence a perspective plan may indicate the size and nature of these items to be included in the targets of the current plan.

A perspective plan is neither definitive nor mandatory. It outlines major trends of development that are desired or expected in the long run. The targets of perspective plans are more general and less binding than those of main plans and are generally expressed in the form of certain growth rates. The most important elements to be considered in the formulation of long-term targets are (i) rate of population growth, (ii) increase of savings rate, (iii) technological developments, (iv) prospective changes in availability of natural resources, (v) rising standards of health, education, and other social and cultural requirements, and (vi) changes in international economic and political relationships.

There are no specific principles deciding the exact number of years a perspective plan should cover or the exact details it should contain. The longer the period, the more uncertain and hazy will be the prediction of the variables. A perspective plan covering a century or more is obviously unthinkable and meaningless, because no one has any idea about the technological developments, the growth rate, the availability of new resources, or the preferences and attitudes of the people which might occur over such a long period. Experience suggests that a perspective plan should cover no more than fifty years and no less than fifteen to twenty years. Between these limits, the exact period must depend on a compromise between the degree of detail to be included and the accuracy required, on the one hand, and the degree of arbitrariness to be avoided, on the other. It also may be possible and advisable to have longer perspective plans for some sectors and aspects than for others.

As in the case of medium-term mandatory plans, perspective plans can also be formulated on a moving basis. But whereas moving medium-term plans are drawn up each year, a moving perspective plan need be drawn up only toward the end of each medium-term plan. The moving medium-term plan gives direction to the formulation of the annual plan, and the moving perspective plan may give perspective to the medium-term plan.

V. Study Area of the Book

1.   *The Main Focus*

This book focuses on the formulation of medium-term plans. It presents methods and discusses techniques required in building models underlying these formulations. The same techniques and methods can be used in reviewing a draft plan and revising its provisions or in evaluating a plan which has already been finalized. Medium-term plans are those to which major planning effort has been devoted, since the movement of the variables in the more distant future is shrouded in haziness, whereas short-term annual plans leave few options or degrees of freedom for planners to make use of. A finite period of five to ten years is the period to which most of the discussion that follows is geared.

2.   *Target Setting*

Any discussion of planning must start with a consideration of what we are planning for. Every effort must be made to delineate and specify the objectives and the goals of a plan. The quality of a plan hinges greatly on the clarity with which the targets are expressed. Chapter two discusses the various methods that can be employed to set plan targets and focuses on the problems and difficulties in formulating the preferences of the planners in quantitative terms.

3. *Plan Types*

Plans may be broadly classified into three categories: feasibility planning, consistency planning, and optimality planning. In feasibility planning, the main concern is to set the magnitudes of targets at levels that can be achieved with the initial available resources. India's First Five Year Plan was mainly a feasibility plan, and so are the first one or two plans of most underdeveloped countries. Chapter three discusses the main consideration in assessing the feasibility of a plan.

As more data becomes available and more experience in planning is gained, the stage is set for consistency planning. A first step in such planning is to draw up an interindustry table detailing the interdependence among industries. Using this table, the level of activity in each sector corresponding to the magnitudes of targets can be obtained, so that the outputs of individual sectors are consistent with each other. The static and dynamic methods of consistency planning are discussed in chapter four.

Optimality is an ideal concept in any situation to which planning in a country can only move directionally. The static and dynamic methods of optimality planning are discussed in chapter five.

4. *Plan Implementation*

The methods of planning discussed in chapters three, four, and five give the physical magnitudes of targets and other plan variables. These magnitudes can be realized through the application of adequate and effective economic policies and measures. This is the subject of chapter six, in which the formal procedures of plan implementation are discussed.

NOTES

1. Wassily Leontief, *The Structure of American Economy, 1919-1931* (New York: Oxford University Press, 1951).

2. George B. Dantzig, "Programming of Interdependent Activities, II, Mathematical Model," in T. C. Koopmans (ed.), *Activity Analysis of Production and Allocation* (New York: Wiley, 1951).

3. T. C. Koopmans, "Analysis of Production as an Efficient Combination of Activities," in Koopmans (ed.), *Activity Analysis.*

4. L. V. Kantorovich, "Mathematical Methods in Organization and

Planning of Production" (Leningrad: Publication House of the Leningrad State University, 1939).

5. The commissions responsible for advising the planning commission (commissariat) on specific aspects of the plan. These commissions are composed mostly of nongovernment officials, namely, industrialists, trade union leaders, and academic experts.

6. The role of these commissions was emphasized in the First Plan as follows: "For the first time, all elements interested in the progress of an industry or a production have found themselves assembled in order to carry out together a common task. The knowledge acquired in common in dealing with common problems greatly facilitates decisions and their understanding once they are taken. In many cases, action results from consultation alone. . . .

"Every branch of activity is promised the possibility of acquiring its production factors and selling its goods on a balanced market. The promise, however, is only kept if everybody plays the game. The promise acts merely as an incentive. It is not binding on anybody. Firms are not relieved of working out their own estimates and taking an attitude to risk. But they can do it in a better informed manner." (Quoted in Joan Mitchell, *Groundwork of Economic Planning* [London: Secker and Warburg, 1966], pp. 195, 196-97.)

7. F. L. Pryor ("Extent and Pattern of Public Ownership in Developed Economies," *Weltwirtschaftliches Archive* [Kiel, 1970], pp. 13, 104) has pointed out that Austria, Finland, and the U.K. have larger publicly owned sectors of industries than does France.

8. No plan can be formulated in such a way that all projects started are completed before the plan's end. However, if a plan is too short, say, two or three years, then a majority of the projects started will remain incomplete when the plan runs out. This would make the problem of drawing up the next plan more complex. At the same time, the plan formulation will be less meaningful in the sense that a major part of the available resources would be committed and allocated to the projects started in the preceding plan.

9. Ragnar Frisch, "General Outlook on a Method of Advanced and Democratic Macro-Economic Planning," memorandum, University of Oslo, Institute of Economics, December 14, 1967, p. 10.

10. Professor Leif Johansen has pointed out that moving planning has been introduced in the U.S.S.R. Professor Frederic L. Pryor indicated that moving planning was also introduced in Czechoslovakia.

11. Albert Waterston, *Development Planning: Lessons of Experience* (Baltimore: The Johns Hopkins Press, 1965), pp. 139-41.

12. In socialist countries, perspective plans include the five-year plans.

CHAPTER TWO

Plan Targets and National Preference

I. Introduction

1. *Targets and Plan*

Targets are an indispensable part of economic plans. It is inconceivable to have a plan without targets; however, targets by themselves do not make a plan. A plan must contain measures and policies to achieve the targets, along with an assessment of resource availability and the structure of the economy.

The character and comprehensiveness of a plan depend, to a large extent, on the nature of the targets and the manner in which they are expressed. An aggregative target like a certain level of national income or employment may or may not be accompanied by comprehensive sectoral breakdown in the plan formulation. But if the targets consist of several specific items, the plan has to be comprehensive enough to meet all target specifications.

2. *Target Setting in Practice*

The system of setting plan targets varies from country to country according to the form of the government and socioeconomic structure. In Communist countries, plan formulation generally starts with the declaration of socialist objectives by the highest organs of the Central Communist Party. These objectives broadly indicate the important national goals regarding total inputs and outputs of key, strategic industries like food grains, steel, and electricity. After some debate and discussion by other

Party organs and leaders, with consequent modifications, if any, the Central Politbureau issues directives to the Central Planning Bureau (CPB), which works out detailed plan targets. These targets are then passed on to lower agencies, starting from the ministries and republics down to the factories with the required disaggregation being effected at each level. The lower agencies modify their own targets, which they had already prepared independently, according to the targets handed down to them from above. In case of conflicts and disagreements, a discussion and bargaining with the immediate higher agency takes place. When a deadlock occurs, the higher agency prevails. The adjusted and modified targets then move up the pyramidal hierarchy with the requisite aggregation at each level to bring about material and other balances. Ultimately the plan targets are finalized by the CPB and presented for approval to the central legislative body.

In countries with a multiparty system of government, the broad objectives of the plan are formulated by the ruling party and are generally included in the platform of that party. These objectives are debated and discussed by the ruling, as well as opposition, parties. In the process, some shifts in the objectives laid down by the ruling party might take place. The modified objectives are then passed on to the planning commission, which sets out tentative targets in concrete terms. The targets are aired in public, debated, and denounced or applauded by various parties, factions, academicians, and interested groups. The planning commission might modify its earlier targets in the light of these discussions and prepare revised targets and a draft plan, which would then be directed for discussion and approval to some powerful council or committee (for example, the National Development Council in India). This council may either accept the draft plan or reject parts of its provisions, requiring the planning commission to revise the draft. In all these processes, lobbying and bargaining by private and public interests go on, and political deals and economic compromises continue to be made. Finally, the revised plan, after having been accepted by councils and committees, is presented for approval by the central legislature or parliament.

In countries with dictatorial forms of government, the plan and its targets may be drawn up by the ruling clique with whatever popular support and compromises it might deem necessary for its self-preservation.

The setting of plan targets in practice, thus, involves all manners of sectional lobbying, political deals, logrolling, and compromises. It is not the purpose of this chapter to discuss these aspects. On the contrary, we will be concerned with the procedures of formulating plan targets on the basis of some straightforward concept of social preference expressed directly by the citizens through their market behavior and utility indices, or indirectly by their representatives. It is understood that the preferences expressed by the representatives such as responsible poltical leaders might be affected by sectional lobbying and political pragmatism. However, these will not be explicitly considered here.

3. *A Preview of the Methods*

The contents of this chapter can be divided into four parts. Section II deals with the fundamental problems and difficulties involved in constructing a national-preference function. Section II and section III, which describes some mathematical forms which such functions can assume, make up the first part. The second part consists of sections IV and V, which discuss the method of setting targets on the basis of individual expenditure behavior and utility preference, respectively. The third part, sections VI and VII, outlines the methods of setting targets in terms of capital stock, derived either from the consumption volumes of the terminal plan year or from the postplan future consumption patterns. In sections VIII and IX, the last part, it is assumed that the national preference is best judged by the political leaders or knowledgeable persons, and methods of setting targets on the basis of information obtained from these leaders and responsible persons are considered.

In discussing some basic methods of target setting, we point out their shortcomings. As can be expected, none of these methods is wholly satisfactory. But whatever the faults of these methods, one or more of them have to be used, depending on the data availability, the type of objectives, and the techniques to be used. Finding an ideal system and method of setting national plan targets suggests the problems associated with an ideal system and form of democracy. Whereas a perfect system for either can perhaps never be evolved, there is always the possibility of finding better and improved approaches.

II. Major Considerations In Target Setting

1. *Preliminary Remarks*

National plan targets are essentially based on social choice. Such choice can be made by one person such as the president or the prime minister of the country; by a group of persons such as the cabinet, a commission, or a committee of technicians and knowledgeable persons; or directly by a large number of or all the individuals of the country, who express their preferences through some voting procedure, for example, market mechanism or some basic premises such as utility indices. However, whoever makes the social choice does it with a view to reflecting social preference as well as possible. The problem of target setting lies in finding appropriate methods to estimate and amalgamate individual economic preferences. The preference of an individual is a function of the utility he expects to derive from different items. The social or national preference has to be derived from aggregation of the individual preferences in some rational way.

2.   *Utility Indices of Individuals*

There is still debate as to whether the utility derived by an individual from a good is cardinally or only ordinally measurable. Though the interpretations of cardinality have not been uniform, it is clear that extreme versions implying measurement of utility in such absolute terms belie all experience. Hence such an interpretation could not be helpful in practice. Moreover, it has turned out that "cardinal utility has had no explanatory power above and beyond ordinal." However, recent empirical researches[1] have shown that some restrictive assumptions on the form of the utility functions have to be imposed to obtain usable results. These restrictions contain some elements of cardinality as stated below.

Let $x_1, \ldots, x_n$ be the amounts of n goods and let ω define the utility function of an individual; then the utility of the n goods to the individual is

$$\omega = \omega(x_1, \ldots, x_n). \tag{1}$$

The assumption of ordinal measurability requires that the individual is able to indicate that out of two n-vectors of goods either one is not preferred to the other or he is indifferent between them. In symbols let $\underline{x}^1 = (x_1^1, \ldots, x_n^1)$, $\underline{x}^2 = (x_1^2, \ldots, x_n^2)$ be two n-vectors with utilities to the individuals $\omega^1 = \omega(\underline{x}^1)$, $\omega^2 = \omega(\underline{x}^2)$; then $\omega^1 \geqslant \omega^2$ or $\omega^1 \leqslant \omega^2$ or $\omega^1 = \omega^2$. For logical reasons, it is also required that the preferences be transitive. "Transitivity" means that of three n-vectors, $\underline{x}^1, \underline{x}^2$, and $\underline{x}^3$, if $\underline{x}^2$ is not preferred to $\underline{x}^1$ and $\underline{x}^3$ is not preferred to $\underline{x}^2$, then $\underline{x}^3$ will not be preferred to $\underline{x}^1$. This implies that if $\omega^1 = \omega(\underline{x}^1) \geqslant \omega^2 = \omega(\underline{x}^2)$ and $\omega^2 = \omega(\underline{x}^2) \geqslant \omega^3 = \omega(\underline{x}^3)$, then $\omega^1 \geqslant \omega^3$. The utility function (1) may be subject to other qualifications. It may be assumed to be single valued and at least twice differentiable. It is generally agreed that the utility of a good increases at a decreasing rate, so that

$$\frac{\partial \omega}{\partial x_j} > 0 \text{ and } \frac{\partial^2 \omega}{\partial x_j^2} < 0. \tag{2}$$

Under these assumptions it can be shown[2] that the preferences of the individual are invariant under a monotonic increasing transformation of ω. This is to say that the quantities demanded by the individual will not change with any other utility function which is a "continuously" increasing function of ω.

Theoretically it is possible to analyze demand using a utility function of the general form (1). Recent advances in empirical research in this field[3] have been successful only on some further assumption about the form of the utility function. One crucial assumption is that the utilities derived from different goods are independent. Utility function (1) then takes on the following additive form:

$$\omega(x_1, \ldots, x_n) = \omega_1(x_1) + \omega_2(x_2) + \ldots, + \omega_n(x_n). \qquad (3)$$

The right-hand side of (3) implies the existence of cardinal utilities. The additive form can be justified[4] on the premise that a utility function can be assumed to exist with a degree of determinateness which allows for only a linear transformation. Or, it can be assumed that only ordinal utility exists implying that any monotonically increasing transformation is legitimate. Independent utilities would then be defined to mean that at least one member of the family of functions which are permissible as descriptions of the preference structure can be written in the additive form.[5]

In section IV, an additive form of utility function will be used to analyze demand projections.

3. *Social Welfare*

Social welfare is represented by social preference. Ideally we ought to be able to derive social preference by aggregating and comparing individual preferences. But the latter depend on individual utilities, which are wholly subjective. As such, no interpersonal comparison of utilities is possible. Hence social-welfare criteria have to be devised by means which do not involve direct interpersonal comparisons.

If interpersonal comparisons cannot be made, "social welfare is no more than a heterogeneous collection of individual welfares." All that can be said is that, if one or more individuals prefer one situation to the other while none prefers the second to the first, then the community ought to prefer the first to the second. This was the concept employed by Pareto[6] in his celebrated principle, now known as the Pareto optimality, which says that a community reaches its maximum welfare when it is not possible to make anyone better off without making anyone else worse off.

Or, in other words, a maximum welfare of the community is reached at a point when it is not possible for any individual to attain a higher level of his preference without at the same time forcing one or more individuals to lower levels of their preferences. It can be noted that there can be more than one, in fact an infinite, number of points where the principle of Pareto optimality will hold.

A broader and more operational method, known as the "compensation principle," was proposed by Bergson[7] in 1938. According to Bergson's criterion, for a community to prefer one state or situation to the other it is not necessary that every individual belonging to the first must be better off or at least must not be worse off than in the second. There may be some individuals who are worse off than they would be in the nonpreferred state, but these individuals can be made better off by payment of compensations from the better-off individuals without the latter's becoming worse off than they would be in the nonpreferred state. Pareto's criterion turns out to be a special case of Bergson's where no compensations would be needed for the community to decide its preferred state. But again there could not be one unique configuration of compensation and, hence, as far as individual welfares or preference levels are concerned, there could be an infinite number of combinations in the preferred state.

Kaldor[8] and Hicks[9] have further relaxed Bergson's criterion by relating it to potential compensation rather than to the actual, as is the case with Bergson. Some of the more recent discussions in this field have been summarized by Arrow[10] and Graaf.[11]

The fact that Pareto and Bergson criteria do not lead to a unique social choice has been formally shown by Lange[12] and Samuelson.[13] Their analysis is summarized in appendix 2.A. It is shown that, in order to have a deterministic optimizing system, a definite welfare function involving ethical notions and value judgments is needed. Therefore, the targets of a national plan cannot be based on considerations of technical conditions and maximization of individual utility functions alone. Some value judgments to replace the interpersonal comparison of utility have to be introduced exogenously.

The question arises whether such a value judgment can be arrived at on some rational basis, as from majority voting or the game-theoretic approach. Majority voting may lead to inconsistent and intransitive preferences, as shown conclusively by Arrow.[14] The game-theoretic approach also does not seem promising. First, solutions of games of more than four persons are often difficult to find. Second, the solutions are generally not unique even when they exist. Last, the difficulties of specifying the payoffs and probabilities are likely to become insurmountable. Arrow's so-called paradox is discussed in appendix 2.B, and some remarks about game theory are given in appendix 2.C.

4. *Joint Welfare Function*

Recently some attempts have been made to derive social preference to represent what is called joint welfare function by Sawyer[15] and Lieberman.[16] Since their procedure appears to be interesting for purposes of national planning, it can be summarized as below.

Let there be three individuals, A, B, and C, and three alternatives, x, y, and z. Let the value to A of a payoff of alternative x to B be denoted by P_{axb}, the value to B of payoff y to C by P_{byc}, and so on. A payoff to another person may not have the same value to an individual which it would have to him if the same payoff is made to himself. The utility or value to A of a payoff x to B, P_{axb} may be a fraction of the value to A of the same payoff x to A himself. Let this fraction be t_{ab}, so that $P_{axb} = t_{ab} P_{axa}$. The symbols t_{ac}, t_{ba}, t_{bc}, t_{ca}, t_{cb} have similar designations. Obviously, $t_{aa} = t_{bb} = t_{cc} = 1$. Joint welfare total (JWT) is defined as the sums of values to each of the individuals derived from a payoff to himself and to others added for each individual. For example, value to A of a payoff x to A is P_{axa}, and the value to A of the same payoff x to B is P_{axb} and the value to A of the same payoff to C is P_{axc} and hence the sum of values to A is $P_{axa} + P_{axb} + P_{axc}$. Similarly to B is $P_{bxa} + P_{bxb} + P_{bxc}$ and to C is $P_{cxa} + P_{cxb} + P_{cxc}$. Hence

$$\text{JWT from } x = (P_{axa} + P_{axb} + P_{axc}) + (P_{bxa} + P_{bxb} + P_{bxc}) + (P_{cxa} + P_{cxb} + P_{cxc})$$
$$= P_{axa} (1 + t_{ab} + t_{ac}) + P_{bxb} (t_{ba} + 1 + t_{bc}) + P_{cxc} (t_{ca} + t_{cb} + 1).$$

Similarly, we can write JWT for alternative y and z by replacing x by y and z.

Out of the three alternatives, the one which has the highest JWT will be preferred. More than one alternative may be chosen by the society if they are feasible according to the rank of the JWT's starting from the highest value.

The method rests on what may be called an altruism scale, which is a measure "for assessing directly the value one places upon the welfare of another in relation to his own." Basically, therefore, a cardinal measurement of utility is involved. The choice of the alternative depends on the sum of utilities or preferences which each individual attaches for himself as well as for each of the other individuals. It can be verified that the collective choice will not be affected under linear transformation of an individual's preferences.

The method appears to avoid direct interpersonal comparison of utilities. But it involves arbitrariness in the units in which the utilities of an individual are measured. There may be some countervailing adjustment due to inclusion of utilities which the individual assigns when the payoff of an outcome accrues to other individuals. Still, the JWT's from the alternative outcomes would remain largely arbitrary and ambiguous, since they require the addition of the values or utilities of different individuals.

Another weakness of the JWT method lies in the cardinal measurement resulting from utilizing the ratios t_{ab}, t_{bc}, ..., and so forth. In practice it may not be possible for an individual to specify these scales in an unequivocal way.

5.   *Intertemporal Preference Function*

So far we have been considering a static preference function. A plan target often has a dynamic dimension. The magnitudes entering the target are set not only with a view to satisfying immediate needs but also with consideration of their effects in the future.

A long-run preference function must include utilities over time, raising problems of intertemporal comparisons. Whether the utility enjoyed by an individual at one point of time is comparable to that at another point of time will depend on whether or not the taste and preferences of the individual have changed. Moreover, it must be considered whether the preferences between periods are complementary or noncomplementary.[17] Only when it is assumed that tastes do not change and, in addition, that noncomplementarity between periods holds can the preferences over time be represented by an additive utility function:

$$\omega = \omega_1 (\underline{x}_1) + \omega_2 (\underline{x}_2) + \ldots, + \omega_t (\underline{x}_t), \qquad (4)$$

where subscripts indicate time.

Both of these assumptions are unrealistic. Tastes do change, and the choices in one period and utility derived thereby affect the choices and utility levels in the following periods. Yet, in dynamic planning models both assumptions often have to be used to insure manageable programs.

Another question to be faced in intertemporal planning models is that of time preference itself. Does an individual prefer a certain amount of utility to be available now to the same amount of utility (however defined) available at a future point of time? Ramsey[18] and some contemporary economists like Harrod[19] and Goodwin[20] have argued that time-preference does not exist. Hence, it is illegitimate to discount future utilities. A majority opinion, however, favors time discounting. Koopmans[21] has shown that if one requires the utility function to give a complete ordering of consumption over an infinite time horizon, time discounting has to be postulated. If time discounting is recognized, an appropriate rate of time discounting has to be sought and specified. Whereas in the past efforts have been made to find a natural, real, or ideal rate of interest, and so forth, the resolution of the problem essentially depends on the intertemporal comparison of utility. This poses a problem as tough as, if not tougher than, interpersonal comparison of utility.

The problem of finding a reliable discounting rate could be neutralized if a cutoff point could be determined. That is, one could say that for a plan to be drawn up in period 0, only the next t periods matter and the following periods can be ignored. Unfortunately, no guides are available to mark off such a truncation. An action taken now affects present as well as future events, changes in the future affect the events occurring in the still more distant future, and so on till infinity. Thus economic actions and policies of today have repercussions on future events and policies in an endless chain. The repercussions may get weaker and more uncertain the further we look into the future, but it is not possible on logical grounds to demarcate a dividing line which would separate a period of interest from others beyond. Any finite time horizon will necessarily be arbitrary.

We conclude this section by stating that construction of any social welfare function involves making interpersonal comparisons or measuring utilities cardinally, and for both no satisfactory methods exist. Intertemporal welfare functions raise, in addition, tough problems of complementarity and time discounting. Plan targets, to the extent that they are required to reflect social welfare, can therefore be estimated only approximatively.

III. Forms of Targets and Preference Functions

1. *Preliminary Remarks*

We have seen that social choice cannot be derived from individual choices without making some value judgments or restrictive assumptions.

Even if we admit meaning to interpersonal comparison of utility, we have to make a choice of different mathematical forms of the social utility function. This might be the sum of the individual utilities, their product, the product of their logarithms, or some other form. As Professor Bergson[22] has pointed out, there are also value judgments implicit even in the choice of a mathematical form in which the social welfare functions ought to be expressed.

In this section we shall state some of the important mathematical forms in which national preferences have been and can be expressed for planning or constructing planning models. In practice, the form of the preference function depends to a large extent on the purpose for which it is formulated, the type of planning to be undertaken, the techniques to be used, and the availability of data.

2.   Fixed Targets

In mandatory national plans, targets are generally fixed. These may be derived by planners from analyses of demand projections, population growth, technological developments, and some important national objectives laid down by the political leaders. Usually the politicians set broad national goals such as growth of national income, capital formation, regional balance, and so forth. The planners work out detailed targets, using all statistical information at their disposal and ensuring that the fixed targets are feasible.

Fixed targets are appropriate for consistency planning and do not preclude optimal planning. Given the initial and fixed terminal values of the target variables, a dynamic optimizing analysis using control theory can be undertaken. We briefly outline such techniques in chapter five.

3.   Linear Form

In recent years a number of efforts have been made to apply programming techniques to national planning. The simplest of these techniques is static linear programming, so called because all the relations are expressed in linear form and all the variables relate to one period. The target function, or what is more commonly called the objective function, is represented in the following way:

$$\omega = \omega(x_1, \ldots, x_n) = w_1 x_1 + \ldots + w_n x_n. \qquad (5)$$

In (5), x's are the target variables and w's are the respective weights attached to these variables, which may be actual prices, shadow prices, or an index of relative importance. If all the x's in (5) are multipled by a constant, the value of the function is multiplied by the same constant. This is a deficiency of targets in linear form, for normally it is expected that the value of the function should increase at a rate lower than that at which the variables increase.

An advantage of linear target functions, when w's are the prevailing prices in the plan period and x's are quantities estimated to be demanded at these prices, is that all the quantities of x's supplied are cleared by definition. But if w's differ from prices, then the plan must contain provisions for disposal of the quantities produced.

4. *Linear-Logarithmic Form*

In the simple linear form of target the marginal value of a good is constant. The linear-logarithmic form has the advantage that the function remains linear in the logarithms of the variables yet satisfies the usual requirement of diminishing marginal utility of a good as quantity increases. The function is written as

$$\omega = \omega(x_1, \ldots, x_n) = w_1 \log x_1 + \ldots + w_n \log x_n. \qquad (6)$$

Differentiating partially (6) with any one of the variables, say x_i, we get

$$\frac{\partial \omega}{\partial x_i} = \frac{w_i}{x_i}, \frac{\partial^2 \omega}{\partial x_i^2} = -w_i x_i^{-2}, \frac{\partial^3 \omega}{\partial x_i^3} = +2 w_i x_i^{-3}. \qquad (7)$$

Thus the marginal welfare of x_i diminishes as x_i increases and thus (6) satisfies the generally accepted behavior of a utility function. It can be seen that a proportional change in x_i's adds a constant amount to welfare.

5. *Nonlinear Forms*

In theoretical and illustrative models of planning, various nonlinear forms of targets have been tried. A frequently used form with some desirable properties is the quadratic, which is written as

$$\omega = \omega(x_1, \ldots, x_n) = \sum_{j=1}^{n} \sum_{i=1}^{n} v_{ij} x_i x_j. \qquad (8)$$

If the variables are separable, implying that the preferences are additive, (8) can be written as follows:

$$\omega = \omega(x_1, \ldots, x_n) = \sum_{j=1}^{n} (u_j x_j + \tfrac{1}{2} w_j x_j^2). \qquad (8a)$$

Under some situations, it is convenient and appropriate to express the preference function as a weighted sum of the squares of differences of the variables x_j from some preassigned values $\bar{x}_j$. Then the preference function to be minimized assumes the following quadratic form:

$$\omega = \sum_{j=1}^{n} w_j (x_j - \bar{x}_j)^2. \qquad (9)$$

It is obvious from (8a) and (9) that the marginal utility of one target item is independent of that of any other. For example, differentiating (8a) we get

$$\frac{\partial \omega}{\partial x_j} = u_j + w_j x_j \qquad j = 1, \ldots, n. \qquad (10)$$

In (8a), w_j must be negative to satisfy the condition of diminishing marginal utility.

6.   *Proportional Targets*

Target variables may be desired to be maximized in a certain proportion. Letting $w_1, \ldots, w_n$ be the proportions in which the variables $x_1, \ldots, x_n$ are desired to be maximized, then these variables can be expressed as

$$w_1 : w_2 : \ldots : w_n = x_1 : x_2 : \ldots : x_n$$

or $\qquad\qquad\qquad\qquad\qquad\qquad\qquad\qquad\qquad\qquad\qquad\qquad$ (11)

$$\frac{x_1}{w_1} = \frac{x_2}{w_2} = \ldots = \frac{x_n}{w_n} = k.$$

The excess of any variable over the amount given by ratio k is assumed not to be valued. The target requires the maximization of the minimum of the ratios $x_1/w_1, x_2/w_2, \ldots, x_n/w_n$. Thus the target can be written as

$$\omega = \omega(x_1, \ldots, x_n) = \min_i \left(\frac{x_i}{w_i} \right).$$

Radner has noted that this type of criteria function is often used in the Soviet Union.[23]

IV. Statistical Demand Analysis and Plan Targets

1. *Preliminary Remarks*

In most mandatory plans, statistical demand analysis has been invariably used, explicitly or implicitly. To begin with, planners may be given some perspectives in form of national priorities and longer-run goals by the politicians and leaders. If the politicians are definite and adamant about a target item, the planners may have to accept it as a datum and include the target value as such. Generally, however, national priorities and perspectives are expressed in loose, flexible terms. It is essential that the politicians indicate the desired rate of growth of real national income and its distribution. If the politicians overestimate or underestimate the potentialities of the economy, they can be advised by the planners so that a maximum feasible rate is agreed upon.

Once the total national income and its distribution are known for the target year, statistical demand analysis can then be applied to estimate the quantities of goods and services which would be demanded. However, demand is determined not only by the income of the individual but also by commodity prices, ethnic composition, education, occupation, taste, customs, and so forth, and only some of these elements can be quantified.

Factors which are not easily quantifiable have to be handled differently. A common way is to classify the population according to the characteristics of such factors, for example, race, occupation, education, climate, and so forth, and then apply usual demand analysis to different strata. Before doing this, it may be desirable to check the significance of each stratification. For this, statistical methods such as analysis of variance can be applied. If some classifications are such that they do not produce any significant difference in consumption behavior, they should be dropped.

If the current relative prices are assumed to remain unchanged, demand analysis can be carried out in terms of real income without considering price variations explicitly. In completely centralized planning, all prices are fixed in advance, and, hence, given the income distribution, demand can be estimated, treating the prices as independent variables or parameters. In semicentralized planning, prices, insofar as they are not fixed by the planners, and quantities supplied and demanded are interdependent.

2.   *Basic Demand Data*

Various types of basic data can be used for the projection of demand. The three most commonly used are (i) cross-sectional data by income from consumer budget surveys, (ii) time series of aggregates for a given area, and (iii) cross-country data relating to area aggregates during a given period of time.

Cross-section data from consumer budget surveys are most frequently used for estimating effect of income on demand. Such data are more convenient to use if they are free from price disturbances. If a budget survey is large enough, it may cover various races, occupations, communities, and the like. Then a separate equation may be fitted to each stratum by cross-classifying the data by income and groups. Various forms of equations have been fitted, including linear, parabolic, logarithmic, log-normal, the Tornquist system of equations, and so forth.[24]

Cross-section analysis of demand projections can be supplemented by time-series analysis. There is no *a priori* reason why the results of the two should tally, since the two analyses study different types of behavior, and, hence, the biases resulting from the specification errors in the two cases may be different. In practice, more reliance can be placed on cross-section data than on time-series data, because the former tend to be free from collinearity complications and allow for a wider range of variation of variables than the latter.

3.   *Methods of Statistical Demand Projections*

Application of cross-section analysis to demand projections rests on the assumption that average future consumption in a prediction period for each income interval will be similar to the present consumption. For this assumption to be acceptable, it must be shown that time does not have a systematic effect on consumption behavior. This can be done by relating more than one set of equally representative cross-section data to different points of time and applying analysis of variance. If it turns out that time does have a systematic effect, then it will be necessary to make use of time-series data. After evaluating the trend factor, one should attempt to check whether it conforms to visible changes in fashion, taste, and so forth. If the value of the trend factor is too big, then the projections of demand on the basis of cross-section data must be adjusted.

Estimation of price effects on demand is very complicated in general and becomes still more difficult when some prices are controlled and managed by state agencies, as is often the case under planning. Price effects can be studied by time-series data. The value of such studies may be marred by the fact that individual income and the price of consumption items increase steadily over time. In regression terms, price elasticities may have reverse signs due to collinearity complications. It is also evident that demand for a commodity depends not only on its own price, but also on the prices of other commodities. Therefore, estimation of indirect as well as direct price elasticities is needed. A method of deriving direct and cross elasticities is discussed in the following section.

Application of statistical demand analysis to underdeveloped countries is significantly impeded by the paucity and low quality of data available. Time series are short and discontinuous, surveys too partial and incomplete. Moreover, a demand pattern estimated from past data may not be a good indication of future patterns because of rapid and radical changes in the economic and social structure of underdeveloped countries. Information on demand patterns in other countries will be helpful only when there are similarities in consumption styles in corresponding groups.

Notwithstanding statistical problems, plan targets have to be derived on the basis of demand analysis and projections. In the last analysis, the overall objective of planning is to chalk out a rational program to meet social preferences over time, and demand analysis and projections can be a potent method of estimating such preferences. In the following section we briefly describe an alternative method of demand projections which is more directly related to utility preference and consumer behavior.

V. Utility Preference and Demand Projections

1. *Why Utility Preference*

In the preceding discussion, statistical methods of deriving demand for individual goods were assumed to rest on observed or observable variables such as prices and incomes which affect levels of demand directly. In this section we consider how to derive demands not from statistical demand analysis but from the basic premises of utility indices. It may be asked: Why do this? Why can't statistical methods based on the tangible and concrete concepts of prices and income suffice?

An answer to these questions has been given by Professor Frisch: "The theory of choice—and particularly the concept of a utility indicator—is assumed to be independent of the particular organizational form of the market. Even if the goods were distributed to the consumers in an entirely different way, not through a market with a budget equation, and so on, the utility indicator would in general exist and may, for instance, be used for estimating the behavior of consumers under specific market forms that may be contemplated in a programming analysis."[25]

Thus utility or preference functions provide a more general approach to demand estimation. Also, as we shall see below, once we get a reliable estimate of the flexibility of marginal utility of money, all the direct and cross-price elasticities can be estimated straight away. We discuss below a simple procedure of demand projection through utility preference.

2.   Johansen's Approach

The estimation of demand from utility functions stems from the classic contributions of Slutsky[26] and the experimentations of Frisch.[27] Recent contributions in this field have been made by Houthakker,[28] Johansen,[29] and Barten,[30] among others. We shall summarize here the result of Johansen's method, which he applied to Norwegian data. Johansen proceeded as follows: First, the equilibrium condition is derived from the budget equation

$$y = \sum_i p_i y_i \qquad\qquad (12)$$

and a utility function of the additive type

$$u = \sum_i u_i(y_i), \qquad\qquad (13)$$

where y is the total income of the group of consumers and y_i is the amount of consumption of commodity i (y and y_i may be considered equivalently per consumer magnitudes).

Using the Lagrange multiplier λ, (13) is maximized subject to (12) to get

$$u_i'(y_i) - \lambda p_i = 0 \qquad i = 1, \ldots, n. \qquad\qquad (14)$$

As we know, λ is the marginal utility of money. The flexibility of marginal utility of money, or the money flexibility, is defined as the elasticity of λ with respect to y, that is, $\dfrac{\partial \lambda}{\partial y} \cdot \dfrac{y}{\lambda}$.

Differentiating (12) and (14) with respect to p's and y, and after some manipulations (shown in appendix 2.D), we get Johansen's main formula:

$$\frac{\partial y_i}{\partial p_j} = \frac{\partial y_i}{\partial y}(\lambda + y_j - \lambda\frac{\partial y_j}{\partial y}) \text{ when } i = j$$

$$\frac{\partial y_i}{\partial p_j} = \frac{\partial y_i}{\partial y}(y_j - \lambda\frac{y_i}{y}) \quad \text{ when } i \neq j.$$

$$(15)$$

In (15), y_j, $j = 1, \ldots, n$, is the amount of commodity j consumed or demanded in the initial stage. The coefficients $\frac{\partial y_i}{\partial y}$, $i = 1, \ldots, n$, giving the rate of change in commodity i demanded due to change in income, can be estimated from empirical observation. Then if we know the value of λ, we can estimate from (15), $\frac{\partial y_i}{\partial p_j}$, the rate of change in the amount of commodity i demanded due to a change in the price of commodity j, (i, $j = 1, \ldots, n$).

The value of λ can be estimated directly, if we have estimates for any one of $\frac{\partial y_i}{\partial p_i}$, $i = 1, \ldots, n$, and $\frac{\partial y_i}{\partial y}$ from empirical observation, given the initial values of y_i's.

It may be that values $\frac{\partial y_i}{\partial p_i}, \frac{\partial y_i}{\partial y}$ are available for more than one good i. If so, we can derive corresponding values of λ. If these values are sufficiently similar, then we can place more confidence in the above procedure. However, if the values of λ differ substantially, then arises a question of which value should be used in the computations. For example, in his computations Johansen obtained the following values of λ for four sectors:

	λ
Agriculture	5.370
Food	4.902
Nonmetallic Mineral Products	10.912
Land Transportation	5.637

The above shows that the values of λ are almost equal for agriculture, food, and land transportation. Johansen finds this very encouraging "since the underlying elasticities for the foods and for travel which produce nearly the same estimate for λ are very different."

However, the value of λ obtained on the basis of data for nonmetallic and mineral products differs very much from others. Johansen ignored this because this sector accounts for a rather small part of the consumers' budget, and the statistical basis for this sector was poor. He chose the value of $\lambda = 5.500$, which corresponds to the value of the marginal flexibility of $\lambda = -1.89$.

All the same, there is some arbitrariness in the procedure outlined above, and further research has been carried out at the Oslo Institute of Economics to find the flexibility of marginal utility of money. This is given briefly in appendix 2.D.

4.   *Concluding Observations*

Estimation of demand derived from theory of choice and preference functions rests on economic principles and methods developed and refined over the last several decades. The chief advantage of the method is that, once a reliable value of money flexibility (flexibility of the marginal utility of money) has been arrived at, the computation of all direct and cross-price elasticities is greatly facilitated and shortened. A pertinent question arises as to whether money flexibility can be assumed to be a constant parameter. The research carried out by Johansen and his associates seems to imply that this is true. This may perhaps be justified if rates of individual price changes, rate of growth of income, and income elasticities all remain constant. However, if these rates differ from period to period, we ought to get different money flexibilities for each period. In order to get a unique value of money flexibility, some sort of averages may have to be used. It is debatable whether the use of such a value would correctly reflect the price elasticities of individual commodities.

So far the application of the method has been developed on the assumption of independence of utilities. The extension of the method to nonindependence of utilities or to general utility functions remains still unattempted. This puts a limitation on the usefulness of the method in practice. It is possible perhaps to define commodities or categories of commodities in such a way that they are independent of each other to some extent. In affluent communities it may be contemplated that perhaps the utility derived by an average consumer from food items is independent of that derived from clothing or shelter because the consumer can afford to have reasonably comfortable levels of each of these. But this may not be true even for necessities in poor countries.

VI. Targets in Terms of Capital Stock

1.   *Why Capital Stock*

The preceding two sections indicated the methods which can be employed in finding the demand for consumption in the successive or final year of the plan. However, having targets set in terms of consumption items alone involves certain risks. If the plan aims at maximizing a function of amounts of consumption only, the rate of capital formation may be too low in the terminal years of the plan, or actual depletion may occur. This may jeopardize the sustained growth of the economy in the postplan years. However, this can be prevented by setting lower bounds on net investment or capital stock.

An alternative is to set the targets in terms of capital stock. In this case, there is the danger that the realization of a certain configuration of capital stock may result in too low a level of national consumption. Again this can be prevented by imposing lower limits on consumption levels. Thus an estimate of the configuration of capital stock is needed for setting the lower bounds in the first case, and for setting the targets in the second. However, one advantage of this alternative approach is that the configuration of capital stock in the final year of the plan can be set in accordance with the desired rate of growth of consumption and income in the postplan years. The postplan years the consumption of which is taken into account in fixing the target may cover the gestation period only. This is discussed in this section. But the capital targets can be fixed by taking into account consumption over a long period in the future, even extending up to infinity. This case is discussed in section VII.

2. *Fixing Terminal Capital Stock*

It will be assumed here that the volumes of consumption items for the target year are given, arrived at from statistical studies or from some social welfare considerations. Let the plan be of T years, starting from year 1, so that the target year is T. Leaving aside for the moment foreign transactions, gestation lags and depreciations, the balance equation is

$$x_i(t) = \sum_{j=1}^{n} a_{ij}x_j(t) + \Delta k_i(t) + c_i(t) \qquad i=1, \ldots, n, \qquad (16)$$

where $x_i(t)$ is the total output, $\Delta k_i(t)$ total investment, and $c_i(t)$ total consumption from sector i in period t. The coefficient a_{ij}, $i,j = 1, \ldots, n$ represents the amount of output of sector i required per unit of output of sector j so that $\sum_{j=1}^{n} a_{ij}x_j$ represents the total intersectoral deliveries from sector i. If the concern were just to produce $c_i(T)$ in the last plan year T, with no consideration to what happens in year $T + 1$, $\Delta k_i(t)$ in (16) will equal zero for t=T. Equation (16) would now become for t=T.

$$x_i(T) = \sum_{j=1}^{n} a_{ij}x_j(t) + c_i(t) \qquad\qquad i=1,\ldots,n. \qquad (17)$$

There are n linear equations in (17) with n unknowns $x_i(t)$. Hence they can be solved by Cramer's rule or by some other method.

The amounts of capital needed for the production of $x_i(T)$, $i = 1$, ..., n can be derived if there are estimates of capital input-output coefficients b_{hi} giving the hth output needed as capital input per unit production of ith output. The amount of capital stock in sector i in year T which has originally come from sector h is

$$k_h(T) = \sum_{i=1}^{n} b_{hi}x_i(T) \qquad\qquad h=1,\ldots,n. \qquad (18)$$

The magnitudes of capital in the terminal year of the plan given by (18) does not provide for any increase in output in year T + 1. In fact, the output in year T + 1 may actually decline due to depreciation. If provision is to be made for the expansion of output in the postplan years, then under the assumption of a gestation lag of one year, it would suffice to allow for expansion in the year following the terminal plan year, (T), with the expectation that this will be repeated year after year. In order to fix the additions to capital stock in year T, let it be assumed that the planners expect, or plan, the volumes of total consumption in year T + 1 to be c_i (T + 1), $i = 1, \ldots,$ n. Given c_i (T + 1), we find x_i (T + 1), $i = 1, \ldots,$ n from (17) for t = T + 1 and k_h (T + 1), h = 1, ..., n from (18), to get

$$\Delta k_h (T) = k_h (T+1) - k_h (T) = \sum_{i=1}^{n} b_{hi}[x_i (T+1) - x_i(T)] \quad (19)$$

$$h = 1, \ldots, n.$$

Replacing Δk_h (T) given by (18) and (19) in (16), we get the total output of commodity i in year T, which will allow for the expected increase in the consumption levels in year T + 1 but not afterwards.

In the above discussion we have assumed a gestation lag of one year since the capital formed in year t begins to yield output in year t + 1. Often it takes more than a year to complete the formation of capital, and the gestation lag is correspondingly longer. Our discussion also did not take into account government expenditure, exports, imports, inventories, depreciation, and so forth. We discuss the determination of capital stock in the terminal year of the plan, taking into account these considerations in appendix 2.E.

3.   Edge Effects

In constructing planning models one often encounters what may be called edginess or edge effects. For example, from putting (18) into (16), we know the total capital stock which must be there in period T, but we do not know how it is formed. It may be that all the investment is made in the final year or in the last two years of the plan; that is, all the capital stock is created towards the end of the plan. This means that productive activity remains constant and investment activity remains almost nil over the earlier years of the plan, but they zoom up toward the end, thus creating sharp edge effects. These effects may occur in the movement of other variables also.

However, the crucial problem most frequently encountered is connected with the formation of capital over the plan years. Sandee[31] was one of the first to deal with this problem. In his ten-year study, "A Demonstration Planning Model for India," he tries to maximize the excess of the aggregate consumption in 1970 over the base year 1960. As his model aims at maximizing excess consumption only in the *final* year of the plan, there are no indicators to determine the size of annual investment outlays. Sandee uses a rule of thumb and assumes that investment increases linearly every year. Denoting the annual constant increment of investment by ΔI and the investment in the base year by $I(o)$,

$$I(t) = I(o) + t\Delta I. \tag{20}$$

Therefore,

$$\sum_{t=1}^{T} I(t) = T\, I(o) + \frac{T(T+1)}{2} \Delta I.$$

Given $\sum_{t=1}^{T} I(t)$, that is, the total investment outlay for the plan period, ΔI and $I(t), t = 1, \ldots, T$ can be obtained.

Chenery and Bruno[32] have adopted a similar approach in their model related to Israel. Instead of investment increasing linearly, they allow it to increase at a constant exponential rate, so that

$$I(t) = I(o)\, e^{gt},$$

where g is the constant rate of growth of investment. Summing over t = o to t = T, we get

$$\sum_{t=o}^{T} I(t) = I(o) \frac{1 - e^{g(T+1)}}{1 - e^g} . \tag{21}$$

Therefore, the fraction of the total investment to be allocated to the terminal year T is given by

$$\frac{I(T)}{\sum_{t=i}^{T} I(t)} = \frac{e^{g(T-1)}}{(1 - e^{gT}) / (1 - e^g)} . \tag{22}$$

Given the total investment for the plan period, g can be obtained from (21), and investment in the terminal period T from (22) Thus when the interest lies in the terminal year of the plan, a device similar to that used by Sandee and Chenery may have to be employed to determine a level of investment in this year consistent with a gradual and smooth increase of investment over the preceding years of the plan. The above method has also been used by Manne and Rudra in "A Consistency Model for India."[33]

Used by Manne and Weisskopf,[34] another way of reducing or removing the edge effect starts with the assumption that investment in each sector grows at a constant rate so that

$$I_{jT} = I_{jt} (1 + g)^{T-t} \tag{23}$$

$$t = 0, 1, 2, \ldots, T$$
$$j = 1, \ldots, n.$$

They do not require that any one of the above relationships hold exactly but rather that they *hold on the average* within each sector. For averaging purposes, they use the following device:

$$I_{jT} = \frac{1}{T} \quad [(1 + g)^T I_{jo} + (1 + g)^{T-1} I_{j1} + \ldots + (1 + g) I_{j(T-1)}]$$

$$j = 1, \ldots, n. \tag{24}$$

Given the values of K(o) and K(t), the spread of investment in each sector for each year of the plan can be worked out.

While a smoothing device of the above types has to be employed often to arrive at (determinate) solutions of planning models, these devices are open to criticism. First, any smoothing device of the above types is liable to be arbitrary. Second, attempts at reducing edge effects which may appear in intertemporal models reduce the dynamic characteristics of the model and turn them into essentially static models. Third, to the extent that these devices are used in optimizing models, they narrow the scope of optimization.

VIII. Fixing Targets by Using a Steady-State Model

1. *Introduction*

Stone and his associates[35] have developed a way to set up targets by using a steady-state model covering the entire future. Their approach rests on two basic facts: first, that what is done now affects to some extent what can be done in the future; and, second, that what will be desired in the future and what facilities will be available to accomplish these desires become less and less clear in the process of imagining times which are more and more remote. Stone sets up a two-part growth model. One part, the long-run, or steady-state, model, is concerned with the rates at which outputs of different products might grow after a transitional period. The other part, the short-run, or transient, model, is concerned with adapting the economy during the transitional period to meet the initial conditions of the steady state of growth.

What is of concern here is how the targets of the transient model are set. The transitional period will be considered as the plan period, and the derivation of the initial conditions of the steady-state model will be considered as the setting of end-of-plan-period targets. The purpose of the steady-state model is to determine the minimum initial stock of assets, which is, of course, the same as the terminal stock of assets of the transitional period. Given the initial assets of the transient period, consumption may be maximized during this period according to some utility function of consumption, with the lower bounds on individual items such that the terminal capital stock for this plan period is achieved. If the problem is not solvable, it is either because the lower bound on consumption during the transitional period has been put too high or because too high a rate of growth for the posttransitional period has been assumed. It may be necessary, then, to adjust the values of the lower bounds on consumption in the transitional period and/or their rates of growth in the steady state and try again until a solution is obtained.

2.   Outline of the Approach

The multisectoral analysis and derivation of the capital stock in the terminal plan year T, which will provide the stream of consumption volumes growing indefinitely at a constant rate in the postplan year, is given in appendix 2.F. Here we can illustrate the derivation by considering an economy of one commodity. Now the balance equation in the terminal plan year can be written

$$x(T) = ax(T) + \Delta k(T) + c(T), \tag{25}$$

where $x(T)$ is the total output, a the current input coefficient, $ax(T)$ the amount of intermediate delivery, $\Delta k(T)$ the net investment, and $c(T)$ the total consumption of the commodity. Our problem is to estimate $\Delta k(T)$ such that it would provide $c(T)(1 + \psi)^t$ consumption in year $T + t$, $t = 1$, ..., ∞, where ψ is the constant rate of growth of consumption.

To start with, we make a provisional first estimate and put $\Delta k(T)^{[1]} = 0$, then we get from (25) the first provisional estimate of $x(T)$:

$$x(T)^{[1]} = \frac{1}{1-a} \, c(T) \tag{26}$$

and
$$x(T + 1)^{[1]} = \frac{1}{1-a} \, c(T)(1 + \psi). \tag{27}$$

From (26) and (27) we get

$$\Delta x(T)^{[1]} = x(T + 1)^{[1]} - x(T)^{[1]} = \frac{\psi}{1-a} \, c(T). \tag{28}$$

Our revised second estimate of $\Delta k(T)$ is

$$\Delta k(T)^{[2]} = b\Delta x(T)^{[1]} = \frac{b\psi}{1-a} c(T), \tag{29}$$

where b is the capital input coefficient.

Putting (29) back in (25), we get the second revised estimate of $x(T)$:

$$x(T)^{[2]} = \frac{1}{1-a} \, (1 + \frac{\psi b}{1-a}) \, c(T). \tag{30}$$

And, as in (28), we derive the second revised estimate of $\Delta x(T)$:

$$\Delta x(T)^{[2]} = \frac{\psi}{1-a} (1 - \frac{\psi b}{1-a}) c(T). \tag{31}$$

As before, we can make the third revised estimate of $\Delta k(T)$:

$$\Delta k(T)^{[3]} = b \Delta x(T)^{[2]} = \frac{b\psi}{1-a} (1 + \frac{\psi b}{1-a}) c(T). \tag{32}$$

Proceeding in this way, we make the final estimate of $\Delta k(T)$:

$$\Delta k(T) = \left[\frac{b\psi}{1-a} + (\frac{b\psi}{1-a})^2 + \dots \right] c(T) \tag{33}$$

$$= \sum_{\theta=1}^{\infty} (\frac{b\psi}{1-a})^\theta c(T).$$

Putting (33) in (25), we get the final estimate of $\Delta k(T)$:

$$x(T) = \frac{1}{1-a} \left[1 + \sum_{\theta=1}^{\infty} (\frac{b\psi}{1-a})^\theta \right] c(T) \tag{34}$$

$$= \frac{1}{1-a} \sum_{\theta=0}^{\infty} (\frac{b\psi}{1-a})^\theta c(T)$$

and, finally, the terminal capital stock:

$$k(T) = \frac{b}{1-a} \sum_{\theta=0}^{\infty} (\frac{b\psi}{1-a})^\theta c(T). \tag{35}$$

The right side of (35) is convergent, if $\frac{b\psi}{1-a} < 1$.

3.   *Brief Observation on the Steady-State Method*

Professor Stone's method of arriving at the terminal investment, output, and consequently capital stock is a major contribution in this field, for it provides a partial answer to one of the knotty questions related to the length of time horizon and truncation point. However, the essential difficulties remain, including such unanswered questions as the following: (i) What are the rates at which the individual components of consumption ought to or will change? (ii) Can these rates be assumed to remain constant? (iii) What criteria were used in arriving at these rates? This question raises the whole issue of the optimal rate of savings and consumption over an infinite horizon for which no satisfactory answer has been found. (iv) Is enough known about the technological changes of the future to use this method with confidence? (v) Are the gestation lags fixed for different sectors and are they uniform within each sector? These questions remain to be studied and solved before Stone's method can be applied in planning models.

However, this method does provide an indication of the appropriate composition of capital structure in the target year, given the current and future techniques of production and the possible or assumed rates of growth of components of future consumption.

VIII. Preference Function

1. *Introduction*

So far we have considered the derivation of plan targets from studies of consumer behavior or individual preferences. The targets were set in terms of fixed levels of consumption or capital stock. These can be used as targets in feasibility or consistency planning, which characterize most of the mandatory national plans. They can also be used in optimality planning where the objective may be to minimize the utilization of resources. However, in optimality planning it is very advantageous to have targets expressed in the form of social or national preference functions. These allow flexibility in preferences and accommodate varying marginal preferences.

We have already discussed the problems involved in deriving social preference functions from individual preferences of the nationals of a country. An alternative procedure would be to assume that social preference can be expressed by a limited number of representatives of the population. They may be responsible political leaders or some other selected knowledgeable persons.

There are two ways of obtaining preferences of the representatives. One, to be discussed first, is through direct, face-to-face interviews. The other is a roundabout method whereby the views of each representative are kept anonymous but are made known to other representatives so as to elicit more considered preferences from them. This method is discussed in section IX.

2. *Linear Preference Function*

Interviewing a responsible person to construct a linear preference function may take the form of asking him to indicate how much of one target variable he considers equivalent to a certain amount of another target variable. Suppose that for the first two target variables, x_1 and x_2, the interviewee states that he is indifferent between v_1 units of the first and v_2 units of the second; then the preference function can be stated in the linear form as $\Phi = \dfrac{x_1}{v_1} + \dfrac{x_2}{v_2}$, expressing the obvious fact that the relative weights of the two variables are in inverse proportion to numbers of their equivalent units. This procedure can be repeated successively by taking the second and third variables, the third and fourth variables, and so on. However, when there are more than two variables in the target, we have to check whether the relative weights are consistent. For example, if the interviewee is indifferent between $1x_1$ and $2x_2$ and again between $1x_2$ and $3x_3$, it should be checked whether he is indifferent between $1x_1$ and $6x_3$ or not. If not, then he should be reminded that his indifferences are inconsistent or intransitive and that he should rethink and revise them to set them right.

Frisch suggests the use of *dichotomic* questions, in which alternative sets of values of two of the variables are compared with a view to fixing two indifferent sets of values. He describes the use of dichotomic questioning in the following way:

> We adopt the rule that no answer "indifferent" shall ever be accepted. Only clear answers "yes" or "no" should be taken into consideration. By changing successively the value of one of the variables in the question, we can obtain an indifference range or threshold range . . . the midpoint of the indifference range will enter the computations.[36]

When more than one person is interviewed, an average of the indifferent sets of values may be taken. For this purpose the geometric average will be appropriate. For example, if v_1^i, v_2^i, $..,v_n^i$ are the quantities of n target goods among which ith person interviewed is indifferent, then the quantities among which all the individuals interviewed may be treated indifferent would be, respectively,

$$\left(\prod_i v_1^i\right)^{\frac{1}{k}}, \left(\prod_i v_2^i\right)^{\frac{1}{k}}, \ldots, \left(\prod_i v_n^i\right)^{\frac{1}{k}} \qquad (36)$$

where $k = \Sigma_i$.

Now if the indifference levels of the n target variables derived from interviewing one responsible person or a group of responsible persons is v_1, $v_2, \ldots v_n$, then the linear preference function can be written as

$$\Phi = \frac{x_1}{v_1} + \frac{x_2}{v_2}, \ldots \frac{x_n}{v_n}. \qquad (37)$$

Van Eijk and Sandee have used a linear preference function derived on the lines stated above.[37]

3.   *Quadratic Preference Function*

In order to avoid constant marginal preferences, the form of the function ought to be nonlinear, whether quadratic or of another form. Perhaps the only economist who has made a serious attempt at constructing such a function from data derived from interviewing responsible politicians is Frisch. We briefly outline in appendix 2.G his method of constructing a quadratic preference function,[38] for which Frisch employs what he calls distributive questions. In such a question, a certain total is assumed given, and the interviewed person is required to state how he would like to see this total distributed over a number of items that together shall make up the given total. This may be related to, for instance, the distribution of gross national product or gross investment.

Denoting the value indicated by the responsible person for the jth component of the ith aggregative item by ϕ_j^{Si} j=1, ..., N and i=1, ..., M, and using what he calls diagonal mean regression, Frisch fits a quadratic function of the following form:

$$F = \sum_j (v_j x_j + \tfrac{1}{2} w_j x_j^2), \qquad (38)$$

where

$$v_j = \frac{\overline{\phi_j}}{\sqrt{m_{jj}}}$$

$$w_j = \frac{-1}{\sqrt{m_{jj}}}$$

and (38 cont'd)

$$\bar{\phi}_j = \frac{\sum\limits_{i=1}^{M} \phi_j^{S_i}}{\sum\limits_{i=1}^{M} S_i}$$

and

$$m_{jj} = \sum\limits_{i=1}^{M} (\phi_j^{S_i} - \bar{\phi}_j)^2$$

$$j = 1, \ldots, N.$$

The derivation of the above formula is briefly described in appendix 2.G. Frisch's method is based on the theory of consumer behavior and uses plausible statistical methods. In optimizing planning models, this may be the method used in the future. However, this method requires too much reliance on the discretion, intelligence, and foresight of politicians. Moreover, it does not eliminate the necessity of making forecasts about future demand for consumption and technological developments. If their preferences or indifferences are to be relevant, politicians must be well informed about future changes in the pattern of consumption and technological developments.

One great advantage of Frisch's method of constructing preference function is that the politicians become intimately involved in the planning process. Besides educating the planners, this procedure may enable them to see the process of planning in better perspective and feel more responsible for its successful implementation.

IX. The Delphi Method[39]

1. *Introduction*

Another method of eliciting and refining group judgment, the Delphi technique, has been recently developed. The rationale for the method is the age-old adage, "two heads are better than one," when exact knowledge is not available.

There are three types of information that can play a role in decision making: (i) knowledge, that is, highly confirmed assertions for which there is a great deal of evidence; (ii) speculation with little or no evidential backing; and (iii) opinion, namely, a broad area of information for which there is some validity but not sufficiently confirmed to warrant being called "knowledge." The methods of dealing with material of the first type, knowledge, are well established except for some problematic details such as the application of statistical measures where underlying distributions are unknown. Speculation is very difficult to apply any systematic analysis to and is best avoided whenever possible. The third type, opinion, is primarily investigated by the Delphi method.

2.   *The Delphi Method*

The usual way of pooling individual opinions is by face-to-face discussion. A great many studies in the past two decades have demonstrated some serious difficulties with this method.[40] The three most serious drawbacks of face-to-face discussion are the following: (i) Influence of dominant individuals—group opinion is highly influenced by the person who talks the most, or who has a dominant personality. There is little correlation between effusive oratory and knowledge. (ii) Semantic noise—most of the communication in a face-to-face discussion is related to individual and group interests rather than to problem solving. This kind of communication may have the appearance of being problem oriented but may often be irrelevant and biasing. (iii) Group pressure for conformity—it has been demonstrated that distortion of individual judgment can occur under group pressure.[41]

These major drawbacks of face-to-face discussion prevent to a large extent the formation of a reliable group opinion. Experiments at the RAND Corporation have shown that, after face-to-face discussion, the group response is less accurate than a simple median of individual estimates (without discussion). The Delphi method is a systematic device to reduce or eliminate the drawbacks of face-to-face discussion in the formation of group opinion.

The Delphi procedures have three main features: (i) anonymity; (ii) controlled feedback; and (iii) statistical group response. Anonymity is effected by the use of questionnaires or other communication channels such as on-line computer communication. This is a way of reducing the effect of dominant individuals, since the respondents do not know each other and the responses remain anonymous.

Controlled feedback is carried out through a sequence of rounds between which a summary of the results of the previous round are communicated to the participants. By reducing semantic noise, this device enables the individual participant to consider the responses of all other participants and thus to become acquainted with other opinions and better informed. It also enables him to reconsider objectively his own response at each round.

Use of a statistical definition of the group response reduces group pressure for conformity, as it is not necessary to have consensus or concurrence among the participants. At the end of the exercise there may still be a spread in the individual opinions. Furthermore, the statistical group response is a device to ensure that the opinion of every participant is represented in the final response.

The Delphi method has several advantages. It requires much less effort for a participant to respond to a well-designed questionnaire than to participate in a conference or to write and present a paper. The feedback can be stimulating and instructive to the participants. The use of systematic procedures with anonymity and feedbacks tends to make the Delphi method very objective, in fact as objective as the formation of group opinion can be. Furthermore, Dalkey says the following:

> And, finally, anonymity and group response allow a sharing of responsibility that is refreshing and that releases from respondents inhibitions. I can state from my own experience, and also from the experience of many other practitioners, that the results of a Delphi exercise are subject to greater acceptance on the part of the group than are the consensuses arrived at by more direct forms of interaction.[42]

2. *The Delphi Method and Target Setting*

The Delphi method can be used in situations where exact knowledge is not available and where decisions have to be based on rational, well-informed, expert opinions. Most often a similar situation is faced in setting plan targets; hence the Delphi technique can be used here, also.

In the preceding section we have seen that in Frisch's method of constructing a preference function, questions are asked to a responsible politician or politicians in face-to-face interviews. This has its own advantages; the planner in the course of asking questions may also educate the politicians and may indicate the pitfalls involved in their thinking and answers. However, in the process of educating politicians, there is also the risk that the planners may influence opinions and possibly make the politicians state what the planners themselves want. This may be advantageous, but then the purpose and objectivity of the inquiry is lost.

The Delphi method can be used in target setting in several ways. One way may be to proceed with the distributive questions of the type discussed in the preceding section. The respondents may include, besides political leaders, academicians, industrialists, and other men of experience and knowledge.

The questionnaire related to the plan targets is to be prepared in specific terms in order to elicit various types of information such as upper and lower limits on the magnitudes of certain target items, the relative or the absolute magnitude of these and other items, the inclusion or noninclusion of some other items, and qualitative aspects of some nonquantifiable items. The questionnaire may also require the respondents to state factors which they consider important and to furnish information regarding the kind of data which would enable them to arrive at a better appraisal of these factors.

After the questionnaire of the type mentioned above has been prepared, it should be distributed to the respondents. When these questionnaires are returned, the results should be analyzed and summarized, the required information should be collected, and the relevant factors suggested should be examined. A second questionnaire should be prepared on the basis of answers received, information required, and relevant factors suggested to be included. This questionnaire, along with the summary and analysis of the first round, should be distributed again to the respondents. The second-round questionnaire may be more detailed than the first one and may contain information to correct misconceptions about empirical factors or theoretical assumptions underlying the first questionnaire. In communicating the summary and analysis of the first-round answers, the identities of the respondents remain concealed.

This procedure of distributing questionnaires and controlling feedback should be continued until the answers of the respondents become fairly stable. The final value of the answer may be determined by using some averaging procedure of the answers in the final round.

Thus the distribution values of the illustration in the preceding subsection may be represented by the average values of the final answers of respondents for each aggregate "summative" item. A preference function along the lines suggested by Frisch can then be constructed.

The Delphi method, with repeated feedback and successive improvement of the questionnaire, makes the elicitation of expert, group opinion more scientific and objective. It may be claimed that there are good chances of reaching better decisions in the general area of informed opinion and value judgments. However, the result will depend on the objectivity and the ability of the respondents and on how far they represent the national preference.

Appendix 2.A

Inevitability of Value Judgments in Formulating a Social Welfare Function

The purpose of this appendix is to show that a social welfare function necessarily involves value judgments.

Let there be k individuals and m commodities. Let x_{ir} be the amount of rth commodity of the ith individual, $(r = 1, \ldots, m)$, $(i = 1, \ldots, k)$. x_{ir} is negative if it is input and positive if it is output.

$$x_r = \sum_{i=1}^{k} x_{ir} \qquad r = 1, \ldots, m. \tag{1}$$

Let the technical production conditions be given by the following function:

$$f(x_1, x_2, \ldots x_m) = 0. \tag{2}$$

Let the utility function of the individual i be given by

$$\omega_i = \omega_i(x_{i1}, x_{i2}, \ldots x_{im}). \tag{3}$$

Utility levels of all other individuals being given the utility of ith individual is maximized by maximizing (3) subject to (2). This gives

$$\frac{\partial \omega_i}{\partial x_{ir}} : \frac{\partial \omega_i}{\partial x_{is}} = \frac{\partial f}{\partial x_r} : \frac{\partial f}{\partial x_s} \quad \begin{array}{l} \text{for } i=1, 2 \ldots, k \\ r=1, 2 \ldots, m \\ s=1, 2 \ldots, m. \end{array} \tag{4}$$

In (1), (2), and (4), there are m + mk variables (m x_r's and mk x_{ir}'s). And there are m equations in (1), 1 in (2) and k(m−1) in (4). Thus the number of equations is (k − 1) less than the number of unknowns. These can only be supplied on the basis of definite assumptions regarding the way in which different individuals enter into the welfare function.

The above conditions are derived, ignoring all the awkward and troublesome aspects associated with rigidities, lumpiness, indivisibilities, and other frictions. They need not be discussed here. The important aspect to note is that we are short of as many equations as there are individuals in excess of unity. The above conditions assure us that we are on one optimum point on the "generalized contract locus," from which there are no possible movements which are advantageous to every individual. But there may exist an infinity of such positions, ranging from a situation in which all the advantage is enjoyed by one individual to one in which all the advantage is enjoyed by another individual. Thus without a well-defined community welfare function—W—involving necessarily an interpersonal comparison of utility, it is impossible to decide which of these points is best. "In terms of a given set of ethical notions which defines a welfare function, the best point on the generalized contract locus can be determined, and only then."[43] To show this formally, let the levels of well-being of different individuals in the system be expressed by writing in an implicit form:

$$F(\omega_1, \omega_2, \ldots \omega_k) = 0. \qquad (5)$$

This means that, if the utility levels of all individuals except that of one individual are specified, this is uniquely determined by (5). The essential shape of this function depends upon the technological and other assumed restraints of the system as well as upon the tastes of different individuals. If we have a given definite welfare function,

$$W = W(\omega_1, \omega_2, \ldots \omega_k), \qquad (6)$$

then we are to maximize (6) subject to (5). The first order condition of equilibrium takes the form

$$\frac{W_i}{W_j} = \frac{F_i}{F_j} \quad i, j, = 1, \ldots, k. \qquad (7)$$

This gives us the missing $(k-1)$ conditions of equilibrium and the equilibrium is seen to be finally determinate. The essence of the dilemma is that, in order to attain a determinate optimizing system, a definite welfare function involving ethical notions and value judgments is needed. There is no escape from it.

Appendix 2.B

Inconsistency of Majority Voting

If all the individuals had identical preferences, the problem of majority preference would disappear; the social and individual choices would coincide. Since this is seldom the case, the social preference has to be the majority preference. That there may not be a consistent majority preference was shown by Condorcet[44] in the second half of the eighteenth century. The paradox of majority voting and social choice, however, was discussed most sharply by Arrow in 1951. His elegant and precise analysis has since been followed by a great many efforts to prove or disprove his thesis. Arrow's analysis can be considered pure in the sense that it does not contain any elements of interpersonal comparisons or cardinal measurability of utilities. By introducing small doses of either of these, some social choice becomes possible. For example, Coleman[45] has attempted to formulate social choice by considering intensities of preferences, and Lieberman[46] and Sawyers,[47] by considering a system of commensuration scales. We examine the latter in the text. Here we outline Arrow's rather well-known paradox.

Arrow first lays down some plausible and persuasive conditions for collective rationality, which can be stated as follows:

(i) Stability of individual orderings. There must be at least three alternatives. The individual preferences between pairs of alternatives must be the same in the admissible set of individual orderings as in any other set of individual orderings.

(ii) Positive association of individual and social orderings. The social ordering must respond nonnegatively to changes in individual orderings.

(iii) Independence of irrelevant alternatives. The elimination of some alternatives must not alter the social ordering.

(iv) Sovereignty of individuals. Individuals can choose freely among all alternatives, and social ordering reflects individual orderings. Or, there is profile of individual orderings for each social ordering.

(v) Nondictatorship. No one individual ordering determines the social ordering, regardless of the orderings of other individuals.

A rather short proof of Arrow's theorem can be given along that sketched by Luce and Raiffa.[48]

Let N be the set of total number of individuals and V the minimal decisive set. Let j be a specific individual in V. Then the set N can be partitioned in three subsets, $N = \{j\} + (V - \{j\}) + (N - V)$. Suppose the preference orderings of the three exclusive sets is as follows for three alternatives, x, y, and z:

$\{j\}$	$(V-\{j\})$	$(N-V)$
x	z	y
y	x	z
z	y	x

Society prefers x against y, that is, xPy, since x is preferred to y by the set V, $V = \{j\} \cup (V-\{j\})$, and V is decisive. And society does not prefer z to y, $z\bar{P}y$, since z is preferred to y only by $(V-\{j\})$, whereas the minimal decisive set is V. Hence by transitivity, xPy, $z\bar{P}y$, so xPz. But j is the only individual preferring x to z. This shows that even if there are two individuals in N and the society must consist of at least two individuals, j is a dictator. By introducing more alternatives, it can be shown that j is a dictator for all pairs. But this is impossible as it contradicts the conditions.

Arrow's position is impeccable under the conditions specified. No rational social ordering is possible on wholly and perfectly *objective* bases of impossibility of both interpersonal comparisons and cardinal utilities. Some criticisms have been raised against Arrow's conditions. A crucial one relates to the independence of irrelevant alternatives. Little has argued that "We have, so to speak, a new world and a new order; and we do not demand correspondence between the change in the world and the change in the order."[49] Arrow[50] has pointed out that decision processes which are independent of irrelevant alternatives have a strong practical advantage, as implied by the electoral system and the decentralized market mechanism. Nonetheless, even the circumstance that the social welfare be identified with majority preference and linked with independence of irrelevant variables implies some value judgments. Furthermore, Luce and Raiffa have stated that Arrow's impossibility theorem can be drawn as a corollary from the theory of decision making under uncertainty.

Appendix 2.C

Game-Theoretic Approach

Game theory deals with decision making in situations involving conflicts of interests. As such it ought to provide the basis for group decisions or social choice. Undoubtedly, the main thrust of research has been in this direction. The number of contributions in the form of papers and books is more than a thousand. A selected bibliography with some comments is given by Schubik[51] in a highly readable book of selections edited by him, *Game Theory and Related Approaches to Social Behavior.* A recent paper by Plott[52] contains a list of contributions which are directly related to group decision making.

Of all the various game theoretic models, cooperative games without side payments are more purposeful in target setting, for these avoid the necessity of interpersonal utility comparisons. Some new results were announced in this field by Aumann and Peleg[53] in 1960. Recently Wilson[54] has utilized their findings in analyzing social choice. A brief sketch of this line of approach is given below.

Suppose that there are m individuals and n alternatives. Suppose further that the social choice is made by majority rule. Any combination of alternatives may be chosen. Let the set of all combinations of alternatives be denoted by S. Let u_i (s) be the utility of sth combination to the ith individual. When decisions are made under risk, it is assumed that each utility function u_i is unique up to a positive linear transformation. In this case, the expected utility to the ith individual from the group choice is

$$u_i(p) = \sum_{s \varepsilon s} p(s)u_i(s),$$

where p(s) is the probability of combination s of alternatives occurring (that is, being chosen). Under majority rule any majority coalition of the individuals can ensure any combination of alternatives. Hence if individuals make their choices under randomization, then the set of individual utilities from different combination of alternatives is

$$H = \{\underline{u}\},$$

where the ith element of $\underline{u}$ represents the expected utility of the ith

individual, viz., $u_i(p) = \sum_{s \varepsilon s} p(s)u_i(s)$.

What would be the social choice of alternatives can be explained in the following way. For any set H of attainable alternatives, a solution V(H) is a subset of H, such that (i) V(H) dominates all other alternatives and (ii) no element of V(H) dominates any other element belonging to it.

A numerical illustration of the solution procedure has been given by Wilson[55] in several of his articles. It has been shown that a solution reached is stable. However, a multiplicity of majority coalitions may form. Which specific solution will result can best be analyzed in terms of historical factors. Each solution is stable in the sense that any alternative outside it is dominated by some alternative contained in it.

The above is a very brief sketch of cooperative games without side payments. In a 1964 survey, Aumann[56] has given an account of research analysis of game-theoretic approach to collective decision making. Some remarks may be made about the prospects of practical application of this approach.

First, as in some other decision-making models, there are the problems of specifying cardinal utilities or preference indices. However, in most game-theoretic models a solution is obtainable only when utilities are associated with probability distribution. In problems of national choice it may be difficult if not impossible to accomplish it.

Second, as it is unthinkable to have a millions-person game theory for national choice, the number of individuals which should take part in any decision making using a game-theoretic approach must be small. Yet games of more than four persons become very difficult to solve, and in certain formulations methods of solutions have not been found. How these individuals should be chosen is, in turn, another decision-making problem. However, the choice of suitable persons is a problem not only in the game-theoretic approach but also is common to some other approaches discussed below.

Game-theoretic models often contain a multiplicity of solutions. In problems of national importance only one solution can be used. In some cases these solutions may form another game which may contain a unique solution; in others this may not be possible. In any case, further assumptions and probably value judgments would be required to find a unique solution if any.

Perhaps a more relevant comment is related to the history of the evolution of the theory. Game theory started as a normative approach and derived elegant results in two-person and zero-sum games. However, not very many decisive results were obtained or are obtainable in n-person games, and so researchers turned more and more toward descriptive theory. But, for decision making regarding national objectives, what is required is normative theory of games. In this respect two-person zero-sum theory is irrelevant, and n-person theory is too inadequate as a basis for national and social choice.

Appendix 2.D

Johansen's Method of Demand Projection

Johansen has presented a simple method of deriving all direct and cross-price elasticities, using what Frisch calls flexibility of money. We shall first outline Johansen's derivation and then discuss Frisch's derivation of flexibility of money. Johansen proceeds as follows:

Let the budget equation be

$$y = \sum_i p_i y_i, \tag{1}$$

where y is the total income of a group of consumers and y_i is the amount of consumption of commodity i (y and y_i may be considered equivalently per consumer magnitudes).

Letting the utility function be of the additive type,

$$u = \sum_i u_i(y_i) \tag{2}$$

Utility maximization under the budget constraint then yields the condition

$$u_i'(y_i) - \lambda p_i = 0 \quad i = 1, \ldots, n, \tag{3}$$

where λ is the Lagrange multiplier and can be interpreted as the utility of money. Solving for y_i's and λ, the result is

$$y_i = y_i(p_1, \ldots, p_n, y) \quad i = 1, \ldots, n \tag{4}$$

$$\lambda = \lambda(p_1, \ldots, p_n, y).$$

Assuming that prices are equal to one in the initial situation, (1) and (3) are differentiated partially with respect to P_j, (j=1, . . . , n) to get

$$\sum_i \frac{\partial y_i}{\partial p_j} + y_j = 0 \tag{5}$$

$$u_i'' \frac{\partial y_i}{\partial p_j} - \lambda - \frac{\partial \lambda}{\partial p_j} = 0 \quad \text{when } i = j \tag{6}$$

and $$u_i'' \frac{\partial y_i}{\partial p_j} \quad \frac{\partial \lambda}{\partial p_j} = 0 \quad \text{when } i \neq j.$$

In (5) it is assumed that total income is independent of prices.

Differentiating equations (1) and (3) with respect to total expenditure y results in

$$\sum_i \frac{\partial y_i}{\partial y} = 1 \tag{7}$$

$$u_i^{''} \frac{\partial y_i}{\partial y} - \frac{\partial \lambda}{\partial y} = 0 \tag{8}$$

or

$$\frac{\partial y_i}{\partial y} = \frac{\partial \lambda}{\partial y} \cdot \frac{1}{u_i^{''}}, \quad i = 1, \ldots n. \tag{8a}$$

As the utility index is arbitrary, any scale of measurement can be chosen. The following normalization is chosen to simplify the formulae:

$$\sum \frac{1}{u_i^{''}} = -1. \tag{9}$$

Now summing (8a) over i's and using (7) we get

$$\frac{\partial \lambda}{\partial y} = -1. \tag{10}$$

Denoting flexibility of the marginal utility of money by $\check{\lambda}$, we have

$$\check{\lambda} = \frac{\partial \lambda}{\partial y} \cdot \frac{y}{\lambda} = -\frac{y}{\lambda}. \tag{11}$$

From equations (6) and (8a) we have, using equation (10),

$$\frac{\partial y_i}{\partial p_j} = -\frac{\partial y_i}{\partial y} \left(\lambda + \frac{\partial \lambda}{\partial p_j} \right) \qquad \text{when } i = j \tag{12}$$

$$\frac{\partial y_i}{\partial p_j} = \frac{\partial y_i}{\partial y} \frac{\partial \lambda}{\partial p_j} \qquad \text{when } i \neq j.$$

By summing (12) over i and substituting from equations (5) and (7), we have

$$\frac{\partial \lambda}{\partial p_j} = y_j - \lambda \frac{\partial y_j}{\partial y}. \tag{13}$$

Substituting equation (13) in (12), we have Johansen's main formula:

$$\frac{\partial y_i}{\partial p_j} = \frac{\partial y_i}{\partial y} \ (\lambda + y_j - \lambda \frac{\partial y_j}{\partial \lambda} \ ) \quad \text{when } i = j$$

$$(14)$$

$$\frac{\partial y_i}{\partial p_j} = \frac{\partial y_i}{\partial \lambda} \ (y_j - \lambda \frac{\partial y_j}{\partial y}).$$

Formulae (14) give all $\partial y_i/\partial p_j$, in terms of $\partial y_i/\partial y$, the quantities y_j consumed in the base year, and the marginal utility of money λ corresponding to the utility index implied by normalization in equation (9).

The value of λ can be obtained in two ways. First, if an estimate for the flexibility of marginal utility of money is available, equation (11) can be used. Second, if estimates of one of $\partial y_i/\partial p_i$ and the corresponding $\partial y_i/\partial y$ are available, the value of λ can be derived from the first equation of (14). Now if we know the quantities $y_1, \ldots y_n$ consumed in the initial period and by empirical observation we estimate the coefficients $\partial \lambda_i/\partial y$ $(i = 1, \ldots, n)$ and one of the coefficients $\partial \lambda_i/\partial p_i$, then we can obtain all the coefficients $\partial y_i/\partial p_i$ from (14). From these, all price elasticities of demands for all individual goods can be derived. The derivatives of demand with respect to prices or the corresponding elasticities can be used to estimate the demand for individual goods in the neighborhood of the point for which these are derived.

Frisch's Derivation of Price Elasticities

Let $x_1, x_2, \ldots, x_n$ be quantities of goods possessed by the representative consumer and let

$$u = u(x_1, x_2, \ldots, x_n) \qquad (1)$$

be an indicator of total utility. Let $p_1, p_2, \ldots, p_n$ be the prices at which the representative consumer can buy the goods and let

$$p_1 x_1 + p_2 x_2 + \ldots + p_n x_n = y \qquad (2)$$

be the budget equation; then the equilibrium of the consumer is given by

$$\frac{u_1}{p_1} = \frac{u_2}{p_2} = \ldots = \frac{u_n}{p_n} = \lambda, \qquad (3)$$

where $u_i = \partial u/\partial x_i \ i = 1, \ldots, n$ and λ is the Lagrange multiplier which equals the marginal utility of money. From equation (2) and the first $n - 1$ equations of equation (3), the demand functions can be written as

$$x_i = x_i(p_1, p_2, \ldots, p_n, y). \tag{4}$$

The demand elasticities with respect to prices are

$$e_{ik} = \frac{\partial x_i}{\partial p_k} \cdot \frac{p_k}{x_i} \qquad \begin{aligned} & i = 1, 2, \ldots, n \\ & k = 1, 2, \ldots, n. \end{aligned} \tag{5}$$

The demand elasticities with respect to income are

$$E_i = \frac{\partial x_i}{\partial y} \; \frac{y}{x_i} \qquad i = 1, \ldots, n. \tag{6}$$

The budget proportions are

$$a_i = \frac{p_i x_i}{y}. \tag{7}$$

Consider the equations that define the marginal utilities as functions of quantities, that is,

$$u_i = u_i(x_1, \ldots, x_n) \quad i = 1, \ldots, n. \tag{8}$$

The inverse functions, that is, the x_i as functions of $u_1, \ldots, u_n$, can be written as

$$x_i = x_i(u_1, \ldots, u_n) \quad i = 1, \ldots, n. \tag{9}$$

Let us denote, as Frisch does, the elasticity of marginal utility of good i with respect to good k by $\tilde{u}_{ik}$, so that

$$\tilde{u}_{ik} = \frac{\partial u_i}{\partial x_k} \cdot \frac{x_k}{u_i} \qquad \begin{aligned} & i = 1, 2, \ldots, n; \\ & k = 1, 2, \ldots, n. \end{aligned} \tag{10}$$

Correspondingly, let us denote the elasticity of good i with respect to the marginal utility of good k by $\tilde{x}_{ik}$, so that

$$\tilde{x}_{ik} = \frac{\partial x_i}{\partial u_k} \cdot \frac{u_k}{x_i} \qquad \begin{array}{l} i = 1, 2, \ldots, n; \\ k = 1, 2, \ldots, n. \end{array} \qquad (11)$$

Differentiating (8) w.r.t. u_k on the assumption that each of the magnitudes $x_1, \ldots x_n$ is a function of $u_1, \ldots u_n$, we get

$$\sum_{s=1}^{n} \tilde{u}_{is} \; \tilde{x}_{sk} = \delta_{ik} \qquad \begin{array}{l} i = 1, \ldots, n; \\ k = 1, \ldots, n, \end{array} \qquad (12)$$

where δ_{ik} is the Kronecker delta, $\delta_{ik} = 1$ when $i = k$, $\delta_{ij} = 0$ when $i \neq k$; equation (12) shows that the matrix $\tilde{u}_{is}$ is the inverse of the matrix $\tilde{x}_{si}$, and vice versa.

The relations between $\tilde{u}_{ik}$ and the second-order derivatives $u'_{ik} = \frac{\partial u_i}{\partial x_k}$ or $u'_{ik} = \partial^2 u/\partial x_i \partial x_k$ are easily seen to be

$$u'_{ik} = \frac{u_i \tilde{u}_{ik}}{x_k} \qquad i, k = 1, 2, \ldots, n. \qquad (13)$$

Similarly, the derivatives $x'_{ik} = \partial x_i / \partial u_k$ are related to the elasticities $\tilde{x}_{ik}$ by

$$x'_{ik} = \frac{x_i \tilde{x}_{ik}}{u_k} \qquad i, k = 1, 2, \ldots, n. \qquad (14)$$

From equations (12), (13), and (14) we get

$$\Sigma u'_{is} \; x'_{sk} = \delta_{ik}. \qquad (15)$$

Hence the matrix x'_{sk} is the inverse of u'_{is} and, consequently, symmetric because u'_{is} is symmetric, since it is a second-order derivative. This means that

$$\frac{u_i \tilde{u}_{ik}}{x_k} = \frac{u_k \tilde{u}_{ki}}{x_i} \qquad i, k = 1, 2, \ldots, n. \qquad (16)$$

If we introduce the equilibrium conditions (3) in (16), we have

$$a_i \tilde{x}_{ik} = a_k \tilde{x}_{ki} \qquad i, k = 1, \ldots, n. \qquad (17)$$

The flexibility of the marginal utility of money, or, shorter, the money flexibility and the partial flexibilities of the marginal utility of money are defined respectively by

$$\check{\lambda} = \frac{\partial \lambda}{\partial y} \cdot \frac{y}{\lambda}$$

$$\lambda_k = \frac{\partial \lambda}{\partial p_k} \cdot \frac{p_k}{\lambda} \qquad k = 1, 2, \ldots n. \quad (18)$$

Now differentiating the equilibrium conditions $u_i/p_i = \lambda$, $i=1, \ldots, n$, with respect to y and p_k, $k = 1, \ldots, n$, the above concepts can be shown to be connected with the demand elasticities by

$$\sum_{s=1}^{n} \bar{u}_{is} E_s = \check{\lambda} \qquad\qquad i = 1, \ldots, n. \quad (19)$$

$$\sum_{s=1}^{n} \bar{u}_{is} e_{sk} = \lambda_k + \delta_{ik} \qquad i, k = 1, \ldots, n. \quad (20)$$

From equation (19) and (20) we get, remembering, that $\bar{u}_{is}$ is the inverse of $\tilde{x}_{si}$,

$$E_i = \check{\lambda} \sum_{s=1}^{n} x_{is} \qquad\qquad (21)$$

$$e_{ik} = \tilde{x}_{ik} + \lambda_k \sum_{s=1}^{n} \tilde{x}_{is}. \qquad\qquad (22)$$

Equation (21) can be written as

$$a_k E_k = \check{\lambda} \sum_{s=1}^{n} a_k \tilde{x}_{ks} \qquad\qquad (23)$$

$$1 = \check{\lambda} \sum_{s=1}^{n} a_s \tilde{x}_{sk}. \qquad\qquad (24)$$

The left-hand side of equation (24) can be obtained by differentiating the budget equation (2) by income y and introducing income elasticities and budget proportions, and the right-hand side, by using equation (17). Hence

$$\check{\lambda} = \frac{1}{\sum\limits_{s=1}^{n} a_s \tilde{x}_{sk}} . \tag{25}$$

Further differentiating the budget equation (2) with respect to p_k and introducing the price elasticities and budget proportions, we get

$$\sum_{s=1}^{n} a_s e_{sk} = -a_k.$$

Using equation (22) in the above we have, after introducing equation (25),

$$\lambda_k = -(a_k + \sum_{s=1}^{n} a_s \tilde{x}_{sk}) \check{\lambda} \tag{26}$$

$$= -a_k (\check{\lambda} + E_k),$$

the last equality being obtained by using (17) and (21). Using equation (26) in (22) and introducing equation (21) we have,

$$e_{ik} = \tilde{x}_{ik} - E_i (a_k + \sum_{s=1}^{n} a_s \tilde{x}_{sk})$$

$$= \tilde{x}_{ik} - E_i a_k (1 + \frac{E_k}{\check{\lambda}}) \quad \text{as in (26)} \tag{27}$$

and

$$e_{ii} = \tilde{x}_{ii} - a_i E_i (1 + \frac{E_i}{\check{\lambda}}). \tag{28}$$

All the above formulae have been derived in a general way without putting any restrictions on the nature of utility of goods. The main assumption of independent utilities or want-independence of goods is now made. Good i is want-independent of all other goods if $\tilde{x}_{ik} = 0$ for all $k \neq$ i. Or, equivalently, good i is want-independent of all other goods if $\tilde{u}_{ik} = 0$ for all $k \neq$ i. It can be easily shown, as Professor Frisch does, that the two definitions are the same. Under independence, equation (21) reduces to

$$\tilde{x}_{ii} = \frac{E_i}{\overset{\vee}{\lambda}}. \tag{29}$$

By introducing equation (29) in (28), we have

$$e_{ii} = -E_i \left(a_i - \frac{1 - a_i E_i}{\overset{\vee}{\lambda}} \right). \tag{30}$$

For $\tilde{x}_{ik} = 0$, we have from equation (27)

$$e_{ik} = -E_i a_k \left(1 + \frac{E_k}{\overset{\vee}{\lambda}} \right). \tag{31}$$

These are the equations which Johansen refers to in his derivation of elasticities described in the text.

Appendix 2.E

Determination of Terminal Capital Stock

In this appendix we derive the terminal capital stock, taking into account inventories, government expenditure, and exports and imports, and introducing gestation lag of more than one year. For the sake of brevity of notations, we use vectors and matrices. Capital letters A and B denote structural matrices of current and capital flows, respectively, and the symbols with bars underneath denote vectors of corresponding elements; for example, $\underline{x}$ is a vector with ith elements $x_i, i = 1, \ldots, n$.

To include the variables explicitly, the macro identity can be expressed as

$$\underline{x}(t) = A\underline{x}(t) + \underline{i}(t) + \underline{r}(t) + \underline{v}(t) + \underline{c}(t) + \underline{g}(t) + \underline{e}(t) - \underline{m}(t). \tag{1}$$

Here $\underline{i}(t)$ stands for new investment, $\underline{r}(t)$ for replacement of depreciated capacity, and $\underline{v}(t)$, $\underline{c}(t)$, $\underline{g}(t)$, $\underline{e}(t)$, and $\underline{m}(t)$ for inventories, private consumption, government use, exports and imports, respectively.

For the sake of simplicity, we assume that the total investment of output of ith sector per unit of output of jth sector b_{ij} consists of three parts, $^1b_{ij}$, $^2b_{ij}$, and $^3b_{ij}$; $^1b_{ij}$ represents the amount of output i needed for investment per unit of output j in a project which will begin to yield in the following year, and $^2b_{ij}$ and $^3b_{ij}$ represent the same magnitude for projects which will begin to produce in the second and third years, respectively. We express these coefficients without association with time, which implies also that techniques of production remain constant. We thus have $B = {}^1B + {}^2B + {}^3B$.

In practice the per unit requirements of output for new investment may be different from replacement so that the b_{ij}'s may be different for the two. For the sake of simplicity again we shall assume that they are similar and put them together and denote $\Delta \underline{k}(t) = \underline{i}(t) + \underline{r}(t)$. Now we can write

$$\Delta \underline{k}(t) = {}^1B[\underline{x}(t+1) - \underline{x}(t)] + {}^2B[\underline{x}(t+2) - \underline{x}(t+1)]$$

$$+ {}^3B[\underline{x}(t+3) - \underline{x}(t+2)]. \tag{2}$$

The inventory accumulation of output i in year t will be assumed to be a proportion of s_{ij} of the increase in output j in year $t + 1$. Thus

$$\underline{v}(t) = S[\underline{x}(t+1) - \underline{x}(t)], \tag{3}$$

where S is the matrix formed of coefficients s_{ij}.

Sectoral consumption, government use, and exports and imports in the postterminal years may be assumed to increase at common constant rates ψ, γ, ε, and μ, respectively, over their levels in the terminal year, so that

$$\underline{c}(t) = \underline{c}(T)(1 + \psi)^{t-T}$$

$$\underline{g}(t) = \underline{g}(T)(1 + \gamma)^{t-T}$$

$$\underline{e}(t) = \underline{e}(T)(1 + \varepsilon)^{t-T} \tag{4}$$

$$\underline{m}(t) = \underline{m}(T)(1 + \mu)^{t-T}.$$

Inserting (2), (3) and (4) in (1), we have

$$\underline{x}(t) = A\underline{x}(t) + {}^1B[\underline{x}(t+1) - \underline{x}(t)] + {}^2B[\underline{x}(t+2) - \underline{x}(t+1)]$$

$$+ {}^3B[\underline{x}(t+3) - \underline{x}(t+2)] + S[\underline{x}(t+1) - \underline{x}(t)] \tag{5}$$

$$+ \underline{c}(T)\,(1+\psi)^{t\text{-}T} + \underline{g}(T)\,(1+\gamma)^{t\text{-}T} + \underline{e}(T)\,(1+\varepsilon)^{t\text{-}T}$$

$$+ m(T)\,(1+\mu)^{t\text{-}T} \qquad t > T. \tag{5 cont'd}$$

A general solution of (5) which is a linear, nonhomogeneous difference equation of order 3 is possible, but we will not attempt it here.

A particular solution of (5) will be the sum of particular solutions with respect to each of the elements in the nonhomogeneous part of (15), namely $\underline{c}(t)$, $\underline{g}(t)$, $\underline{e}(t)$, $\underline{m}(t)$. In order to find a particular solution of $\underline{x}(t)$ with respect to $\underline{c}(t)$, assume $\underline{x}(t) = \underline{q}\psi\,(1 + \psi)^{t\text{-}T}$ and substitute it in (5). Deleting the terms $\underline{g}(T)\,(1 + \gamma)^{t\text{-}T}$, $\underline{e}(T)\,(1 + \varepsilon)^{t\text{-}T}$ and $\underline{m}(T)\,(1 + \mu)^{t\text{-}T}$, and retaining only $\underline{c}(T)\,(1 + \psi)^{t\text{-}T}$ of the elements of the nonhomogeneous terms, we get

$$\underline{q}_\psi = [I - A + (^1B + S)\psi + {}^2B(1 + \psi)\,\psi$$

$$+ {}^3B(1 + \psi)^2\,\psi]^{-1}\,c(T). \tag{6}$$

We can find particular solutions to $\underline{x}(t)$ with respect to $\underline{g}(t)$, $\underline{e}(t)$, and $\underline{m}(t)$ similarly.

A particular solution of (15) is, therefore,

$$\underline{x}(t) = [I - A + (^1B + S)\psi + {}^2B(1 + \psi)\psi$$

$$+ {}^3B(1 + \psi)^2\,\psi]^{-1}\underline{c}(T)\,(1 + \psi)^{t\text{-}T}$$

$$+ [I - A + (^1B + S)\,\gamma + {}^2B(1 + \gamma)\,\gamma$$

$$+ {}^3B(1 + \gamma)^2\gamma]^{-1}\underline{g}(T)(1 + \gamma)^{t\text{-}T}$$

$$+ [I - A + (^1B + S)\varepsilon + {}^2B(1 + \varepsilon)\,\varepsilon$$

$$+ {}^3B(1 + \varepsilon)^2\varepsilon]^{-1}\underline{e}(T)\,(1 + \varepsilon)^{t\text{-}T}$$

$$+ [1 + A + (^1B + S)\mu + {}^2B(1 + \mu)\,\mu$$

$$+ {}^3B(1 + \mu)^2\mu]^{-1}\underline{m}(T)\,(1 + \mu)^{t\text{-}T}$$

$$t = T + 1, T + 2, T + 3. \tag{7}$$

Using (7) back in (1), we get $\underline{x}(T)$ in terms of government use, exports, consumption, and imports, of which the first two may be assumed given exogenously, and the last two may be constrained from below and/or above. The total capital stock in the terminal period can be derived by multiplying the vector of total output by the matrix of capital coefficients:

$$\underline{k}(T) = B\underline{x}(T). \tag{8}$$

$\underline{k}(T)$ thus derived takes into account the growth of output that would be required in the postterminal years over the period of gestation lags.

Appendix 2.F

Expansion of Output and Investment in a Steady-State Model of Exponential Growth in Consumption

The balance equation in the terminal plan year is

$$x_i(T) = \sum_{j=1}^{n} a_{ij} x_j(T) + \Delta k_i(T) + c_i(T)$$

and

$$\Delta k_i(T) = \sum_{j=1}^{n} b_{ij} [x_j(T+1) - x_j(T)] = \sum_{j=1}^{n} b_{ij} \Delta x_j(T)$$

$$c_i(T+t) = c_i(T) (1 + \Psi_i)^t \quad \begin{matrix} i = 1, \ldots, n \\ t = 1, \ldots, \infty. \end{matrix}$$

Using matrix notation, the above can be written

$$\underline{x}(T) = A\underline{x}(T) + \Delta\underline{k}(T) + \underline{c}(T) \tag{1}$$

$$\Delta k(T) = B\Delta\underline{x}(T) \tag{2}$$

$$\underline{c}(T+t) = \underline{c}(T) (I + \hat{\Psi})^t. \tag{3}$$

Here $\hat{\Psi}$ is a diagonal matrix with Ψ_i's on the diagonal.

As in the text, let a first tentative estimation of $\Delta\underline{k}(T)$ be $\Delta\underline{k}(T)^{[1]}$ $= \underline{0}$; then from (1) we get the first approximative estimation of $\underline{x}(T)$,

$$\underline{x}(T)^{[1]} = (I - A)^{-1} \underline{c}(T) \tag{4}$$

and
$$\underline{x}(T+1)^{[1]} = (I - A)^{-1} \underline{c}(T)(1 + \hat{\Psi}). \tag{5}$$

From (4) and (5), a second approximative estimation of $\underline{\Delta k}(T)$ and corresponding approximations of $x(t)$ and $x(T+1)$ are

$$\underline{\Delta k}(T)^{[2]} = B(I - A)^{-1} \hat{\Psi} \underline{c}(T) \tag{6}$$

$$\underline{x}(T)^{[2]} = (I - A)^{-1} [I + B(I - A)^{-1} \hat{\Psi}] \underline{c}(T) \tag{7}$$

$$\underline{x}(T+1)^{[2]} = (I - A)^{-1} [I + B(I - A)^{-1} \hat{\Psi}] \underline{c}(T)(1 + \hat{\Psi}). \tag{8}$$

Using (7) and (8) and (2), we have a third approximative estimation of $\Delta k(T)$,

$$\underline{\Delta k}(T)^{[3]} = B(I - A)^{-1} \hat{\Psi} [I + B(I - A)^{-1} \hat{\Psi}] c(T) \tag{9}$$

$$= B(I - A)^{-1} \hat{\Psi} + [B(I - A)^{-1} \hat{\Psi}]^2 \underline{c}(T). \tag{10}$$

Proceeding in this manner, we get the final estimate of $\underline{\Delta k}(T)$,

$$\underline{\Delta k}(T) = \sum_{\theta=1}^{\infty} [B(I - A)^{-1} \hat{\Psi}]^{\theta} \underline{c}(T). \tag{11}$$

Putting (11) in (1) and (2), we can find $\underline{x}(T)$ and $\underline{k}(T)$.

Appendix 2.G

Quadratic Preference Function

To illustrate the construction of the quadratic preference functions by Professor Frisch, consider Table 2.1, which records the results of the distributive questions.

Table 2.1 gives different values of a component for alternative values of the summation item derived from the preferences expressed by the politicians. Thus the jth component of the summative item is

$$x_j = \phi_j^S \quad j = 1, \ldots, N, \text{ for any one of the alternative}$$
$$\text{values of the summative item, (1)}$$

and

$$\sum_j \phi_j^{S_i} = S_i \qquad i = 1, \ldots, M. \qquad (2)$$

Table 2.1

Preferred Values of Components of Summative Items

Values of the Summative Item	S_1 . . . S_i . . . S_m				
	1 . . . i . . . m				
1	$\phi_1^{S}{}_1$ . . .	$\phi_1^{S}{}_i$ . . .	$\phi_1^{S}{}_m$		
.					
.					
.					
a	$\phi_a^{S}{}_1$ . . .	$\phi_a^{S}{}_i$ . . .	$\phi_a^{S}{}_m$		
.					
.					
.					
j	$\phi_j^{S}{}_1$ . . .	$\phi_j^{S}{}_i$ . . .	$\phi_j^{S}{}_m$		
.					
.					
.					
β	$\phi_\beta^{S}{}_1$ . . .	$\phi_\beta^{S}{}_i$ . . .	$\phi_\beta^{S}{}_m$		
.					
.					
.					
N	$\phi_N^{S}{}_1$ . . .	$\phi_N^{S}{}_i$ . . .	$\phi_N^{S}{}_m$		

Values of the Components of the Summative Items

Frisch prefers dollar values to percentages as the unit of measurement of the main item and its components, and suggests that any information gathered in terms of percentages be converted accordingly. If some of the $\phi_j^S i$'s remain constant for $i = 1, \ldots, M -$, the affix j will be called irregular and the corresponding "variable" will simply be omitted from the preference function.

The basic principle underlying the construction of the preference function is the realization of the marginal or tangency conditions for "choice" equilibrium. The preference function can be written, excluding irregular variables, as

$$F = \Sigma \left(v_j x_j + \frac{1}{2} w_j x_j^2 \right). \tag{3}$$

If none of the distribution numbers are at their interview bounds, we must have for any value of S

$$F_1 = F_2 = \ldots, = \ldots = F_N. \tag{4}$$

In addition, we have the budget condition, $\sum_j x_j = S$. $\tag{5}$

If v_j and w_j are given as in the usual economic theory, (4) and (5) will determine the equilibrium point. Here it is necessary to adopt the opposite viewpoint, that the quantities are given as functions of v_j and w_j, which are unknowns. Writing (4) in full we have, excluding irregular variables,

$$v_1 + w_1 \phi_1^S = v_2 + w_2 \phi_2^S = \ldots = v_N + w_N \phi_N^S. \tag{6}$$

Picking out any two of the expressions with, say, affixes a and β, we get

$$(v_a - v_\beta) + w_a \phi_a^S - w_\beta \phi_\beta^S = 0, \tag{7}$$

where a and β are any two regular affixes.

According to Frisch, equation (7) can be interpreted as a requirement that a linear relation shall exist between the two variables ϕ_a and ϕ_β over the range of variation S. In order to determine the coefficients $(v_a - v_\beta)$, w_a and w_β, since there is nothing to determine the choice between a and β, the regression in question would necessarily have to be one that treats the two affixes symmetrically.

The ordinary regression of ϕ_a on ϕ_β or the inverse cannot be performed. Frisch uses what he calls *diagonal mean regression,* which can be written in the present case as

$$\frac{\phi_a - \overline{\phi}_a}{\sqrt{m_{aa}}} = \frac{\phi_\beta - \overline{\phi}_\beta}{\sqrt{m_{\beta\beta}}} \quad , \tag{8}$$

where

$$\overline{\phi}_j = \frac{\sum\limits_{i=1}^{M} \phi_j^{S_i}}{\sum\limits_{i=1}^{M} S_i} \qquad j = 1, \ldots, N \tag{9}$$

$$m_{jj} = \sum\limits_{i=1}^{M} (\phi_j^{S_i} - \overline{\phi}_j)^2 \quad j = 1, \ldots, N. \tag{10}$$

Alternately, (8) can be written as

$$\frac{\overline{\phi}_a}{\sqrt{m_{aa}}} - \frac{\overline{\phi}_\beta}{\sqrt{m_{\beta\beta}}} + (\frac{-1}{\sqrt{m_{aa}}}) \phi_a - (\frac{-1}{\sqrt{m_{\beta\beta}}}) \phi_\beta = 0. \tag{11}$$

Comparing the coefficients of 1, ϕ_a, and ϕ_β in (11) and (7), we see that $(v_a - v_\beta)$, w_a, and w_β can be put proportional to

$$\frac{\overline{\phi}_a}{\sqrt{m_{aa}}} - \frac{\overline{\phi}_\beta}{\sqrt{m_{\beta\beta}}} , \quad \frac{-1}{\sqrt{m_{aa}}} , \text{ and } \frac{-1}{\sqrt{m_{\beta\beta}}} .$$

Thus the following may be taken as a set of special solutions:

$$v_j = \frac{\overline{\phi}_j}{\sqrt{m_{jj}}} \tag{12}$$

$$w_j = \frac{-1}{\sqrt{m_{jj}}} . \tag{13}$$

In (12) and (13) the square roots are taken as positive, and the sign of w_j is determined so as to express the principle of declining marginal utility. Frisch then proceeds to find general solutions and other properties of his approach. These refinements and details cannot be included here.

NOTES

1. The literature on measurability of utility is copious, with varying degrees of sophistication and abstraction. Some important references and brief discussions are available in R. G. D. Allen, *Mathematical Economics* (New York: Macmillan, 1956), pp. 670-76. Two eminent contemporary economists who hold that utility is cardinally measurable are R. F. Harrod and R. Frisch; see Ragnar Frisch, "Dynamic Utility," *Econometrica* 32 (July-October 1964).

2. This has been shown in mathematically oriented textbooks on micro-economics. See J. M. Hendersen and R. E. Quandt, *Microeconomic Theory* (New York: McGraw-Hill, 1958).

3. Leif Johansen, "A Multisectoral Study of Economic Growth," *Contributions of Economic Analysis* XXI (Amsterdam: North Holland, 1960); A. P. Barten, "Consumer Demand Functions under Conditions of Almost Additive Preferences," *Econometrica* 32 (January-April 1964).

4. Leif Johansen, "A Multisectoral Study. . . . "

5. R. G. D. Allen, "The Nature of Indifference Curves," *Reveiw of Economic Studies* I (February 1934).

6. Vilfredo Pareto, *Manuel d'Économie Politique* (Paris: M. Giard, 1927).

7. A. Bergson, "A Reformulation of Certain Aspects of Welfare Economics," *Quarterly Journal of Economics* LII (February 1938).

8. N. Kaldor, "Welfare Propositions of Economics and Interpersonal Comparison of Utility: A Comment," *Economic Journal* 49 (September 1939).

9. J. R. Hicks, "The Foundations of Welfare Economics," *Economic Journal* 49 (December 1939).

10. K. J. Arrow, *Social Choice and Individual Values* (New Haven: Yale University Press, 1963).

11. J. de V. Graaf, *Theoretical Welfare Economics* (Cambridge: University Press, 1967).

12. O. Lange, "The Foundations of Welfare Economics," *Econometrica* 10 (July-October 1942).

13. P. A. Samuelson, *Foundations of Economic Analysis* (Cambridge: Harvard University Press, 1947).

14. K. J. Arrow, *Social Choice. . . .*

15. Jack Sawyer, "The Altruism Scale: A Measure of Cooperative, Individualistic, and Competitive Interpersonal Orientation," *American Journal of Sociology* 71 (January 1966).

16. Bernhardt Lieberman, "Combining Individual Preferences into a Social Choice," in Ira R. Buchler and Hugo G. Nutini (eds.), *Game Theory in Behavioral Sciences* (Pittsburgh: University of Pittsburgh Press, 1969).

17. G. Debreu, "Topological Methods in Cardinal Utility Theory," in K. J. Arrow et al. (eds.), *Mathematical Methods in the Social Sciences*, proceedings, Stanford Symposium on Mathematical Methods in the Social Sciences, 1959 (Stanford: Stanford University Press, 1960); T. C. Koopmans, "Stationary Ordinal Utility and Impatience," *Econometrica* 28 (April 1960).

18. F. P. Ramsey, "A Mathematical Theory of Saving," *Economic Journal* 38 (December 1928).

19. R. F. Harrod, "Second Essay in Dynamic Theory," *Economic Journal* 70 (June 1960).

20. R. M. Goodwin, "The Optimal Growth Path for an Under-developed Economy," *Economic Journal* 71 (December 1961).

21. T. C. Koopmans, "Stationary Ordinal Utility . . . . "

22. A. Bergson, "A Reformulation . . . . "

23. Roy Radner, *Notes on the Theory of Economic Planning* (Athens: Center of Economic Research, 1963), p. 50. Radner cites B. Wards, "Kantorovich on Economic Calculation," *Journal of Political Economy* 68 (December 1960). In a preview of this book, Professor R. W. Campbell of Indiana University has pointed out that this method is really not used in practice in the U.S.S.R.

24. See "Analysis and Projections of Consumption Demand: Methodological Notes" in *Industrialization and Productivity*, Bulletin 9. This is a simple, though sketchy, survey on the methodology of projections of consumption demand and gives ten different types of functions with their limitations and merits. These functions and their statistical derivations are not discussed here, as these are standard content in textbooks on econometrics.

25. R. Frisch, "General Theory of the Kernel Model," memorandum, University of Oslo, Institute of Economics, February 7, 1958, p. 95, fn. 2.

26. E. E. Slutsky, "On the Theory of the Budget of the Consumer," *Giornale degli Economisti* 51 (July 1915).

27. Ragnar Frisch, "A Complete Scheme for Computing All Direct and Cross Elasticities in a Model with Many Sectors," *Econometrica* 27 (April 1959).

28. H. S. Houthakker, "Additive Preferences," *Econometrica* 28 (April 1960).

29. Leif Johansen, "A Multisectoral Study . . . . " Also, Leif Johansen (in collaboration with Harvard Alstadheim and Asmund Langsether), "Explorations in Long Term Projections for the Norwegian Economy," *Economics of Planning* 8 (1968).

30. A. P. Barten, "Consumer Demand Functions . . . . "

31. J. Sandee, *A Demonstrations Model for India* (Calcutta: Indian Statistical Institute, 1960).

32. H. B. Chenery and M. Bruno, "Development Alternatives in an Open Economy: The Case of Israel," *Economic Journal* 72 (March 1962).

33. Alan S. Manne and Ashok Rudra, "A Consistency Model of India's Fourth Plan," *Sankhya*, Series B, 27 (1965).

34. A. S. Manne and T. E. Weiskopf, "A Dynamic Multisectoral

Model," Research Center in Economic Growth, Memorandum No. 57, December 1957 (Stanford: Stanford University Press, 1957).

35. Cambridge, Department of Applied Economic Research, *A Complete Model of Economic Growth*. No. 1 in *A Program of Growth* (London: Chapman and Hall, 1962).

36. Ragnar Frisch, "Numerical Determination of a Quadratic Preference Function for Use in Macro-Economic Programming," memorandum, University of Oslo, Institute of Economics, February 14, 1957.

37. C. J. van Eijk and J. Sandee, "Quantitative Determination of an Optimum Economic Policy," *Econometrica* 27 (January 1959).

38. Ragnar Frisch, "Numerical Determination . . . . "

39. The inclusion of this section was suggested by Professor R. W. Campbell of Indiana University. This writer is, however, responsible for the decision to include this method. The method may be said to have been originated with the papers (i) Olaf Helmer and Nicholas Rescher, "On the Epistemology of the Inexact Sciences," Management Science 6 (October 1959); (ii) Norman Dalkey and Olaf Helmer, "An Experimental Application of the Delphi Method to the Use of Experts," *Management Science* 9 (April 1963); and (iii) T. J. Gordon and Olaf Helmer, *Report on a Long-Range Forecasting Study* (Santa Monica, Calif.: The Rand Corporation, 1964).

40. H. H. Kelley and J. W. Thibaut, "Experimental Studies of Group Problem Solving and Process," in Gardner Lindsey (ed.), *Handbook of Social Psychology*, 2 (Reading, Mass.: Addison-Wesley, 1954).

41. S. E. Asch, "Effects of Group Pressure upon the Modification and Distortion of Judgments," in Eleanor E. Maccoby et al. (eds.), *Readings in Social Psychology*, 3d ed. (London: Holt, Rinehart and Winston, 1958).

42. Norman C. Dalkey, *The Delphi Method: An Experimental Study of Group Opinion.* (Santa Monica, Calif.: RAND Corp., 1964).

43. P. A. Samuelson, *Foundations of Economic Analysis.*

44. Marquis de Condorcet, *Essai sur l'application de l'analyse à la probabilité de décisions rendues à la pluralité des voix* (Paris, 1785).

45. James S. Coleman, "The Possibility of a Social Welfare Function," *American Economic Review* 61 (December 1966).

46. Bernhardt Lieberman, "Combining Individual Preferences . . . . "

47. Jack Sawyer, "The Altruism Scale . . . . "

48. R. Duncan Luce and Howard Raiffa, *Games and Decisions* (New York: Wiley, 1957).

49. I. M. D. Little, "Social Choice and Individual Values," *Journal of Political Economy* 60 (October 1952).

50. K. J. Arrow, *Social Choice.*

51. Martin Shubik, *Game Theory and Related Approaches to Social Behavior* (New York: Wiley, 1964).

52. Charles R. Plott, "Recent Results in the Theory of Voting," mimeographed, Purdue University, 1970.

53. R. J. Aumann and B. Peleg, "Von Neumann–Morgenstern

Solutions to Cooperative Games without Side Payments, *Bulletin of the American Mathematical Society* 66 (May 1960).

54. R. Wilson, "A Class of Solutions for Voting Games," Paper 156, Stanford University, Graduate School of Business (Stanford: Stanford University Press, 1968).

55. Ibid.

56. Robert J. Aumann, "A Survey of Cooperative Games without Side Payments," in Martin Shubik (ed.), *Essays in Mathematical Economics* (Princeton, N. J.: Princeton University Press, 1967).

CHAPTER THREE

Plan Feasibility

I. Basic Considerations

1. Introductory Remarks

Most plans start with a formulation of targets to be achieved during a fixed plan period. In mandatory plans most targets are fixed in absolute magnitudes such as millions of tons of steel, millions of tons of food grains, millions of jobs, or level of national income. The list of targets is followed by detailed descriptions of the availability of resources and the potentials in mining, agriculture, and industry. Often, but not in all cases, the plans contain some description of the production structure. Finally, the plans state the various measures and policies to be adopted to achieve the targets, given resource availabilities and the structure of the economy.

The relevant information and data regarding targets, structure, and resource availabilities are seldom adequate in any country, and therefore, national plans are generally formulated on the basis of less than adequate data. In the analysis and evaluation of a plan, the inadequacy of relevant information and data is felt even more, since not all the available information and data used are contained in the plan document itself.

Whatever the state of the data and the targets being presupposed, a plan can be formulated and evaluated with three major considerations in view: feasibility, consistency, and optimality. A plan is said to be feasible if its targets are achievable with the given resource availabilities and production structure. It is consistent if the activities of each sector are planned in such a way that no bottlenecks or excesses are likely to arise. It is optimal if there are no alternative ways to raise the value of the targets.

The three aspects are separable but interrelated. Feasibility of a plan requires that the plan has been formulated in a consistent way. But a consistent plan is not necessarily feasible. However, any consistent plan can be made feasible by reducing the level of the targets. Consistency is thus a necessary, but not sufficient, condition for feasibility.

As another example, feasibility and consistency are both prerequisites for optimality. A plan cannot be optimal until and unless it is both feasible and consistent. Nevertheless, it is useful to treat these three aspects as separable and consider them one by one.

The purpose of this chapter is to examine feasibility and its ramifications. After clarifying a few crucial points in section I, we give a brief and simple technical discussion of feasibility in section II. This is followed by a discussion in section III of the main elements of plan feasibility at aggregative levels which should be checked in the formulation of an actual national plan. In sections IV and V an attempt is made to outline disaggregative levels of feasibility. Section VI contains some observations on complementarity and substitution in the context of plan feasibility. Section VII contains an outline of the Chenery-Bruno model for Israel, an excellent example of plan feasibility developed at an aggregative level.

2. *Resource Stretchability*

Basic to the information regarding the availability of resources is their stretchability. This issue is a very common one, though it has not been given adequate consideration in formal discussions. For example, production can be carried out in one, two, or three shifts; thus the same machines and buildings can produce varying amounts of output per month or per year, depending on the number of shifts they are worked. Capital-output ratios will change drastically if production is carried out in two or three shifts instead of one. Also related to this ratio is a factor that may be called "capital fatigue," in that the life of a capital item may be reduced if it is operated in two or three shifts instead of one.

A pertinent example is provided by the case of transportation facilities. During a plan period, targets may possibly be achieved by overstraining and overstretching these facilities. But overuse may take its toll in the postplan years if adequate provisions are not made for the upkeep of existing facilities and for adequate expansion to meet future growth.

Stretchability is also relevant to labor. Even if labor is classified according to skill and training, the same number of workers can do more work if they work overtime or six days instead of five. Even without working longer hours, they can be more productive if they are sincere, serious, and hardworking, though there is a limit beyond which labor resources cannot be strained.

A stretchability factor is present in natural resources, too. Oil, minerals, forests, and the like can be exploited over a shorter or longer period of time. Thus a plan may be made feasible by overexploiting natural resources at the expense of serious repercussions in the postplan periods. An assessment of feasibility, therefore, has to be qualified by considerations of stretchability and overuse.

3.   *Annual Plans*

Though national plans generally cover three to seven years and extend up to ten years or more, often the main plan is broken down into parts, and a fraction of the overall targets is assigned to each year of the plan. Breaking up the plan into annual plans leaves open a number of decisions: What should be the size of the annual targets, and what part of the resources should be allocated to the successive annual plans? What investment projects should be started, in which year, and how fast should they be completed? Decisions regarding these and many other similar questions can affect overall plan feasibility.

It is not absolutely necessary that each annual plan be feasible with the same degree of strictness as the underlying long-run plan. If each annual plan is feasible, then the whole plan will necessarily be feasible, but the converse need not be true. The experience gained in the first few annual plans may enable the planners to rephase the plan in such a way that the plan as a whole becomes feasible. It may turn out that the first or second annual plan will show that the plan targets have been set too high and that the plan should be revised well in advance of its termination to preclude the possibility of its failure as a whole. In short, though the feasibility of an entire plan depends largely on the feasibility of its components, formulation of the latter may be eased by the fact that each annual plan may have experimental leeway attached to it.

4.   *Private Sector Aspects*

The formulation of a feasible plan in a mixed economy with a sizable private sector may involve some additional problems. Presumably, though not necessarily, relevant data and information for the private sector may not be as adequate as for the public sector. Moreover, the behavior of the private sector after the introduction of planned policies may not be as certain as the performance of the public sector under plan directives and other measures. In particular, mobilization and utilization of resources can be predicted less firmly for the private sector than for the public. The part of the plan pertaining to the private sector must be guesswork to an extent, depending on the best available forecasts of resource availabilities and output decisions.

5. *Price Aspects*

Closely connected with the presence of the private sector is the management and behavior of prices. Although even in the presence of a private sector, commodity as well as factor prices can be fixed by the government and consumption and investment thereby controlled to an extent, policy tools are likely to become difficult to manage and make effective when prices become unstable despite some controls. In practice, governments tend to be more effective in prohibiting undesirable private-sector decisions than in inducing desired decisions.

A plan, which may be feasible if prices remain stable or move according to the plan, may become unfeasible if prices become unstable or diverge from their planned course. Reliable forecasting of prices is a very difficult problem, the more so when the period covered is longer than one or two years.

6. *Other Exogenous Factors*

Uncontrolled activities of the private sector and unregulated movements of prices are therefore a kind of half-way house with respect to possible influences by planning or governmental agencies. In addition, certain other factors such as natural and climatic conditions, political developments, or international affairs are largely outside the control of these agencies. Insofar as these factors can be correctly predicted, their repercussions can be taken into account in the formulation of the plan. But unexpected and unpredictable changes can make an otherwise feasible plan unfeasible. Since these factors are uncontrollable by planning agencies and cannot be predicted, it becomes a nice question—perhaps a semantic one—whether the formulation of the plan is faulty if it becomes unfeasible because of exogenous factors or has been booby-trapped through no fault of its own.

II. Concept of Feasibility in Theoretical Programming

1.   *Intratemporal Feasibility*

As noted earlier, three sets of information are involved in plan formulation: a preference function, technological or production possibilities, and resource availability.

In order to bring out the principle of feasibility clearly, we shall assume that the targets are given in absolute amounts of each commodity, namely, x_j, $j = 1, \ldots, n$. Let the amount of each resource given in the beginning of the period be denoted by b_i, $i = 1, \ldots, m$. The production function for producing commodity j is denoted by F^j, $j = 1, \ldots, n$. Let q_{ij} be the amount of factor i going into the production of commodity j. Then

$$x_j = F^j (q_{1j}, \ldots, q_{ij}, \ldots, q_{mj}) \qquad (1)$$
$$j = 1, \ldots, n.$$

The targets are feasible with the resources initially given if the values of q_{ij} satisfying equation (1) are such that they also satisfy the following inequality:

$$\sum_{j=1}^{n} q_{ij} \leqslant b_i \qquad i = 1, \ldots, m. \qquad (2)$$

In (1), the q_{ij}'s are variable. If any set of them exists which satisfies both (1) and (2), then the targets and the plan are feasible.

To illustrate, we shall now specialize the production function F and assume that the factors needed for the production of a commodity constitute a fixed proportion of the amount of the commodity. Thus assume that

$$a_{ij} = \frac{q_{ij}}{x_j} \text{ is a constant} \qquad (3)$$

$$i = 1, \ldots, m$$
$$j = 1, \ldots, n.$$

This now replaces (1) as a production function, which now takes the following form: $\min_{i} (\frac{q_{ij}}{x_j})$. Substituting for q_{ij} in (2) we have

$$\sum_{j=1}^{n} a_{ij}\, x_j \leqslant b_i \qquad\qquad i = 1, \ldots, m. \qquad (4)$$

Thus, given a's as technical coefficients of production, b's as initial resources, and x's as targets, the plan is feasible if (4) holds.

We can illustrate the above by an elementary diagram. We assume that there are two commodities and three resources, so that in place of (4) we have

$$a_{11}x_1 + a_{12}x_2 \leqslant b_1$$

$$a_{21}x_1 + a_{22}x_2 \leqslant b_2 \qquad\qquad (5)$$

$$a_{31}x_1 + a_{32}x_2 \leqslant b_3.$$

We plot (5) in Figure 3.1. Any point lying within or on the boundary of the area ABCDO satisfies (5) and hence is feasible. Thus given the b's (the initial resources) and the a's (the constant technical coefficients of production), the x's (the target values) are feasible if they satisfy (4) or (5), that is, if the values of the target variables correspond to a point lying in the feasible region ABCDO. In Figure 3.1, points x^1 and x^2 are feasible, but x^3 is infeasible.

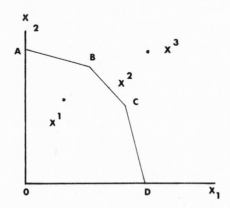

Fig. 3.1. Feasibility Region

2. *Intertemporal Feasibility*

Figure 3.1 can be extended to give an elementary illustration of

intertemporal feasibility (see Figure 3.2). Assume that two of the
resources are accumulated (capital) amounts of the two commodities and
that the third is a nonproduced natural resource. We shall not explicitly
show this resource. In order not to crowd the diagram, we shall consider
only two periods, just enough to illustrate the problem. Let $x(2)$ denote
the target volumes of the two commodities at the end of year 2. Let the
accumulated amounts of the two commodities at the end of year 0 be
denoted by the point $\underline{b}$ (0).

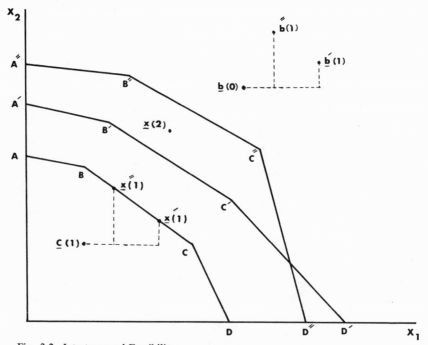

Fig. 3.2. Intertemporal Feasibility

Let ABCD be the production frontier corresponding to the resource
point $\underline{b}$ (0). Any point on this frontier gives the maximum combination of
the two commodities that can be produced in the sense that neither of
them can be increased without decreasing the other. Let point $\underline{c}$ (1) be the
vector of planned and predicted consumption (including capital depreciation) in year 1. To illustrate, let us choose two points $\underline{x}'$ (1) and x'' (1).

The excess of production of the two commodities over the planned
or predicted level of their consumption is accumulated for the formation
of capital. Adding to $\underline{b}(0)$, we get the two resource vectors $\underline{b}'$ (1) and
$\underline{b}''$ (1) corresponding to the points $\underline{x}'$ (1) and $\underline{x}''$ (1). In year 2 then, we
shall have two production frontiers. A' B' C' D' and A'' B'' C'' D'',

corresponding to $\underline{b}'$ (1) and $\underline{b}''$ (1), respectively. The target x(2) is seen now to be feasible with respect to one frontier but not to the other. Thus it is shown that the feasibility of the target in the terminal year depends on the choice of points on the production frontier in the first year and the choice of frontiers and the points thereon in the following years.

3. *Major Considerations in Intertemporal Feasibility*

The above diagram, though simplistic, pinpoints the main consideration that the feasibility of the terminal targets of a plan covering several years depends on the annual allocations of resources. However, the freedom to allocate resources is subject to several limitations. First, the projects already started in preplan years may have to be completed, unless they are too inefficient in the framework of the current plan. That may require allocating a substantial portion of the investible resources to projects already committed. Second, the allocation of investment will have to be such as to produce the "desired" vector of consumption. Finally, the choice of alternatives is conditioned by technological changes, considerations of economies of scale, changing world conditions, and a host of other factors and circumstances continuously unfolding. The problem of intertemporal feasibility lies in taking measures in advance to meet future exigencies.

III. Feasibility at the Aggregative Levels

1. *Preliminary Remarks*

A plan has to be feasible at aggregative as well as at sectoral levels. Feasibility at the aggregative level can be established only very roughly, since accurate estimates of many of the relevant parameters may not be available. The coefficients related to the aggregative levels are the weighted averages of the corresponding coefficients of their components. However, the data required for computing coefficients related to the components may be lacking and may be difficult to obtain. The aggregative coefficients also may be derived from time-series analyses if such series are available. One observed advantage of coefficients related to the aggregate quantities is that they are more stable than those related to components or sectors. Therefore, in drawing up a plan it is easier and safer to ensure first that the plan is feasible at the aggregative levels.

In this section we shall outline some rough methods for establishing plan feasibility with respect to crucial variables at the aggregative levels.

2. Output Target in Relation to Capital

Most plans set a target rate of annual growth of national income over the plan period in terms of the prices of the base year. Given the national income in the base year, the total planned increase in the national income in the final year can be calculated. To check whether the planned rate of the national income is feasible, we need at least two pieces of information: the total investment target for the whole plan and the marginal capital-output ratio for the economy as a whole.

Assume Y_o is the initial income figure, the targeted rate of growth is 100r percent, and the plan is to run for t years. Targeted income in year t is then $Y_t = Y_o (1 + r)^t$. The increase in income in year t over the initial year is $\Delta Y_t = Y_t - Y_o$.

Let Δk_t be total investment planned for the whole period of the plan and σ the marginal capital-output ratio. Then a minimum test that the plan is feasible in the aggregate with respect to capital is

$$\Delta Y_t \cdot \sigma \leqslant \Delta k_t. \tag{6}$$

Any formulation of a national plan must satisfy the very general feasibility test (b). In those cases in which the target values of Δk_t and ΔY_t are given but the plan does not explicitly state the value of σ, the implicit value of σ is ΔY_t divided by ΔK_t. The feasibility test then takes the form of checking whether the resulting value of σ lies within reasonable or acceptable limits according to subsidiary, independent, or comparative information.

Some plans specify their income targets in per capita terms. Since every national plan implies a certain rate of population growth, the end-period income Y_t and the plan-period rise ΔY_t can be easily derived. Let the initial population be N_o, its growth rate n, and the initial per capita income y_o. It follows that

$$Y_t = N_t y_t = N_o (1 + n)^t y_o (1 + r')^t$$

$$\Delta Y_t = Y_t - Y_o = N_o y_o [(1 + n)^t (1 + r')^t - 1],$$

where y_t is the per capita income in year t and r' is the targeted rate of growth of per capita income. The elementary test (6) can then be applied as before.

3. Employment Target

Plans in underdeveloped countries often contain employment among their targets. If the figure of the employment target is given and if a capital-labor ratio is known, the feasibility of the plan can be checked with respect to employment. Letting η be capital-labor ratio and ΔN_t the employment target, the plan is feasible if

$$\Delta N_t \eta \leqslant \Delta K_t,$$

where ΔK_t is the planned amount of investment in year t.

The value of η can be obtained from the labor-output ratio ζ and the capital output σ, since $\eta = \sigma/\zeta$.

4. Savings Target

Plans generally contain targets about resource availability. The crucial element of this target is the size of real savings. Private savings depend on the size and distribution of income, condition of the market, and profit opportunities. Public savings depend on tax revenues, retained earnings from public enterprises, government borrowing, and government expenditure on current account.

The savings target will be feasible if the following holds:

$$S_t \leqslant \text{private saving} + \text{public saving}$$

$$\text{or} \quad S_t \leqslant [Y_t - T_t - C_o - v_t(Y_t - T_t)] + [T_t + B_t - G_t]$$

$$\leqslant Y_t - C_o - v_t (Y_t - \tau_t Y_t) + B_t - G_t, \tag{8}$$

where S_t is the total planned domestic savings, Y_t the total income in year t of the plan, C_o the total consumption and Y_o the total income in the initial year of the plan, v_t the marginal propensity to consume, τ_t the rate of taxation, B_t the total borrowing, G_t the government consumption, and T_t the tax revenue.

5. Foreign Aid

Foreign aid may fill either of two gaps: foreign exchange or savings. The adequacy of foreign aid, therefore, is to be checked with respect to the greater of the two. Foreign loans and assistance are functions of diverse economic and noneconomic factors prevailing or expected to prevail in the borrowing and lending countries. Let us suppose that the most probable aid that can be envisaged in plan year t is $\overline{F}_t$. Then the plan would be feasible with respect to foreign exchange if $\overline{F}_t$ is greater than or equal to the deficit in the balance of payments, that is,

$$\overline{F}_t \geqslant q_t \, \Delta K_t + m_t Y_t + m'_t x_t - E_t, \qquad (9)$$

where q_t is the fraction of capital imported from abroad, m_t the average propensity to import goods for consumption, m'_t the ratio of intermediate goods imported to the value of total output. E_t is the value of total exports in year t.

In order to make a rough estimate of the adequacy of foreign aid to fill the savings gap, we have to compare savings with the investment required in plan year t. If we assume a gestation lag of one year, the investment required in year t will be

$$I_t = \sigma(Y_{t+1} - Y_t) = \sigma Y_o \, (1+r)^t r, \qquad (10)$$

where σ is the capital-output ratio as before and r is the planned rate of growth of income.

The foreign aid will be adequate to fill the savings gap if

$$\overline{F}_t \geqslant I_t - S_t. \qquad (11)$$

S_t can be derived as shown above. For plan feasibility $\overline{F}_t$ must satisfy both (9) and (11). These statements are very simple, but some quite interesting work has been done on the basis of such relations.[1]

6.   *Deficit Financing*

Another crucial check of plan feasibility is related to deficit financing. In plan countries like India, deficit financing has been defined as "Government spending in excess of government receipts in shape of taxes, earnings from state enterprises, loans from the public, deposits and funds and other miscellaneous sources."[2] The criterion of what constitutes an act of deficit financing should, by and large, be whether or not the transaction in question tends to increase the supply of money. Withdrawals from cash balances[3] and increases in floating debt normally tend to increase it. However, short-term borrowing cannot be treated as if at a par with long-term borrowing; similarly the borrowings from the Central Bank, commercial banks, and the public have different effects on the creation of money. Further, it may be noted that a decline in cash balances or an increase in short-term debt may be offset by a corresponding withdrawal from foreign exchange reserves.

Limits to the creation of money through deficit financing are set by the degree of inflation that the planners and policy makers deem tolerable. All development programs involve some general price rise; but too large an increase may disrupt all plan estimates and calculations, in addition to bringing undue hardship to the citizens. A speedy economic development program accompanied by a price inflation of about 2 percent per annum is generally considered tolerable.

Deficit financing as defined above comes very close to creation of new money or activation of inactive money. By using Cambridge equation of quantity of money, a rough assessment of the plan feasibility with respect to deficit financing can be made. Let r be the planned rate of growth of real income, and let the tolerable limit of rate of inflation be v percent per annum. Then the feasible limit of deficit financing in plan year t is

$$
\begin{aligned}
(DF)_t &= \frac{1}{\Upsilon} \; (Y_t \, (1 + v) - Y_{t-1}) \\
&= \frac{1}{\Upsilon} \, Y_0 (1 + r)^{\, t-1} (v + r + vr),
\end{aligned}
\tag{12}
$$

where Υ is the income velocity of money. $(DF)_t$ gives the amount of deficit financing that can be resorted to without the rate of inflation becoming intolerable.

7. *Income Redistribution*

Most plans, especially those in underdeveloped countries, have income redistribution as one of their targets. This objective is difficult to quantify and express in quantitative terms; one way may be to classify nationals in income groups and to set targets of maximum and minimum per capita disposable income for each group. An important factor to be considered here is that a more egalitarian income distribution may have an adverse effect on the rate of savings. Up to a point, employment can be increased without curtailing savings, but after that limit one can be raised only at the cost of the other.[4] This problem arises because after a critical point marginal productivity falls below wage rate as employment increases. An income redistribution target is feasible if it does not involve employment, wage, and tax rates beyond their acceptable upper or lower limits and at the same time yields the planned rate of savings.

8.   *Concluding Remarks*

In the preceding paragraphs, we have pointed out the basic facts related to plan feasibility at the aggregate level and have stated simple relations which must hold in each plan year in order to ensure plan feasibility. A cruder but a more workable method would be to express these relations for the plan period as a whole, by summing both sides of the inequalities over t. Evidently, if the inequalities hold for each year, they will hold for the plan period as a whole. However, the reverse may not and need not be true. It may be more difficult to formulate a plan in such a way as to ensure basic plan feasibility for each plan year than to plan the period as a whole. In any case, overall feasibility is of more concern than annual feasibility.

In the preceding discussion we have expressed the inequalities for each plan year as though they were independent of other years. It hardly needs to be stressed that feasibility in a plan year is interdependent with that of other years. We shall not discuss this aspect at any length, as the discussion is bound to be loose. However, such feasibility is an essential element of consistency and optimality models, as we shall discuss intertemporal consistency and optimality models in chapters four and five.

IV. Disaggregative Tests of Feasibility—A General View

1.   *Preliminary Remarks*

Theoretically speaking, if an economy is divided into separate sectors and if the volume of final demands (consumption + addition to capital stock, skills, and infrastructure + exports) for each sector is specified, the total output required of each sector can be estimated from a relevant input-output matrix. Once the total output for each sector is known, the amounts of different resources needed in each sector can be estimated.

A planning commission or agency seldom has all the information and coefficients needed for these purposes. First, sectoral divisions often are not exhaustive in the sense that the sectoral targets do not cover all the output of the economy; a substantial part may be left without any specific targets. Even if the amounts of production for the omitted part are estimated, it will be relatively difficult to decide the amount of resources needed because the coefficients of production, even if available, may be still less reliably known. Therefore, one may be obliged to be content with only rough checks of feasibility for sectors for which reliable data are not available. However, for key sectors, adequate and fairly reliable data and coefficients may be available; and the feasibility of the targets of these sectors may be checked with greater accuracy.

2. *Limitation of Skills*

It may not be necessary to check the adequacy of every resource with respect to the targets of a plan. Some resources may be known to be available in abundant quantities, and for them feasibility tests may be dispensable. A typical example is unskilled labor in most backward countries. Another example in some countries may be arable land, while in others foreign exchange may be no problem.

In most underdeveloped countries, moderately and highly skilled labor is in short supply and so are managerial and entrepreneurial skills. Although it is relatively easy to apply feasibility checks for moderately skilled workers in factories and firms if the methods of production are known, that cannot be done for teachers, nurses, and other similar-grade workers in the social services. Here there are typically no fixed or known coefficients of the requirements of workers per unit of service, and worker supply can be judged only with reference to rather loose norms, for example, pupil-teacher ratios or the number of patients per doctor. The difficulties are compounded when checking feasibility with respect to highly skilled workers and high-level managers and entrepreneurs for whom problems of indivisibility are added to the above considerations. A given number of managers, for example, may be adequate for different levels of output if they are employed in different sizes of plants.

3. *Shortage of Types of Capital*

If total output by sectors is specified and technical coefficients are known, the required magnitudes of different types of capital items can be derived. Probably no planning commission has details about every capital item, but many may have information about major items for which an adequacy check can be made. For the rest, one has to inquire whether they can be created with the residue of total planned investment after allowing for the items whose quantities have been accounted for. When alternative techniques are available, adequacy of capital items can be checked only after optimal techniques have been chosen.

4.   Land Resources

Land as a factor of production is mainly important for agriculture. Both agricultural output and land reclamation targets are typically included in national development plans. Increases in agricultural output, of course, are a function not only of additional land reclaimed but also of the use of fertilizers, better seed varieties, improved farming methods and equipment, expanded irrigation, and so forth. To add to the complications, these elements do not bear a fixed relationship to the agricultural output since substitution possibilities are more or less continuous. Therefore, additional or new inputs to changes in agricultural output may be an uncertain undertaking. The magnitude of uncertainty surrounding the relative contributions of inputs can be kept within tolerable limits and estimates which relate increases in outputs to increases in nonland inputs may be available. The remaining planned output then has to be related to increases in land area reclaimed, including multiple cropping. If the area is adequate according to the available ratios and after allowance for other inputs, the plan is feasible in this respect. But, since land-output ratios differ according to the quality of land, a rather comprehensive survey of lands under cultivation may have to be made before adequacy can be determined. The same situation arises in the case of other natural resources.

5.   Infrastructure

Infrastructure is another factor which must be considered in checking the feasibility of a plan. It includes transportation, communication, electricity supply, health and education, maintenance of law and order, and so forth. Since various infrastructural means, competing and complementary, can be used for abetting real income or output, depending on its composition and technology, there may be no exact relationship between amounts of goods produced and infrastructural services needed. A detailed survey of the methods, nature, and location of economic activities is a prerequisite for estimating the adequacy or inadequacy of such items. In the case of transportation, some rough coefficients can be worked out in terms of railroad capacity per unit of output. The adequacy of a planned extension in railroad services can thereby be checked with respect to the planned increases in total outputs and their delivery routings. Another very rough test can be applied when there is no under- or overutilization of the existing capacity at the beginning of the plan; in such a case additional outlays for such facilities can be fixed according to the ratio of expenditures to total value of output in previous years, with due consideration to any improvements that are being planned. Electricity requirements can be worked out fairly accurately from production targets; the adequacy of the planned supply can be checked more reliably than is possible for other items of the infrastructure.

The adequacy of items such as health, education, and other welfare projects cannot be checked without setting certain norms, which may vary widely and which must ultimately be decided by politicians or their constituents. Health and education facilities, though often expandable at rapid rates, typically involve long-term impacts and targets. Benefit-cost analyses of such processes, therefore, need to have central attention placed on their special time horizons.

V. Detailed Tests of Feasibility—Technical Approaches

1. *Preliminary Explanations*

In this section an attempt is made to present a brief, formal description of detailed tests of feasibility as summarized in Table 3.1. The details and degree of disaggregation introduced here are for illustrative purposes only. For simplicity and brevity, details have been kept to the minimum. (The symbols in Table 3.1 are presented below.)

Suppose an economy can be divided into n sectors and that the targets of final goods (consumption, exports, additions to capital stock, skills, and infrastructure) for each sector are either given or can be worked out from the information given in the plan. Capital goods and infrastructure are divided into finished and nonfinished components. Similarly, skills may be categorized as being of higher or lower levels. Such subdivisions may well be strategic from the viewpoint of feasibility and other evaluation aspects of a plan. Thus even if real savings in a period equal finished plus nonfinished capital, the amount of productive capital which increases capacity in the next period is only equal to the finished part. Furthermore, since work has to be continued on the unfinished part, a portion of investment must be committed to this purpose; and only the remainder can be allocated to new investment projects.

Another important detail to be introduced is the differentiation of capital goods produced in each sector with respect to their destinations,

Table 3.1

Matrix of Main Feasibility Variables

Delivering Sectors	Receiving Sectors (1)	...	Receiving Sectors (n)	Total	Consumption	Capital Finished	Capital Unfinished	Inventory	Skill Finished Semi-skilled	Skill Finished Highly skilled	Skill Finished Managerial	Skill Unfinished Semi-skilled	Skill Unfinished Highly skilled	Skill Unfinished Managerial	Infrastructure Finished	Infrastructure Unfinished	Exports	Grand Total
(1)	x_{11}	...	x_{1n}	W_1	C_1	ΔK_1	$\bar{K}_1$	V_1	ΔS_1^s	ΔS_1^h	ΔS_1^m	$\bar{S}_1^s$	$\bar{S}_1^h$	$\bar{S}_1^m$	ΔH_1	$\bar{H}_1$	E_1	X_1
⋮	⋮	⋮	⋮															
(n)	x_{n1}	...	x_{nn}	W_n	C_n	ΔK_n	$\bar{K}_n$	V_n	ΔS_n^s	ΔS_n^h	ΔS_n^m	$\bar{S}_n^s$	$\bar{S}_n^h$	$\bar{S}_n^m$	ΔH_n	$\bar{H}_n$	E_n	X_n
Total	U_1	⋮	U_n		C	ΔK	$\bar{K}$	V	ΔS^s	ΔS^h	ΔS^m	$\bar{S}^s$	$\bar{S}^h$	$\bar{S}^m$	ΔH	$\bar{H}$	E	X

Value Added

	(1)	...	(n)	Total
Rents and interests	y_1^l	⋮	y_n^l	Y^l
Wages of unskilled workers	y_1^u	⋮	y_n^u	Y^u
Wages of semi-skilled workers	y_1^s	⋮	y_n^s	Y^s
Salaries of highly skilled workers	y_1^h	⋮	y_n^h	Y^h
Profits and surplus	y_1^m	⋮	y_n^m	Y^m

Aggregate	Sector n	⋮	Sector 1			Resource Availability
Y	Y_m	⋮	Y_1	Total of Value added	Other Costs	
Z^t	Z^t_n	⋮	Z^t_1	Indirect taxes	Other Costs	
Z^m	Z^m_n	⋮	Z^m_1	Imported intermediates	Other Costs	
Z^d	Z^d_n	⋮	Z^d_1	Depreciation	Other Costs	
Z^r	Z^r_n	⋮	Z^r_1	Gov't transfers (negative)	Other Costs	
Z	Z_n	⋮	Z_1	Total of Other Costs		
X	X_n	⋮	X_1	Grand Total U + Y + Z		
L	L_n	⋮	L_1	Land	Domestic Factors of Production	$\bar{L}$
S^u	S^u_n	⋮	S^u_1	Unskilled — Labor	Domestic Factors of Production	$\check{S}^u$
S^s	S^s_n	⋮	S^s_1	Semiskilled — Labor	Domestic Factors of Production	$\check{S}^s$
S^h	S^h_n	⋮	S^h_1	Highly skilled — Labor	Domestic Factors of Production	$\check{S}^h$
S^m	S^m_n	⋮	S^m_1	Entrepreneurial & Managerial — Labor	Domestic Factors of Production	$\check{S}^m$
K	K_n	⋮	K_1	Capital	Domestic Factors of Production	$\check{K}$
H	H_n	⋮	H_1	Infrastructure	Domestic Factors of Production	$\check{H}$
K^m	K^m_n	⋮	K^m_1	Capital	Imported	$\check{K}^m$
X^m	X^m_n	⋮	X^m_1	Intermediate goods	Imported	

that is, the sectors in which they are going to be used. Capital capacity in any sector can be increased only by the amount of finished capital goods produced for this sector in the preceding period (excluding imported capital and industrial shift of capacity). Of course, this detail may not provide all that is needed for checking feasibility exactly, for example, if one sector produces several capital items for another sector. However, taking all the individual items into account separately is almost an impossible task, and the classification suggested here by sectoral aggregates may be largely adequate.

In agriculture, production is often recorded as a single sector in available input-output models, even though agriculture produces a variety of products requiring very different types of land. On the other hand, to classify land by type of produce may be difficult; the same land can often produce different types of products, and, as stated before, there is no exact relationship between land inputs and outputs. Hence tests of the adequacy of land by crude methods may be sufficient as well as unavoidable.

Labor can be usefully classified in at least four categories: unskilled, semiskilled, highly skilled, and entrepreneurial-managerial. Since it is usually very difficult to distinguish each type of skill by industrial sector, a fair test of feasibility can be accomplished by checking whether the domestically available semiskilled and highly skilled workers plus those from abroad are adequate for the output targets. The amount of imported skill is likely to be negligible even though it may be critical in some circumstances. Therefore, it is ignored in Table 3.1.

Although there are several categories of infrastructure and for a strict check of feasibility each type must be distinguished, we express them together for convenience and brevity. Infrastructure is a form of capital which can be treated as wholly domestic.

Intermediate imported goods should be recorded separately. First, they are not primary inputs but require foreign exchange in the same way as capital imports. Second, for checking the feasibility of the total gross domestic product (GDP) against the factors of production, imported intermediate goods have to be deducted from the GDP.

Goods imported for consumption are included in the imported intermediate goods, since there can seldom be such a good which does not go through a domestic sector such as transportation, retailing, and other services before it is consumed.

Financial aspects of planning are discussed at some length in chapter six. Here we merely make formal recognition of the fact that domestic income flows are generated corresponding to the physical activities carried out in the economy. The pattern of domestic income flows determines the size of savings and consumption. We make a rather standard classification of value added into rents and interests, wages and salaries, and profits and surplus. Other costs of production are divided into indirect taxes, imported intermediates, depreciation, and government transfers.

No explicit reference is made in the table to replacement of capital equipment, skill, or infrastructure. For simplicity, replacements are lumped with additions, though in reality the components may be different. Depreciation is treated as an *ex post* deduction at the end of the production period. Estimates of depreciation, replacement, and additions are crucial for estimating capacity in the following period. This process will be described briefly at the end of this section.

In planned economies the state at its various levels engages in productive activities in several sectors. Ideally the sectors should be divided between private and public. This division is particularly advantageous for planning because the private and public sectors differ substantially in the degree of convenience and certainty with which they can be managed and controlled. Further, the two may require different instruments and policies for their respective plan executions. For the sake of brevity and clarity, this subdivision has not been undertaken.[5] For checking physical feasibility as such, this subdivision is not essential. Given the techniques, only the total amounts of different types of resources and the magnitudes of the elements of the target are relevant. The summation over the rows of the table can be in physical terms, but over the columns only in value terms. For the sake of convenience we assume that each commodity is defined in such a unit that its value equals one dollar.

2. *Symbols Used in Table 3.1*

The following symbols are used in Table 3.1:

x_{ij} the amount of the ith commodity going into the production of the jth commodity

W_i the total of the intersectoral deliveries of the ith row, $W_i = \sum_j x_{ij}$

U_j the total of the intersectoral deliveries of jth column $U_j = \sum_i x_{ij}$

C_i the total consumption of the output from sector i

$$C = \sum_i C_i$$

Δk_i the additions to capital stock from the output of sector i in finished form ready to be used as capital in the following period

$$\Delta K = \sum_i \Delta K_i$$

$\tilde{K}_i$ the additions to capital stock from the output of sector i in unfinished form not ready to be used as capital in the following period

$$\tilde{K} = \sum_i \tilde{K}_i$$

V_i the additions to inventory from the output of sector i

$$V = \sum_i V_i$$

ΔS_i^s the additions to finished semiskill originating in sector i

ΔS_i^h the additions to finished high skill originating in sector i

ΔS_i^m the additions to finished managerial skill originating in sector i

$$\Delta S^s = \sum_i \Delta S_i^s, \quad \Delta S^h = \sum_i \Delta S^h, \quad \Delta S^m = \sum_i \Delta S_i^m$$

Symbols topped by ˜ rather than preceded by Δ represent additions to different types of skill in unfinished stages which cannot be used for further production in the following period.

ΔH_i the additions to finished infrastructure originating in sector i

$\tilde{H}_i$ the additions to unfinished infrastructure originating in sector i

$$\Delta H = \sum_i \Delta H_i, \quad \tilde{H} = \sum_i \tilde{H}_i$$

E_i the total exports from sector i

$$E = \sum_i E_i$$

$\phi_i = C_i + \Delta K_i + \tilde{K}_i + V_i + \Delta S_i^s + \Delta S_i^h + \Delta S_i^m + \tilde{S}_i^s + \tilde{S}_i^h + \tilde{S}_i^m +$

$\Delta H_i + \tilde{H}_i + E_i$

y_j^l the rents and interests accruing in sector j

y_j^u the wages of unskilled workers accruing in sector j

y_j^s the wages of semi-skilled workers accruing in sector j

y_j^h the salaries of highly skilled workers accruing in sector j

y_j^m the profits and surpluses accruing in sector j

Y_j the total value added in sector j

$$Y_j = y_j^l + y_j^u + y_j^s + y_j^h + y_j^m$$

$$\sum_j y_j^\theta = Y^\theta \quad \theta \text{ for } l, u, s, h, m$$

$$Y = \sum_j Y_j = Y^l + Y^u + Y^s + Y^h + Y^m$$

z_j^t the amount of indirect taxes realized from sector j

z_j^m the value of imported intermediate goods used in sector j

z_j^d the value of depreciation occurring in sector j

z_j^r the value of government transfer in sector j

Z_j the total of other costs in sector j

$$Z_j = z_j^t + z_j^m + z_j^d + z_j^r$$

$$z^t = \sum_j z_j^t \text{ and similarly for m, d, r.}$$

$$Z = \sum_j Z_j = z^t + z^m + z^d + z^r$$

$$X_i = W_i + \phi_i = U_i + Y_i + Z_i$$

$$X = \sum_i X_i \text{ or } \sum_j X_j$$

L_j the total amount of land resources specific to sector j at the beginning of the year

$$L = \sum_j L_j$$

S_j^θ the total amount of labor of type θ specific to sector j available at the beginning of the year

$$S^\theta = \sum_j S_j^\theta$$

$\check{S}^\theta$ the amount of retirement of labor of type θ during the year

Here $\theta = u, s, h, m$. The superscript u stands for unskilled labor, s for semiskilled, h for highly skilled, and m for managerial.

K_j the total amount of capital specific to sector j available at the beginning of the year

$$K = \sum_j K_j$$

H_j the total infrastructure relevant to sector j available at the beginning of the year. Most infrastructure cannot be categorized by sector. It is done here as a formality.

$$H = \sum_j H_j$$

K_j^m the imported capital specific to sector j

$$K^m = \sum_j K_j^m$$

X_j^m the imported intermediate goods of the type of sector j

$$X^m = \sum_j X_j^m$$

$\check{K}, \check{H}, \check{K}^m$ denote the depreciated amounts of capital, infrastructure, and imported capital, respectively.

It should be noted that in order to keep the table manageable the additions to capital, inventory, skills, and infrastructure by the sectors of their destination or utilization have not been specified. However, depreciation has been classified by sector.

3.   *Physical Tests in the Aggregate and by Sectors*

We can now attempt a detailed, but still rough and crude, check of intratemporal feasibility. It is assumed that the values of the items of final demand such as consumption, additions excluding replacements to capital, skill, and infrastructure, and exports are given by sectors and in the aggregate as targets. Availability of primary inputs in the beginning of the period such as land and different types of labor, capital, and infrastructure specific to each sector and in the aggregate are assumed to be known and given, as are the amounts of capital and intermediate goods to be imported and utilized during the period.

Consider a plan year t, and suppose that the overall plan target is divided into annual components. We further assume that these components consist of the elements of the final deliveries for all sectors. If the overall figures for some sectors are not given, they will have to be derived from other plan magnitudes. Final deliveries consist of consumption, additions (including replacement to capital, finished and unfinished), inventories, skills of various types (finished and unfinished), infrastructure (finished and unfinished), and exports. Let us suppose that the annual targets for the plan year under consideration are set in terms of items of the final deliveries, denoted by ϕ_i's. Let us further suppose that the ratios of intermediate deliveries to total sectoral output are constant, denoted as usual by

$$a_{ij} = \frac{x_{ij}}{X_j} \qquad i, j = 1, \ldots, n. \tag{13}$$

Therefore, $W_i = \sum_j a_{ij} X_j$

and $\qquad X_i = \sum_j a_{ij} X_j + \phi_i.$ \hfill (14)

There are n linear equations in (14) in n unknowns X_j's, and they can be solved to find the values of the unknowns.

In order to check the feasibility of targets with the resource availabilities, we have to deduct from the total sectoral output X_j required of sector j the imports of intermediate goods of the type of sector j, not necessarily used in sector j, denoted by X_j^m in Table 3.1. Thus the total output of a sector j required to be produced domestically is $X_j - X_j^m$, $j = 1, \ldots, n.$

In order to check the feasibility of targets with the resource availabilities, we assume that the factor input-output coefficients are given or can be estimated.

Let λ_j denote the land required per unit of output in sector j, $j = 1,$ $\ldots, n.$ Then the physical feasibility of targets with respect to land for producing corresponding sectoral outputs can be expressed as follows:

$$\lambda_j (X_j - X_j^m) \leqslant L_j \qquad (15)$$

or for the economy as a whole by

$$\sum_j \lambda_j (X_i - X_j^m) \leqslant \sum_j L_j = L. \qquad (15a)$$

For checking the feasibility of the targets with respect to different kinds of labor, let ξ_j^θ denote the amount of labor of type θ per unit of output of sector j. The feasibility of the targets of sector j with respect to labor of type θ can be expressed as follows:

$$\xi_j^\theta (X_j - X_j^m) \leqslant S_j^\theta \qquad (16)$$

and for all the sectors of the economy as a whole by

$$\sum_{j=1}^{n} \xi_j^\theta (X_j - X_j^m) \leqslant \sum_{j=1}^{n} S_j^\theta = S^\theta. \qquad (16a)$$

If b_j denotes the amount of capital required per unit of output of sector j, the feasibility of the targets with respect to capital can be expressed as follows:

$$b_j(X_j - X_j^m) \leqslant K_j + K_j^m \qquad (17)$$

and for all the sectors of the economy together by

$$\sum_{j=1}^{n} b_j(X_j - X_j^m) \leqslant \sum_{j=1}^{n} K_j + \sum_{j=1}^{n} K_j^m \leqslant K + K^m. \qquad (17a)$$

If we also had a breakdown of capital by the sector of origin so that we had estimates of different commodities to be used as capital in the year under consideration, we could apply an alternative check of feasibility with respect to capital. Let k_{hj} represent the amount of the capital item which originates in sector h but is used in sector j, so that $\sum_{h=1}^{n} k_{hj} = K_j$

$j=1, \ldots, n$. Let $\sum\limits_{j=1}^{n} k_{hj} = {}^{o}K_{h}$ denote the total amount of capital originating from sector h. Further, let b_{hj} represent the amount of output from sector h required as capital per unit of output of sector j. The adequacy of capital originating from sector h and utilized in sector j can be expressed as follows:

$$b_{hj}(X_j - X_j^m) \leqslant k_{hj} \qquad (18)$$

or for the economy as a whole by

$$\Sigma b_{hj}(X_j - X_j^m) \leqslant k_{hj} = {}^{o}K_{h}. \qquad (18a)$$

Finally, let ζ_j represent the amount of infrastructure per unit of output in sector j. Then the feasibility of the targets with respect to infrastructure for sector j can be expressed as follows:

$$\zeta_j (X_j - X_j^m) \leqslant H_j \qquad (19)$$

or for the economy as a whole by

$$\sum\limits_{j=1}^{n} \zeta_j (X_j - X_j^m) \leqslant \sum\limits_{j} H_j = H. \qquad (19a)$$

These relationships comprise a crude but useful set of tests of physical sectoral feasibility.

4. Feasibility of Consumption

A crucial check of the feasibility of consumption may be made with respect to the income generated. In Table 3.1, value added has been classified into five categories. For a more accurate estimate a greater number of classes corresponding to regional, ethnic, and other groupings would be required.

Let τ^θ be the rate of direct taxes imposed on Y^θ, the total value added by and hence income accruing to income group θ. Let $v_{\theta j}$ be the propensity of the income group θ to consume the commodities from the jth sector. Then the availability of consumption goods from each sector will be adequate if

$$\sum_{\theta} v_{\theta j} (1 - \tau^{\theta}) Y^{\theta} \leqslant C_j - {}^g C_j \quad j = 1, \ldots, n, \qquad (20)$$

where ${}^g C_j$ is the government consumption of goods from sector j. Government consumption may be assumed to be given exogenously.

5. *Intertemporal Feasibility*

The preceding discussion of feasibility pertained to one production period, specifically to one annual plan. Intertemporal feasibility pertains to the possibility of achieving targets with the resources available at the beginning of the preceding period plus additions and replacements made less the depreciation that occurred in that period. Given the targets for each period, the feasibility of the plan for successive periods can be checked as before, after making adjustments in the availability of resources owing to additions, replacements, and depreciation.

For example, the amount of domestic capital available at the beginning of period t+1 is given by

$$K(t + 1) = K(t) + \Delta K(t) - \check{K}(t). \qquad (21)$$

Similarly, the availability of different types of labor and infrastructure in successive periods can be obtained.[6]

VI. Complementarity, Substitution, and Plan Feasibility

1. *Complementarity and Feasibility*

All feasibility tests have to be qualified by the degree of complementarity and substitution among inputs. In the presence of strict complementarity, tests of feasibility are simpler and in some respects straightforward, since a target is feasible only when the amounts of each and every factor input are equal to or greater than those required for the production of the target according to a fixed input-output ratio. The proportion of a target that will be realized is determined by the most limited primary input, that is, the one permitting the smallest output. Most of the preceding discussion deals with annual plans for which the assumption of strict complementarity may be most realistic, since if the feasibility of a medium-term plan is checked year by year, taking into consideration the marginal shifts of techniques, this assumption may still be applied. However, if a medium- or long-term plan is considered as a whole, the assumption of strict complementarity becomes less plausible.

Coefficients related in incremental levels of output over time may be different from those of previous outputs in view of changes of techniques and tastes, even over fairly short periods. If coefficients adjusted for marginal changes are available and known or can be estimated well enough, the feasibility of sectoral output targets over time can again be checked with respect to the available resources.

2. *Substitution and Plan Feasibility*

The preceding discussion implies that the techniques to be used have been decided on before we embark on the study of feasibility. If the resources, capital stock, and skills created in the preplan period can be combined with only a limited number of techniques, the choice will be restricted accordingly. However, since factor proportions vary with the alternative techniques, the extent of such variation depends on the number and dispersion of alternative techniques.

As an extreme case, we can assume (i) that incremental resources and skills are freely mobile and malleable and (ii) that the production structure is such that it allows continuous possibilities for substitution along a continuous production function for each product, that is, that substitution can involve small amounts of the available factors. In this case it will not be necessary and possible to check whether or not a single plan target is feasible, but the feasibility of the plan targets as a whole can be checked. This is because the factors can be substituted for one another.

The validity of the check for the overall feasibility of the plan targets rests on how well the above two assumptions depict reality. If they do within tolerable limits, the problem of the feasibility of the targets can perhaps be attacked by using continuous functions. Usually production functions with a constant elasticity of substitution equal to unity or some other number have been assumed to describe the productive activity of an economy.[7] In recent decades a good deal of empirical and theoretical research has been carried out around these functions. However, it is far from settled whether these functions of the Cobb-Douglas or CES variety can justifiably be applied to incremental amounts of factor inputs and outputs for short- or medium-term analysis and projections.

Professor Johansen[8] has used a Cobb-Douglas–type function for combining incremental amounts of factors in making sectoral projections for the Norwegian economy. He assumes labor and capital to be substitutable factors of production, though he adopts the usual hypothesis of fixed production coefficients for intermediate deliveries. His estimations of growth rates are close to the actual rates. Johansen's method, however, is based on the assumption of full employment in the base and subsequent years, a condition which is not true of most underdeveloped countries. Hence Johansen's approach cannot be used directly for formulating feasible development. In countries with sizable rates of unemployment the supply of labor considerably exceeds demand; hence the full-employment equilibrium analysis may not be tenable.

3.   *Limited Scope for Substitution*

Experience shows that in underdeveloped countries the actual scope for factor substitution in short- or medium-term plans is very limited. Alternative methods of production are available only in a limited number of industries, and the number of such alternatives tends to be very small.[9] The assumption of widespread substitution in the context of planning in most underdeveloped countries is not realistic. It is more realistic to work with a limited number of alternative techniques available for productive activity in individual sectors. However, the difficulties of specifying alternative techniques in practice should be fully recognized.

An attempt to check the feasibility of plan targets when alternative techniques of production in each sector are available requires programming techniques which are discussed in chapter five. A rough method of trial and error would consist of checking a few main combinations of techniques. If the plan targets are feasible with respect to any one of the combinations, then the plan is feasible.

In reality, factor inputs tend to be specific. A capital item is created to produce a specific good, and a skilled worker can be employed in the activity requiring his skill. Unskilled laborers can be employed in alternative uses where no particular skill is required, but they are not in short supply in most underdeveloped countries (or in some developed countries). Infrastructure poses special problems in that it is a joint input for all types of productive activities; hence it may be a major exception. However, its gestation period tends to be long, so that again for short- and medium-term plans the approach outlined in the preceding sections is, to a large extent, relevant.

VII. An Illustrative Feasibility Model

1.   *Introduction*

As noted above, mandatory national plans tend to be primarily feasibility plans, even though a great deal of effort goes into achieving consistency and, lately, optimality. In a sense, all open-ended growth models can be taken as feasibility models.

In recent years, however, Chenery[10] and his associates have formulated a class of simple aggregative models which can be applied under conditions of scarce and crude data. Such models are helpful also because they can pinpoint main limitational elements. As an illustration, we discuss here the Chenery-Bruno model of Israel, which comes very close to being what we would consider a feasibility planning model.

Chenery and Bruno include two types of control variables to determine the range of feasible programs. The first consists of policy instruments which are subject to what the authors term indirect control by the government, as in the case of the exchange rate or the level of foreign borrowing. The second type may vary within limits set by institutional factors but may or may not be directly influenced by government policy. Some variables may identify objectives as well as instruments. In their model, Chenery and Bruno use the classification of variables as shown in Table 3.2.

The Chenery-Bruno model is a comparative static model which attempts to study the limiting factors in the final year of a plan on the basis of the values of the variables in the initial year and the expected changes in the intervening period.

2.   *The Chenery-Bruno Model*

The model consists of twelve equations: seven structural, three limitational, and two definitional. The equations are as follows:

The aggregate production function,

$$V_n = V_o + \bar{\beta}\,(\overline{K}_o - \overline{K}_n) + \beta\,(K_n - K_o), \qquad (22)$$

where V_n is the gross national product in year n, K_n the total capital stock, and β an output-capital ratio or the average product per unit of increase in the capital stock. Subscripts o and n represent the initial and final year of the plan, and $\overline{K}_o$ and $\overline{K}_n$ the initial and final unused capacity, respectively. $\overline{\beta}$ is the average product obtainable per unit of unused capacity. The second term in the equation allows for the possibility of reducing the level of excess capacity $\overline{K}$, which is a significant factor in Israel, as in many underdeveloped countries.

Labor demand,

$$L_n = \lambda_o (1 - l)^n V_n, \tag{23}$$

Table 3.2

Classification of Policy Variables

Variables	Objectives.		Policy instru- ments .	Institu- tional limits.
	Fixed.	Variable:.		
1. Gross national product (V)		X		
2. Private consumption (C)		X		
3. Public consumption (G)	X			
4. Foreign capital inflow (F)		X	X	X
5. Unemployment rate (u)	X			
6. Savings rate (s)			X	X
7. Exchange rate (r)			X	
8. Rate of increase in labour productivity (l)				X

Hollis B. Chenery and Michael Bruno, "Development of Alternatives in an Open Economy: The Case of Israel," *Economic Journal* 72 (March 1962), p. 84. (Reprinted by permission.)

where L_n is the total demand for labor in the final year, λ_o the average labor input per unit of output in the initial year, and l the annual rate at which it decreases. The value of l includes effects of both substitution and technological changes and is estimated statistically from past trends.

Import demand,

$$M_n = \mu_c^r C_n + \mu_g^r G_n + \mu_i^r (I_n + R_n) + \mu_e^r E_n. \tag{24}$$

M_n is the demand for imports, C_n the private consumption, G_n the government current expenditure, I_n the total investment not including replacement, R_n the replacement, and E_n the exports, all in the final year. The coefficients μ^r represent the total imports required directly and indirectly per unit of each type of demand at exchange rate r. The use of a higher exchange rate would result in additional import substitution and a decrease in the import coefficients.

Replacement,

$$R_n = R_n (K_n, K_{n-1}, \dots). \tag{25}$$

R_n, the replacement of capital, depends on the age and estimated life of the capital stock. No concrete relationship is established for replacement.

Savings,

$$S_n = S_o + s(V_n - V_o). \tag{26}$$

Gross domestic savings in the final year S_n is the sum of gross domestic savings in the initial year S_o and the excess of V_n over V_o multiplied by the marginal propensity to save s. The marginal propensity to save s is an analytical catchall representing the combined effects of tax policy, changes in income distribution, and other policy measures that affect savings.

Labor supply,

$$N = N_o (1 + \gamma)^n. \tag{27}$$

The supply of labor in the final year N_n is determined from the labor supply in the initial year N_o by assuming increases at an exponential rate γ, when the natural increase in the existing population is combined with immigration.

Exports,

$$E_n = \sum_i E_i (r, P_{ei}, t). \tag{28}$$

The level of total exports E_n is the sum of the individual commodities and services exported; each is assumed to depend on the effective exchange rate r, the foreign prices P_{ei}, and the time t needed to penetrate new markets.

The seven equations above describe the structural relationship of the economy. The three that follow are balance or equilibrium equations which specify three major resource limitations or bottlenecks:

Savings-investment equilibrium,

$$S_n + F_n = I_n + R_n. \tag{29}$$

S_n is the total domestic savings in the final year, and F_n the total foreign capital inflow.

Balance-of-payments equilibrium,

$$M_n = E_n + F_n. \tag{30}$$

Employment equilibrium,

$$L_n = (1 - u)N_n, \tag{31}$$

where the proportion unemployed u is specified as an objective.

The last two equations are definitional:
Total net capital formation,

$$\sum_{t=0}^{t=n-1} I_t = K_n - K_o.$$

In order to express the model in terms of initial- and final-year values only, an approximation of the following form is needed:

$$I_n = \rho(K_n - K_o). \tag{32}$$

Here ρ depends on the rate of growth of investment and the length of the planning period. Some assumption of this type is needed to make I_n

determinate in order to provide a complete description of the structure of the economy in the final year.

Gross national product,

$$V_n = C_n + G_n + I_n + R_n + E_n - M_n. \tag{33}$$

Eliminating variables, the above equations can be reduced to the following four equations involving the objective and instrument variables only. The first three correspond to the three equilibrium conditions for labor, capital, and foreign exchange. They express the gross national product of the final year as a function of the limitational factors of labor, capital, and foreign exchange, respectively:

$$V_n = \left[\frac{N_o (1 + \gamma)^n}{\lambda} \right] \frac{(1 - u)}{(1 - l)^n}, \tag{34}$$

$$V_n = \frac{[\rho/\beta \overline{V}_o + S_o - R_n] - sV_o + F_n}{\rho/\beta - s}, \tag{35}$$

$$V_n = \frac{(1 - \mu_e)E_n + (1 - \mu_c)F_n + (\mu_e - \mu_g)G_n + [(\mu_i - \mu_c)(\rho/\beta \overline{V}_o - R_n)]}{\mu_c + (\mu_i - \mu_c)\rho/\beta}, \tag{36}$$

where $S_o = s_o V_o$ and $\overline{V}_o = \overline{\beta}(\overline{K}_o - \overline{K}_m) + V_o$.

The fourth equation gives the sum of private consumption and government current expenditures as a function of the gross national products in the initial and final years and the marginal propensities to save in the initial and final years:

$$C + G = (1 - s)V_n + (s - s_o)V_o. \tag{37}$$

Substituting statistical estimates in the reduced form of the model yields these specific equations for Israel for the period 1959-60 to 1964-65:

Full-employment equilibrium,

$$V_n = 4,999 \frac{(1 - u)}{(1 - l)^5}. \tag{34a}$$

Savings-investment equilibrium,

$$V_n = \frac{2,700 + F_n - 4,010\, s}{0.608 - s}.$$ (35a)

Balance-of-payments equilibrium,

$$V_n = 3.73\, F_n - 0.38\, G_n + 5,440.$$ (36a)

Total consumption,

$$C_n + G_n = (1 - s)V_n + (s - 0.10)\, 4,010.$$ (37a)

3.   *Feasible Combinations of Instrument Variables*

A feasible program is defined as a set of values for the policy variables for which equations (34) to (37) are satisfied and no controlled variable falls outside the predetermined range. The authors assume three values for the controlled variables: a minimum value, representing a pessimistic assessment of future possibilities; an intermediate value, usually based on past trends or a specific forecast; and a maximum or most optimistic value, beyond which the likelihood of further increase is too small to be considered for planning purposes. Government expenditure and unemployment level are assumed to be fixed objectives; hence they are given only one value. The limits assumed are as shown in Table 3.3.

Now we can find the set of feasible development programs that satisfy the equations of the reduced model and fall within the limits set for the control variables. The feasibility aspect is shown most simply by two-dimensional graphs showing V on the horizontal axis and one of the control variables, S, E, or F on the vertical axis. Since l is independent of the other control variables in the model, the V axis is marked off according to the value V takes on for different assumptions about the value of l, savings volume S, exports E, and foreign capital inflow F. The set of all feasible programs is shown by the shaded areas in Figures 3.3, 3.4, 3.5, and 3.6. In Figure 3.3 savings rates are constant, but total savings is a linear function of the gross national product.

The vertices of the feasible area can be determined by finding the points of intersections at which two variables are at one of their respective limits and the other two are within theirs. The solutions for the six vertices are given by points 1 through 6 in Table 3.4.

Table 3.3

Controlled Variables

Assumption	Effective exchange rate,[1] r.	Foreign capital inflow,[2] F.	Marginal savings rate, s.	Growth in labour productivity, l.	Unemployment level, u.	Government current expenditure, G.
a	2·5 I£/$	240	0·165	3%	0·05	1,010
b	3·0	330	0·25	4%	0·05	1,010
c	3·5	480	0·30	5%	0·05	1,010

[1]The corresponding exports are E_a = 1,000, E_b = 1,150, E_c = 1,400.
[2]The capital inflow in dollars is: (a) \$150 million; (b) \$220 million; (c) \$285 million. Conversion is made at the official rate of 1·8 I£/\$. A reduction of 30 million I£ has been made from the pound equivalent at the existing exchange rate of 1·8 I£/\$ to allow for a 20% fall in prices of citrus exports.

Hollis B. Chenery and Michael Bruno, "Development of Alternatives in an Open Economy: The Case of Israel," *Economic Journal* 72 (March 1962), p. 92. (Reprinted by permission.)

Of the four remaining points in Table 3.4, point 10 represents the case when no foreign capital inflow is allowed; exports are taken at their middle value of 1,150 and l at its lowest value of 0.03. At this point the balance of payments is the limiting factor, and the savings limit is redundant. In this unrealistic case, the GNP would rise only 9 percent above its initial (1959) level. Point 10 can be obtained from equation (15) or (15a). Its value is lower than the 18 percent increase that would be possible if savings were available at the lowest rate of savings of 0.165. Point 9 is obtained from (14) or (14a) by putting F_n = 0 and s = 0.165.

If we allow foreign capital to increase, keeping the same export level, we will move along E_b from point 10 to point 8, where the GNP reaches 5,290. At this point the savings boundary S_a is intersected, and the point can be determined by solving (14) for F_n = 250, s = 0.165. At this point investment requirements have been rising more than import needs, making the minimum savings level the more restrictive factor. This situation is evident from the figures. If we now move along S_a we reach point 6, which is the intersection of l_a with S_a. This point can be determined by first finding V_n from (34) for $l_a = l$ = 0.03 and u = 0.05 and

Table 3.4

Selected Solutions to the Model

Point.	Supply.			Resource use.				Savings.	Controlled variables.				
	V+F.	V.	M.	G.	C.	I+R.	E.	S.	s.	F.	r.	l.	u.
Base year.	5,095	4,010	1,085	750	2,860	940	545	400		540	a		0.05
Solution 1	6,290	5,810	1,490	1,010	4,100	1,180	1,010	700	0.165	480	c	0.04	0.05
2	6,610	6,130	1,610	1,010	4,230	1,370	1,130	890	0.231	480	c	0.05	0.05
3	6,460	6,130	1,670	1,010	4,080	1,370	1,340	1,040	0.300	330	c	0.05	0.05
4	6,050	5,810	1,590	1,010	3,860	1,180	1,350	940	0.297	240	c	0.04	0.05
5	5,760	5,520	1,480	1,010	3,750	1,000	1,240	760	0.238	240	c	0.03	0.05
6	5,870	5,520	1,440	1,010	3,860	1,000	1,090	650	0.165	350	c	0.03	0.05
7	6,140	5,810	1,550	1,010	3,950	1,180	1,220	850	0.248	330	c	0.04	0.05
8	5,540	5,290	1,400	1,010	3,670	860	1,150	610	0.165	250	c	0.03	0.095
9	4,730	4,730	1,290	1,010	3,200	520	1,290	520	0.165	0	c	0.03	0.19
10	4,360	4,360	1,150	1,010	3,060	290	1,150	290	0.420	0	c	0.03	0.25

Hollis B. Chenery and Michael Bruno, "Development of Alternatives in an Open Economy: The Case of Israel," *Economic Journal* 72 (March 1962), p. 94. (Reprinted by permission.)

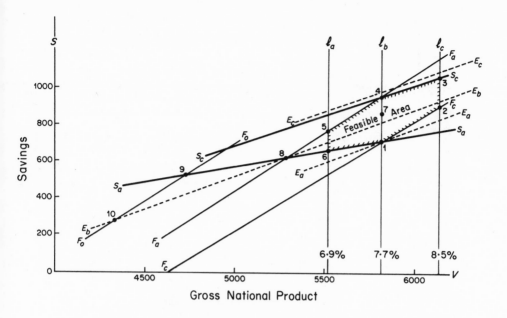

Fig. 3.3. Limits on S-V Axes. (Hollis B. Chenery and Michael Bruno, "Development of Alternatives in an Open Economy: The Case of Israel," *Economic Journal* 72 [March 1962], p. 95. Reprinted by permission.)

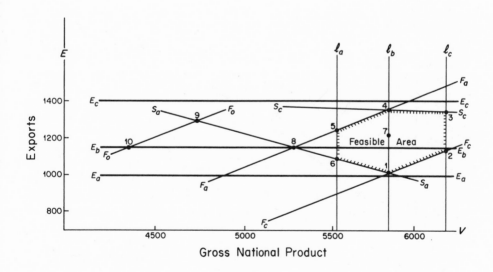

Fig. 3.4. Limits on E-V Axes. (Hollis B. Chenery and Michael Bruno, "Development of Alternatives in an Open Economy: The Case of Israel," *Economic Journal* 72 [March 1962], p. 95. Reprinted by permission.)

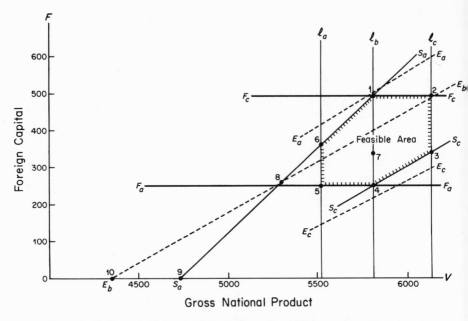

Fig. 3.5. Limits on F-V Axes. (Hollis B. Chenery and Michael Bruno, "Development of Alternatives in an Open Economy: The Case of Israel," *Economic Journal* 72 [March 1962], p. 96. Reprinted by permission.)

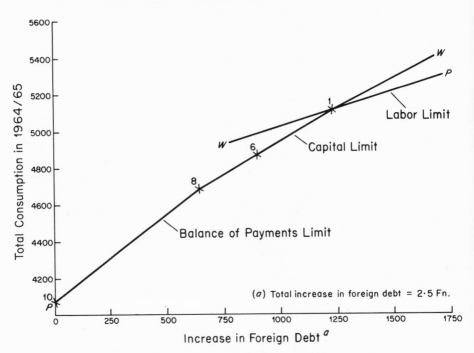

Fig. 3.6. Welfare Analysis. (Hollis B. Chenery and Michael Bruno, "Development of Alternatives in an Open Economy: The Case of Israel," *Economic Journal* 72 [March 1962], p. 100. Reprinted by permission.)

then finding the intersection of S_a and V_n from (35) for F = 330. Point 6 is one of the vertices of the feasible area. Moving along the lines representing the lowest or highest levels of control variables, we can trace the boundary of the feasible area.

The dual role of foreign capital in supplying both savings and foreign exchange can be seen more clearly from Figure 3.5. When there is no foreign capital inflow, that is, F = 0, the gross national product is more severely limited by the shortage of foreign exchange than by the level of savings, as shown by the positions of points 10 and 9 on the axis representing V. As V increases, import requirements increase less rapidly than investment requirements, and the two become equally restrictive at the intersection of S_a and E_b at point 8. As V increases further the shortage of savings is more restrictive than the supply of foreign exchange at the present savings rate of s_a.

The last equation (37a) is used to estimate total consumption. The productive possibilities of the economy are summarized in equations (34a), (35a) and (36a). Assuming values for the remaining control variables (s_a = 0.165, E_b = 1,150, l = 0.04), we can determine the total consumption as a function of foreign borrowing. The following production possibility curve (it may be more appropriate to call it a consumption possibility curve) is constructed from equation (37) and the data in Table 3.4. Up to point 8, growth is limited by the import restriction. Between point 8 and point 1 the increase in F permits a further increase in investment and the GNP, but, beyond point 1, the GNP is constant because full employment has been reached, and the increase in foreign borrowing will be used only to increase consumption. The three segments of the P – P curve correspond to the three equilibrium equations of the model, each of which is binding over one of the segments.

4. *Some Observations*

The Chenery-Bruno model consists of three separate models represented by equations (34), (35), and (36), respectively. Equation (34) determines the level of output (GNP) with respect to the level of employment and labor productivity, equation (35) determines it with respect to the availability of capital, and equation (36) with respect to the availability of foreign exchange. It is obvious that (34) is independent of (35) and (36) since the independent variables λ, u, and l do not appear as variables in (35) and (36). Equations (35) and (36) are interconnected since the instrument variable F_n is common to both. That is so because foreign loans and aid determine the availability of both capital and foreign exchange. Moreover (35) and (36) are both capital models and so depend on capital output coefficients, whereas (34), which is purely a labor model, does not.

Because (34) is independent, it is convenient to take employment as a target which fixes the value of the GNP corresponding to labor productivity l. The feasibility of the GNP thus derived can be checked with respect to savings, exports, and foreign exchange using equations (35) and (36), which contain these variables.

The Chenery-Bruno model focuses attention on the two crucial bottlenecks arising from shortages of capital and foreign exchange. These two bottlenecks along with that caused by a shortage of skill and managerial ability constitute the three major obstacles to the development of underdeveloped countries. The authors may not have considered the last one in their paper since it is not a serious bottleneck in Israel.

One interesting feature of the model is the treatment of foreign aid which fills either the savings gap or the foreign exchange gap, demonstrating the strategic importance of foreign aid in the development planning of underdeveloped countries.

Another important aspect of the model is the introduction of labor productivity and unutilized capacity, making the approach more realistic.

The Chenery-Bruno model offers a good illustration of feasibility considerations at the aggregate level. This type of model can be roughly applied to most underdeveloped countries where detailed input-output tables are not available or, if available, are not reliable. With some extensions and elaborations, similar models have been applied to other underdeveloped countries by Chenery and his associates.[11]

NOTES

1. P. N. Rosenstein Rodan, "International Aid for Underdeveloped Countries," *Review of Economics and Statistics* 43 (May 1961).

2. Planning Commission, Government of India, *Second Five Year Plan* (1956), p. 83. "In India, where the normal practice is not to rely on the central bank for subscription to new issues of long-term securities and where short-term debt of the government is largely held by the central bank, a deficit measured in terms of withdrawals of cash balances and net increases in floating debt gives, on the whole, a reasonably reliable indication of the impact of the budget on money supply." (Ibid., p. 84.)

3. Cash balances may refer to commercial banks' cash reserves in

excess of statutory requirements as well as to idle cash balances belonging to individuals.

4. J. C. Fei and Gustav Ranis, *Development of the Labor Surplus Economy: Theory and Policy* (Homewood, Ill.: Irwin, 1964).

5. To start with, sectors were divided between private and public, as were the items of final demand and the primary inputs. But the table became too unwieldy, and hence the subdivision was not employed.

6. For the sake of avoiding repetition of equations similar to (34), we do not represent the availability of different types of labor and infrastructure in the text.

7. These are the well-known functions of the Cobb-Douglas type or Constant Elasticity of Substitution (CES) variety. The first was discovered by P. H. Douglass in collaboration with C. Cobb; see Paul H. Douglas, *The Theory of Wages* (New York: Macmillan, 1934). The second was developed by K. J. Arrow, H. B. Chenery, B. S. Minhas, and R. M. Solow, "Capital-Labor Substitution and Economic Efficiency," *Review of Economics and Statistics* 43 (August 1961).

8. Leif Johansen, *A Multisectoral Study of Economic Growth* (Amsterdam: North Holland, 1960).

9. During the summer of 1961 the writer had an opportunity to work at the Indian Planning Commission and intended to work out some sort of accounting or shadow prices for the Indian economy. It was a great surprise to learn from one of the most active and able members of the Commission that the consideration of alternative techniques is largely of an academic nature and that in practice (at least for Indian planning at that time) the question of alternative techniques hardly arose.

10. H. Chenery and I. Adelman, "Foreign Aid and Economic Development: The Case of Greece," *Review of Economics and Statistics* 48 (February 1966); H. Chenery and M. Bruno, "Development Alternatives in an Open Economy: The Case of Israel," *Economic Journal* 72 (March 1962); H. Chenery and A. MacEwan, "Optimal Patterns of Growth and Aid: The Case of Pakistan," *Pakistan Development Review* 6 (Summer 1966); H. Chenery and A. Strout, "Foreign Assistance and Economic Development," AID Discussion Paper No. 7 (June 1965); H. Chenery, "Foreign Assistance and Economic Development," *American Economic Review* 56 (September 1966).

11. See n. 10 above.

CHAPTER FOUR

Plan Consistency

I. Introduction

1. *Definition and Importance of Consistency*

Plan consistency means that various elements of the plan are compatible and are designed to move in harmony with each other. More specifically, consistency implies that supplies of goods and services equal the demands for them in successive plan periods and that no undue excesses and shortages occur. A broader definition of consistency would require the plan to be compatible with the environmental, social, and political conditions prevailing in the country. This may be termed external consistency, in contrast to the preceding, narrower definition, which may be called internal consistency. Though external consistency is important, we shall restrict our discussion to internal aspects.

2. *Feasibility versus Consistency*

Plan feasibility refers basically to magnitudes of targets relative to amounts of initially given or anticipated resources. Feasibility tests link targets directly with resource availabilities.

Plan consistency, in contrast, is basically concerned with the interlinking intermediate states and processes which connect resources to targets. In particular, consistency brings into focus the balancing of intersectoral and interregional activities. It is understood, therefore, that for an accurate feasibility check, consistency analysis is a prerequisite.

3.   *Major Aspects of Consistency*

The following are some major considerations in plan consistency.

(i) Accounting identities. The fulfillment of accounting identities or balance equations is central to consistency. A key to such identities is that total output by sectors must equal the intermediate deliveries plus final demand, where the latter equals the sum of private and government consumption, private and government investment, inventories, replacement, and exports minus imports. This is the familiar starting point for input-output models to be discussed below.

(ii) Dynamic consistency. Whenever a plan covers several years, productive activity in any year is linked not only to that year's targets but to the targets and resource availabilities of the succeeding years. Input-output consistency planning should also seek to take account of the postplan period even if only approximately.

(iii) Investment lags. Investments in the construction of physical capital or in upgrading human resource capabilities are spread over multiple periods in most cases. Such gestation lags vary with types of capital items and skills. In order to achieve greater accuracy, therefore, investments should be subdivided and related to the year in which they would fructify or begin to produce output.

(iv) Technological changes. To make a consistency model more realistic, coefficients of intersectoral flows should reflect engineering realities with technological changes taken increasingly into account the longer the plan period.

(v) Regional balance. Regions of an ecomomy differ in factor endowments, market conditions, and the starting configuration of productive activities. Comprehensive consistent planning must encompass such variations whether or not it aims at increasing regional parity. Realization of regional targets, in turn, requires not only regional subplans but also interregional consistency.

(vi) Economies of scale. Strict adherence to consistency may preclude realization of advantages of economies of scale. Therefore, in order that economies of scale may be achieved, some excess capacity may have to be allowed in some sectors. However, such excesses may be considered technically necessary and compatible with consistency.

4.   *Approaches to Consistency Planning*

Two main approaches to consistency by planners have been through material balances and input-output analysis. Material balances have been widely used in formulating actual national plans in the socialist countries of Eastern Europe. As will be discussed, the method essentially consists of trial-and-error procedures based upon experience and estimated prospects. Though the approach is rough and ready, it allows a good deal of freedom for adjustment to economies of scale, technological change, substitution possibilities, and similar considerations often difficult to incorporate in more tightly structured methods.

One such class of methods, input-output analysis, has been the main vehicle of consistency planning models throughout the world. Though no national plan has yet been wholly formulated on the basis of an input-output analysis, the experiments with the construction of input-output tables and their analysis has yielded valuable insights into the interdependence of sectors and regions, the magnitudes of interregional and intersectoral commodity flows, and the role of capital coefficients. The extent of such contributions has been conditioned, however, by the degree of reliability of basic data and estimates.

5. *Plan of the Chapter*

This chapter discusses the basic methods of formulating consistent plans and consistency planning models. Section II gives a very brief account of material balances used in actual formulation of national plans in Soviet-type economies. Section III gives an elementary treatment of input-output methods and also describes approaches which have been developed to modify the static form of such analyses to make them more realistic.

In section IV, the intertemporal consistency models are developed under various assumptions regarding consumption targets and with ramifications such as introduction of foreign trade and aid, gestation lags, technological changes, and interregional analysis. The methods of solution of the models are given in the chapter appendices.

The final section briefly outlines the Manne-Rudra model of the Indian economy as an illustration of intertemporal consistency planning.

II. Balances

1. *Preliminary Remarks*

In Soviet-type economies, plan consistency has been and is still achieved through the system of material balances. Since a system of material balances cannot cover all items required by an industry, it cannot be the sole instrument of operational planning. A system of financial balances has, therefore, been used from the very beginning for accounting purposes, though not with much success.

Since practice regarding the system of balances varies among different countries of the Soviet Bloc and has been changing over time, the present brief description is intended to bring out some main features only.

2. Main Features

The use of balances, begun in 1923–24 in the U.S.S.R. after a period of coexistence of the state and private sectors terminated in the ultimate victory of the former, now constitutes the foundation of planning in all socialist countries. The essential purpose of the method is to bring into balance the supply and demand of material and of financial and labor resources.

The planning system in socialist countries is characterized by (i) perspective (long-term) plans and (ii) the current (short-term) plans. The former generally mean the five-year plans, and the latter are the annual plans which are drawn up on the basis of the five-year plans. Balances are set up in more or less the same manner for both types of plans except that in the perspective plans balances reflect the major aspects in the economy such as the determination of the relative size of each sector, the amount of capital investment and its sector distribution, and the utilization of labor resources. The perspective plan sets forth the control figures which represent the basic parameters and coefficients used in short-term planning. For arriving at the control figures, structural shifts, moderniza-tion of industries, and regional developments are investigated.

In the Soviet Union the perspective plans are drawn up by the State Planning Committee of the U.S.S.R. (Gosplan). The control figures of the plan are sent to the union ministries and agencies and to the state planning committees of the union republics. These bodies draw up their plans within the framework of the control figures and set their own control figures for the individual enterprises. Each enterprise makes up its own plan based on the control figures and directives received. These are sent up the hierarchy for aggregation and amalgamation at different levels and finally into the Gosplan.

Balances are used more extensively and firmly in the formulation of annual plans, as is to be expected, since these are the operational units. The following brief account relates to the Soviet Union. Similar procedures are used in other socialist countries with some variations and uncertain reforms.

In the Soviet Union, annual preparatory statistical work at all levels, based on plan performance in the previous year and part of the current year, precedes the setting of the annual input and output targets for the next year. The Soviet Council of the National Economy prepares "control figures," or tentative targets, for different strategic sectors, including the output of a limited number of significant commodities. As Bergson points out, these control figures are "formulated with due regard for targets set in the long-term plan then in effect and for general directives issued by the Council of Ministers on behalf of or jointly with the highest party organs."[1] After the release of the control figures, all agencies exercising operational control—the ministries, republics, and enterprises—are expected to review their earlier estimates and projections. At the same time, the figures are elaborated into more detailed targets of inputs and outputs for lower agencies. These detailed figures then move upward from lower to higher agencies in aggregated terms. The highest (Gosplan) undertakes to ensure a balance between the various output and requirements, negotiating with different ministries if necessary to rectify imbalances. Finally, after its approval by the Party and government, the plan is passed on to the ministries as operational directives. Various procurement contracts are signed between user and supplier agencies at all levels, and arrangements are made regarding specifications, delivery dates, prices, and the like, though these do not form part of the plan.

Some 800 to 1,000 important materials, production, and distribution are annually planned by the central Soviet planning organ. Another five to six thousand materials are distributed by the main administrations for interrepublic deliveries of the U.S.S.R. Council of the National Economy. This has been found necessary to overcome the tendencies of the republics and their subsidiary regional economic councils to place regional needs ahead of national need for materials.

3. *Problems Faced in Implementation*

When, as often happens, divergencies occur between supplies and requirements of industrial materials, the provisional targets have to be revised. But since in most cases industrial products are interdependent, revisions in targets pertaining to the balance of one product call for further revisions in others, and these in turn for still others, and so on, in a chain-like fashion. Various methods have been used to bring about consistency at an early point. One main concern has been simply to limit the secondary effects. This has been done in diverse ways such as (i) adjusting end industrial products not related to productive uses elsewhere, (ii) changing input norms of users, and (iii) changing input norms of suppliers by changing their production targets.

A word is necessary about input norms, which play an important role in effecting a balance among industrial materials. Such norms are arrived at on the basis of statistical analysis of past plan performance, and negotiations among agencies at different levels. Because of this, but also because they are adjusted to avoid secondary effects, they become to an extent artificial. Arbitrariness may occur whether supplies may exceed requirements or, as is more likely to happen, requirements exceed supplies. In the latter situation, the arbitrary nature of the decisions will be somewhat mitigated so far as the shortfalls in supplies arise from the padding of input norms by enterprises, regional economic councils, republics, and ministries. Often by setting input norms below the previous average, pressures to realize a "reserve of productivity" are created. But since it is not easy to discover when the norms are padded, needed downward revisions may not occur, and errors in materials balances may not be eradicated.

Another problem faced in applying the method of material balances is the degree of fineness of commodity breakdowns. If the supplies and requirements of individual enterprises are to be balanced exactly, each target should be broken down into minute details and specifications. This is an enormous task whose dimensions can be judged from the fact that each year the chief administration for ferrous metal sales had finally to issue some half-million production and delivery orders to subordinate enterprises. It can be expected that further imbalances pertaining to the specifications of the materials and the delivery dates, and so forth, to individual firms have to be rectified. The tremendous amount of detail that must be handled can be gauged from the following example:

> In all, some 9,000 varieties of ball bearings are in production. Requisitions for this material alone by one auto factory from the First Government Ball Bearing Factory were processed by fourteen agencies. In the circumstances, some 430 pounds of documents were generated.[2]

As stated above, when a deficit in the supply of a material arises, an effort is made to correct the imbalance in a way that avoids secondary effects by adjusting the level of an appropriate end product target or the user's and supplier's input norms. To enlarge the output of a deficit material would otherwise require additional output increases of various kinds in a series of an interminable number of rounds. In Soviet planning, when a need arises to trace secondary effects, the calculations are generally stopped after three or four rounds. In most cases, this amount of iteration captures about 80 to 90 percent of the total secondary effects, which get smaller with successive iteration.[3]

4.   *Recent Improvements*

With the development and extensions of input-output analysis, a powerful mechanism for tracing all balance input requirements exhaustively and simultaneously was provided. In fact, recent descriptions of efforts at balancing supplies and demand appear to be paraphrases of the standard principles of input-output analysis. Even the nomenclature "material balances" is being replaced by "intersectoral balances," as in a recent account by Fedorenko.[4] These balances are prepared both for accounting and for purposes of planning and both for the country as a whole and for regions. From these balances a number of basic calculations are derived, such as volume and composition of planned final products, planning coefficients describing direct use of materials, volumes of gross outputs of individual sectors, and their coordination with capital investment and labor utilization. In this way, global economic and sectoral proportions are coordinated for the most important types of production. Such planning intersectoral balances were constructed in physical terms for the U.S.S.R. as a whole for 1962–70, the number of individual products increasing from 346 in 1962 to 600 for the years 1966–70.

A special place is given to the balances of economic regions. These are constructed in aggregate monetary terms on the basis of production plans of individual enterprises in the form of input-output tables. This makes it possible to achieve consistency in the planning indicators linking the enterprises and sectors of the economic regions.

Intersectoral balances in the U.S.S.R. involve a clear distinction between intermediate and final products and between material production and the so-called nonproductive sphere. Intermediate includes "material expenditures of objects of labor" (that is, use of produced goods) in the various sectors of material production. Nonproductive use relates to all activities which do not produce any material product.

In socialist terminology, final products include (i) personal consumption by the population of material production; (ii) social consumption in the nonproductive sphere (that is, expenditure of the output of the material production sphere in the fields of health, education, science, culture, social welfare, the sphere of administration, sciences, and housing); (iii) capital investment and capital repairs of "basic real fund"; increase in circulating production funds, inventories, and reserves; (iv) increase of cattle in agriculture, new trees in forestry, and long-lasting plants in agriculture; and (v) balance of exports and imports.

The second stage of planning intersectoral balances requires the creation of "normative bases," or norms. This is one of the most important and complex problems in the construction of balances. The difficulty concerns the absence of a statistical base adequate to calculate a large number of coefficient of "direct expenditure," that is, direct use or utilization. Factors taken into account in calculating coefficients are (i) technological changes, (ii) organizational changes, (iii) shifts in industrial location, and (iv) price changes.

Intersectoral balance is formulated irrespective of administrative jurisdiction. For instance, electrical energy generated in an enterprise producing textiles is represented in a sector called electrical energy rather than in textiles. In planning, however, the concept of adminstrative sectors is employed and classified by enterprise. This makes it necessary to convert pure intersectoral balances into administrative counterparts. This is done by means of a detailed product decomposition of all administrative sectors.

It is thus observed that the system of material balances practiced in the Soviet Union and other socialist countries is gradually approaching, through refinement and logical extension, the system of input-output structure developed in the Western countries, though the socialist dialectic still persists.

From the very beginning, too, the central authorities in the Soviet Union and other socialist countries have made use of parallel financial balances. The household income and expenditure determines the supply of consumer goods to the households, the incomes to be earned are derived from the manpower balance, and the wage funds are those ratified in the financial balance.[5] However, application of financial balances in the Soviet-type economies has not yet resulted in procedures which enable short-term money transition to be identified with physical flows with sufficient precision.

III. Methods of Static Input-Output Analysis

1. Introduction

We have already used some basic notions of input-output analysis in chapters two and three. After summarizing the fundamental relations and underlying assumptions, we shall outline some useful manipulations of the structure in this section.

Some of the methods discussed below modify the input-output structure in such a way that the solutions become easier and also more realistic. Others are interesting also from the administrative point of view.

They show how under certain conditions policies can be administered to a sector or groups of sectors without having repercussions in other sectors.

2.   Static Input-Output Analysis and Its Underlying Assumptions

The output of an industry goes either for intermediate use by other industries or for final use. Ignoring the subdivisions of the final use, the outgoings or deliveries of the output of an industry can be expressed as

$$x_i = \underbrace{\frac{x_{i1} + \ldots + x_{ij} + \ldots x_{in}}{\text{intermediate use}}} + \underbrace{\phi_{in}}_{\substack{\text{final} \\ \text{use}}} \tag{1}$$

$$i = 1, \ldots, n,$$

where n is the number of industries or the number of industrial classifications (sectors) in the economy. The jth element on the right-hand side denotes the amount of intermediate use of output from industry i by industry j, (i, j=1, ... , n). If we divide x_{ij} by x_j the total output of industry j, we get $a_{ij} = \dfrac{x_{ij}}{x_j}$ the amount of commodity i required per unit of output of sector j. Substituting $a_{ij} x_j$ for x_{ij}, we can rewrite (1) as

$$x_i = a_{i1} x_1 + \ldots + a_{ij} x_j + \ldots + a_{in} x_n + \phi_i \tag{2}$$

$$i = 1, \ldots, n.$$

Given the values of ϕ_i's as plan targets in physical terms, the total physical output of each sector can be derived, encompassing all the interdependencies exhaustively, by solving the system of n equations for n unknowns x_i's. The values of x_i's give the amounts of total output of each sector which are in balance with each other. This is what the Russian and East European planners had been trying to arrive at through iterations in the system of material balances, before the above systematic formulation of input-output analysis was developed by Leontief[6] in the West and became increasingly used in Socialist planning.

The underlying assumptions of input-output structure are these: (i) each sector produces a well-defined commodity or group of commodities, which is not produced by any other sector; (ii) at a point of time each sector uses only one method of production, which implies that the set of inputs per unit of output of a sector is unique; (iii) only the level of output of a sector determines the magnitudes of inputs from other sectors; (iv) as a result of assumptions (i) and (iii), the "total effect of carrying on several types of production is the sum of the separate effects."[7] This implies additivity of productive activity and rules out economies and diseconomies of scale.

The input-output system (2) with one and only one coefficient for each combination of an input and an output does not allow any substitution of inputs, and there is only one set of equilibrium prices associated with it. This is true even when the magnitudes of the components of final use change. This can be intuitively realized by the fact that ϕ_i's are the constants of the system and they do not affect the relationships between the commodities which are fixed any way.[8]

From the definition of a_{ij}, it is evident that $a_{ij} \geqslant 0$. Moreover, in equilibrium the total value of inputs in sector j can at most equal the value of its total output. Hence $\sum_i x_{ij} \leqslant x_j$, both sides being expressed in value terms. Dividing through by x_j, $\sum_i a_{ij} \leqslant 1$. With $a_{ij} \geqslant 0$ and $\sum_i a_{ij} \leqslant 1$, the equations have unique solutions which are positive if the ϕ_i's are positive. These results can be checked by actual iteration.[9]

The set of equations in (2) can be solved by Cramer's rule or by one-by-one elimination of variables. The former is equivalent to inversion of the matrix of coefficients a_{ij}; the latter leads to the Gaus Seidel iteration method. These two methods are lucidly explained in Chenery and Clark, *Interindustry Economics*.[10] Another method of approximation, advanced by Waugh,[11] involves summing a matrix power series. In this method the solution can be obtained to the required degree of accuracy without using Cramer's rule or inversion of matrices. The method also provides means of checking the accuracy of computations.

3. *Independence of Sectors and Groups of Sectors*

In input-output analysis, a system of general independence, in which every sector has a direct connection with every other sector, is assumed. In practice, however, it is observed that this interdependence of industries is limited. Some industries may draw their inputs from a limited range of other industries, and some groups of industries tend to form blocks with a great deal of buying and selling within groups but relatively little between groups.

Chenery and Clark have discovered that, by an appropriate adjustment and interchange of sectors, input-output tables can be approximated roughly by a triangular form.[12] The pattern they have attempted to fit to the interindustry flows of each country is that of one-way interdependence, as can be described by the system of equations (3) for five sectors as follows:

$$x_1 = a_{11} x_1 \qquad\qquad\qquad\qquad\qquad + \phi_1$$

$$x_2 = a_{21} x_1 + a_{22} x_2 \qquad\qquad\qquad + \phi_2$$

$$x_3 = a_{31} x_1 + a_{32} x_2 + a_{33} x_3 \qquad\qquad + \phi_3 \qquad (3)$$

$$x_4 = a_{41} x_1 + a_{42} x_2 + a_{43} x_3 + a_{44} x_4 \qquad + \phi_4$$

$$x_5 = a_{51} x_1 + a_{52} x_2 + a_{53} x_3 + a_{54} x_4 + a_{55} x_5 + \phi_5.$$

Sequences like raw cotton-textiles-clothing fit nicely into such an arrangement, but circular relations like coal-steel-mining equipment-coal do not.

  If an input-output table can be represented in a triangular form as above, with values of the elements above the diagonal being very insignificant or zeros, the value of the total output of sectors affected by a change in a component of the final deliveries can be easily derived. Whenever a sector's final delivery has changed, only this sector and those recorded below it will have altered outputs. As the outputs of sectors appearing above this sector are known and unaffected, the change in the output of the sector whose final delivery had changed can be immediately obtained. And, by successive substitution, the changed outputs of the remaining sectors can be estimated without any need for inverting the matrix. Further, since the policy changes introduced in a sector do not affect the sectors appearing earlier in the triangular pattern, the effects of a policy change in a certain sector need to be traced only in respect to sectors lying below it.

  If the groups of sectors formed completely independent blocks without any interblock deliveries, the computing work of input-output analysis is again greatly simplified. Let us consider an economy of five sectors, the first three sectors being completely independent of the last two sectors.

$$x_1 = a_{11} x_1 + a_{12} x_2 + a_{13} x_3 \qquad\qquad + \phi_1$$

$$x_2 = a_{21} x_1 + a_{22} x_2 + a_{23} x_3 \qquad\qquad + \phi_2 \qquad (4)$$

$$x_3 = a_{31} x_1 + a_{32} x_2 + a_{33} x_3 \qquad\qquad + \phi_3$$

$$x_4 = \qquad\qquad a_{44}\, x_4 + a_{45}\, x_5 + \phi_4$$

$$\text{(4 cont'd)}$$

$$x_5 = \qquad\qquad a_{54}\, x_4 + a_{55}\, x_5 + \phi_5$$

System (4) can be divided into two completely independent systems, since there are no intersectoral deliveries between the first three sectors and the last two sectors. The two structures are completely independent and can be solved separately. Each of them is easier to solve and analyze. Though in reality completely independent blocks of sectors in an economy seldom exist, an underdeveloped economy can be roughly divided into two blocks, one the traditional agricultural sector and the other the non-traditional, or modern, industrial sector.

If a certain amount of buying and selling among blocks, which cannot be ignored, does take place, this can be studied under some simplifying assumptions. First, it can be assumed that the amount of goods available for absorption by industries outside the block is dictated by supply considerations. Thus, in our illustration, the availability of the products of any of the first three sectors to the last two sectors may be represented by a certain proportion of that sector's output, and vice-versa. This can be expressed in our simple illustration in the following way:

$$x_1 = a_{11}\, x_1 + a_{12}\, x_2 + a_{13}\, x_3 + a_1\, x_1 + \phi_1$$

$$x_2 = a_{21}\, x_1 + a_{22}\, x_2 + a_{23}\, x_3 + a_2\, x_2 + \phi_2 \qquad\qquad (5)$$

$$x_3 = a_{31}\, x_1 + a_{32}\, x_2 + a_{33}\, x_3 + a_3\, x_3 + \phi_3$$

and

$$x_4 = a_{44}\, x_4 + a_{45}\, x_5 + a_4\, x_4 \qquad + \phi_4 \qquad\qquad (5a)$$

$$x_5 = a_{54}\, x_4 + a_{55}\, x_5 + a_5\, x_5 \qquad + \phi_5$$

where a_i, $i=1, \ldots, 5$, denotes the proportion of the output of ith sector supplied to the other block of sectors. The system of equations belonging to the two blocks then can be solved independently.

Second, it can be assumed that the demand for the product of each sector in one block by the other block is a proportion of the total output of all the sectors in that block. Thus the demand for the product of one of the sectors of the second block by the sectors of the first block is a proportion of the total output of the first block, so that

$$x_4 = a_{44} x_4 + a_{45} x_5 + a_4 (x_1 + x_2 + x_3) + \phi_4$$

$$x_5 = a_{54} x_4 + a_{55} x_5 + a_5 (x_1 + x_2 + x_3) + \phi_5$$

$$(x_1 + x_2 + x_3) = (a_{14} + a_{24} + a_{34}) x_4 + (a_{15} + a_{25} + a_{35}) x_5 + \phi_1 + \phi_2 + \phi_3.$$

This can be solved for x_4, x_5, and $x_1 + x_2 + x_3$ by the usual methods.

Ghosh[13] has applied the simplified analyses outlined above to the input-output table of the United Kingdom for 1948 prepared by the Department of Applied Economics at Cambridge. He found that the average error introduced by the partial approach may be considered quite tolerable.

The methods stated above are interesting for the study and analyses of underdeveloped economies where partly independent blocks of sectors do exist. When this is the case, modifications may be carried out within the block, and levels of output may be estimated by studying the interdependence of the sectors by block, ignoring the remaining sectors. Also, more or less independent policies can be formulated and pursued in respect of individual blocks. In some underdeveloped countries it is convenient to lump together some sectors such as those related to agriculture or oil and study the interdependence between this aggregated sector and other important sectors. This may also be necessitated by the paucity of detailed data.

4.   Sector Limitations

Individual sectors of an input-output system may be subject to various types and degrees of limitations. We shall discuss here two extreme cases. First is the one in which a sector need not expand or contract with the system, that is, the output level of the sector may not have to change with the vector of final use. The second case is that in which the output level of a sector cannot be increased beyond a certain level.

In the first case, sectors are divided into two parts, one including those whose outputs are freely imported and exported and the other including the remaining sectors whose outputs cannot be imported. The sectors belonging to the first category are called international sectors and the others, national sectors. A change in the requirement of goods produced by the international sectors may not require a change in the level of operation of international sectors, but a change in the requirement of goods produced by the national sectors must be accompanied by a corresponding change in the level of operation of these sectors.

Let us suppose that, in our example, the first three sectors are international and the last two are national. Since the goods of the international sectors can be imported, the production level of these sectors to be produced domestically can be fixed. But the production level of national sectors, for meeting the domestic production of goods of national as well as international sectors, has to be realized. If we assume that the levels of output of the international sectors to be produced domestically are fixed at x_1^*, x_2^*, x_3^*, the balance equations for the national sectors can be written as follows:

$$x_4 = a_{41} x_1^* + a_{42} x_2^* + a_{43} x_3^* + a_{44} x_4 + a_{45} x_5 + \phi_4$$
$$\tag{7}$$
$$x_5 = a_{51} x_1^* + a_{52} x_2^* + a_{53} x_3^* + a_{54} x_4 + a_{55} x_5 + \phi_5.$$

Solving the above for x_4 and x_5, the levels of output of the domestic sectors compatible with the production levels of international sectors can be obtained. The advantage of this method is that it allows freedom in fixing the output levels of international sectors and thus facilitates the planning of national sectors. In usual input-output models, if one sector expands, other sectors must also expand correspondingly, and there is no mechanism to draw down the exports of the international sectors to feed the expansion of domestic sectors. The above method relaxes the rigidity of common input-output models.[14]

The second case relates to a situation which is often met in practical planning. The capacity of some sectors is limited because of physical or technical conditions in the economy, and they cannot produce more than certain maximum levels of output. If the capacity output of such sectors is known and given, the total output levels of other sectors and the final deliveries of the capacity-limited sectors can be derived, given the final demand for the nonlimited sectors.

As an illustration, let us suppose that the first three sectors of our five-sector economy are limited by given capacity outputs of x_1, x_2, and x_3, and let the amounts of output for final use for the remaining two unlimited sectors be ϕ_4^u and ϕ_5^u. The total outputs of the unlimited sectors can be written as follows:

$$x_4^u = a_{41} x_1 + a_{42} x_2 + a_{43} x_3 + a_{44} x_4^u + a_{45} x_5^u + \phi_4^u$$

$$\tag{8}$$

$$x_5^u = a_{51} x_1 + a_{52} x_2 + a_{53} x_3 + a_{54} x_4^u + a_{55} x_5^u + \phi_5^u.$$

This can be solved for x_4^u and x_5^u. The levels of final use of the capacity limited sectors are

$$\phi_1 = x_1 - a_{11} x_1 - a_{12} x_2 - a_{13} x_3 - a_{14} x_4^u - a_{15} x_5^u$$

$$\tag{9}$$

$$\phi_2 = x_2 - a_{21} x_1 - a_{22} x_2 - a_{23} x_3 - a_{24} x_4^u - a_{25} x_5^u$$

$$\phi_3 = x_3 - a_{31} x_1 - a_{32} x_2 - a_{33} x_3 - a_{34} x_4^u - a_{35} x_5^u.$$

It may turn out that one or more of ϕ_1, ϕ_2, and ϕ_3 are negative or less than the minimum amount required for final use as a target. Then, if these deficits cannot be met from imports, the final deliveries of unlimited sectors may have to be adjusted to allow for the residue of minimum final demand required from the capacity-limited sectors.

A straightforward application of input-output analysis ignores the capacity limitations of individual sectors. An application of the above modified procedure will make the estimation of the volumes of sectoral outputs as well as the setting of plan targets more realistic.

IV. Dynamic Consistency Planning

1.   *Targets in Terms of Consumption Levels*

We have already described the system of balances used for consistency planning in the Soviet-type economies. We shall outline now consistency planning models which can be formulated on the basis of dynamic input-output analysis. These models can be designed to fit various targets set in terms of levels of final deliveries.

First, we shall consider targets consisting of levels of consumption of individual sectors. Other details such as external transactions, gestation lags, and technological progress will be introduced later.

Often, plan targets may be fixed in terms of levels of consumption to be provided in the terminal year of the plan or in each year of the plan. If the targets are set only for the terminal year of the plan, the levels of output and investment in the earlier plan years may be arbitrary. It is necessary, however, to have minimum levels of consumption in each plan year. Let the minimum level of consumption of output from sector i in the year t be $c_i(t)$, $i=1, \ldots n$ and $t=1, \ldots, T$.

In order that a $c_i(t)$ level of consumption of commodity i in year t be realized, the total output of commodity i in that year, $x_i(t)$, must be such that, after deducting deliveries for current and capital inputs, a level $c_i(t)$ of the commodity is left, that is,

$$x_i(t) - \sum_{j=1}^{n} a_{ij} x_j(t) - \Delta k_i(t) = c_i(t), \tag{10}$$

where $\Delta k_i(t)$ is the delivery from the output of sector i for capital formation or additions to capital stock. We assume here that $x_i(t)$ represents the net value of output. We assume further that output set aside for capital formation in year t is installed and begins to produce output in year t+1. Under the assumption of full capacity utilization which is implied here, this means that $\Delta k_i(t)$ must be adequate to produce the excess of net output in year t+1 over that in year t, that is,

$$\Delta k_i(t) = \sum_{j=1}^{n} b_{ij} (x_j(t+1) - x_j(t)), \tag{11}$$

where b_{ij} is the amount of output from sector i required as capital per unit of output from sector j.

Substituting (11) into (10), we get

$$x_i(t) - \sum_{j=1}^{n} a_{ij} x_j(t) - \sum_{j=1}^{n} b_{ij} (x_j(t+1) - x_j(t)) - c_i(t) = 0. \tag{12}$$

This is a system of n nonhomogeneous linear difference equations of degree one. Solutions of the system are given in the chapter appendices.

The minimum levels of consumption to be provided in successive plan years can be decided on the basis of demand analysis or on some simpler assumptions. One of the simplest assumptions is that minimum levels of consumption of sectoral outputs grow at a common constant rate. In this case,

$$c_i(t) = c_i (1 + \psi)^t, \tag{13}$$

where c_i is a base level of consumption of the output of sector i. The solution of this case is given in appendix 4.A. A less restrictive assumption would be that the minimum levels of consumption grow at constant rates which are not necessarily equal. In this case,

$$c_i(t) = c_i (1 + \psi_i)^t. \tag{14}$$

The most general case, of course, is the one in which the levels of all $c_i(t)$ are free to change at varying annual rates. In this case,

$$c_i(t) = c_i \pi_t (1 + \psi_i(t))^t. \tag{15}$$

Appendix 4.B discusses a method of solution to the general consumption planning model where the consumption levels of individual sectors can be given any values.

2.   *Intertemporal Consistency Planning with Foreign Trade*

Exports can be affected, to some extent, by changes in taxes and exchange rates, by export promotion policies, or by establishing and strengthening trade relations with other countries through trade agreements. Largely, however, the level of exports tends to be beyond the control of the exporting country. We assume here that the rate of growth of exports and the availability of foreign aid and loans are exogenously given.

Imports can be divided into two parts: complementary and competitive. Complementary imports are those which cannot be produced domestically but which the country must obtain to carry out its planned productive activities. Therefore, these form constant proportions of sectoral outputs. Competitive imports relate to goods which can be produced domestically and hence their volumes to be imported can be fixed by the policy makers. The distinction between complementary and competitive imports is not fixed. Some goods which were not previously produced by a country may begin to be produced. Some other goods may be produced up to a certain limit, beyond which they have to be imported.

The balance equation including exports and imports can be written as follows:

$$x_i(t) = \sum_j a_{ij} x_j(t) + \sum_j b_{ij}(x_j(t+1) - x_j(t)) + c_i(t) + e_i(t) - m_i(t). \tag{16}$$

In the above equation, $e_i(t)$ represents the volume of exports of the ith sector in year t, assumed to be exogenously given. The total volume of imports of the ith sector in year t is represented by $m_i(t)$. If the import of the ith sector is complementary, it will be the sum of total sectoral outputs multiplied by the proportion of the import of the ith sector required per unit of sectoral outputs. In this case,

$$m_i(t) = \sum_j \acute{m}_{ij} x_j(t), \tag{17}$$

where $\acute{m}_{ij}$ is the proportion of import of the ith sector required per unit of output of sector j. The coefficient $\acute{m}_{ij}$ may be modified according to the proportion in which the imports are planned to be substituted from domestic production. If the exports and consumption are assumed to grow exponentially at rates ε and ψ, respectively, then (16) can be rewritten as follows:

$$x_i(t) = \sum_j a_{ij} x_j(t) + \sum_j b_{ij} (x_j(t+1) - x_j(t)) + c_i(1+\psi)^t$$

$$+ e_i(1+\varepsilon)^t + \sum_j \acute{m}_{ij} x_j(t). \tag{18}$$

The solution of the model is given in appendix 4.C.

3.   *Consistency Models of Investment Planning*

Investment planning involves several crucial aspects which need to be considered. Three most important among these are (i) gestation lags, (ii) depreciation and replacement, and (iii) technological changes.

(i) Gestation lags. If all the projects were completed in the year in which they were started, the problem of gestation lag would assume little importance. In fact, the majority takes more than a year to be completed, and many of them take four or five years. All the investment in a year, therefore, does not begin to produce output in the following year, but only that part which is used in projects that are completed in the current year. Part of the current year investment may be used in projects to be completed in the following year which will begin to produce output in the second year; yet another part may be used in projects which will be completed in the second year and will begin to produce output in the third year; and so on.

If we assume for the sake of simplicity a constant gestation lag for all projects, say of three years, and further assume that investment is uniformly spread over the gestation lag, then the current year investment from ith sector becomes

$$\Delta k_i(t) = \frac{1}{3}\sum_j b_{ij}\,(x_j(t+1) - x_j(t)) + \frac{1}{3}\sum_j b_{ij}\,(x_j(t+2) - x_j(t+1))$$

$$+ \frac{1}{3}\sum_j b_{ij}\,(x_j(t+3) - x_j(t+2))$$

$$= \frac{1}{3}\sum_j b_{ij}\,(x_j(t+3) - x_j(t)). \tag{19}$$

The solution of this model is given in appendix 4.D.

In reality, however, gestation lags of projects are not equal, and investments from sectors are not uniformly spread over time. Suppose for the sake of simplicity now that the investments from sector i are used in projects subject to gestation lag of two years only; then

$$\Delta k_i(t) = \sum_j b_{ij}^{(1)}\,(x_j(t+1) - x_j(t)) + \sum_j b_{ij}^{(2)}\,(x_j(t+2) - x_j(t+1)),$$

$$\text{where } b_{ij} = b_{ij}^{(1)} + b_{ij}^{(2)}. \tag{20}$$

Here $b_{ij}^{(1)}$ represents the investment from sector i per unit of output of sector j in projects that will begin to yield outputs in year $(t+1)$, and $b_{ij}^{(2)}$ those in year $(t+2)$.

Replacing $\Delta k_i(t)$ by the right-hand side of equations (19) and (20), in the balance equation (10), we can formulate a consistency model with gestation lags. Solutions of models with heterogeneous gestation lags are given in appendix 4.E.

(ii) Depreciation, replacement, and inventories. Every year some capital depreciation, which may or may not be replaced in full, takes place. If the demand for the goods produced by the depreciated capital does not fall, full replacement will take place, but, if it falls, then the replacement may be correspondingly less than the depreciation.

Depreciation in individual sectors may assume different patterns depending on the life of capital equipment and rates of obsolescence. The loss of productive capacity, however, is not directly measurable by the amount of actual depreciation of the individual elements of plant and capital equipment. It is determined by the highest proportion by which any one of the elements has depreciated. For instance, if the productive capacity of one element of plant or capital equipment has depreciated by half and other elements by less than that, the overall production capacity is at least reduced by half. The restoration of worn-out elements, however, need not be accompanied by a corresponding replacement of other elements of the capital equipment which have not been worn out. These considerations make a realistic formulation of the replacement of depreciated capacity quite difficult. It is, therefore, usual to make some simplifying assumptions in the representation of depreciation and replacement. For example, a simple assumption introduced in some models is that all capital equipment in a sector has a constant life and that it remains in operation at full productive capacity for a definite number of years and then it is scrapped. Similarly, plants in individual sectors may be assumed to have a constant life which may be different, in most cases longer, than that of capital equipments. In most cases, replacements may be completed within a year, but, in some cases, they may have gestation lags of more than a year. Let the depreciated capacity in sector j in year t be represented by $x_j^D(t)$, and let $\acute{\rho}_j(t)$ be the proportion to be restored in year t. Then the amount of output from sector i that goes for replacement (assuming that all replacement takes place in the year in which the capacity is depreciated) is given by

$$\Sigma \, \Upsilon_{ij}(t) \, \acute{\rho}_j(t) \, x_j^D(t), \tag{21}$$

where $\Upsilon_{ij}(t)$ is the proportion of output i required to restore unit capacity in sector j in year t. An alternative formulation would be to relate the capacity restoration to total sectoral output in year t. Letting $\rho_j(t)$ denote the proportion of total capacity of sector j to be restored in year t, the amount of output from sector i that goes for replacement is given by

$$\sum_j \, \Upsilon_{ij}(t) \, \rho_j(t) \, x_j(t). \tag{22}$$

Change in the size of inventories depends on various circumstances and expectations. It may not be easy to take into account all these in formulating a model. However, in practice, a good part of inventories is related directly to the size of sectoral output. Therefore, it can be roughly assumed that change in inventories in a sector is a fixed proportion of the change of the sectoral output in that year.

The change in inventories of sector i in year t can thus be represented by

$$v_i(t) \quad \Delta x_i(t),$$

where $\Delta x_j(t) = x_j(t+1) - x_j(t)$.

(iii) Technological changes. When techniques change, the current and capital input-output coefficients may become variable and a function of time. Thus the balance equation representing technological changes along with a two-year gestation lag, capacity restoration, and inventory changes can now be written as follows:

$$x_i(t) = \sum_j a_{ij}(t)\, x_j(t) + \sum_j b_{ij}^{(1)}(t)\, \Delta x_j(t) + \sum_j b_{ij}^{(2)}\, \Delta x_j(t+1)$$

$$+ \sum_j \Upsilon_{ij}(t)\, \rho_j\, x_j(t) + v_i(t)\, \Delta x_i(t) + c_i(t)$$

$$+ e_i(t) - m_i(t) \qquad\qquad (23)$$

$$i=1, 2, \ldots n.$$

The solution of model (23) can be undertaken on the lines of the solution of model (20) in Appendix 4.E.

4.   *Interregional Consistency Planning*

Regions of a country differ in their resource endowments, development levels, and preferences. When plans specify separate sets of targets for individual regions, an interregional consistency analysis is therefore required in addition to the sectoral one. That is, the delivery of a good from sector i to sector j, x_{ij}, has further to be qualified according to its movement from a region r to another s denoted by $_{sr}x_{ij}$. Except for this specification, a simple interregional consistency planning model follows the procedures outlined above. The simple balance equation pertaining to sector i of region r is

$$_r x_i = \sum_{s,j} {}_{sr}x_{ij} + \sum_{s,j} \Delta_{sr}k_{ij} + \sum_s {}_{sr}c_i. \qquad (24)$$

In an interregional model, we have to define sets of interregional coefficients besides intersectoral ones. Let $_{sr}a_{ij}$ denote the intermediate delivery from sector i of region r per unit of output of sector j of region s. Let $_{sr}b_{ij}$ denote the delivery from sector i of region r required as capital per unit output of sector j of region s. The balance equation can now be written as follows:

$$_r x_i = \sum_{s,j} {}_{sr}a_{ij} \, _s x_i + \sum_{s,j} {}_{sr}b_{ij}\Delta \, _s x_j + \sum_s {}_{sr}c_i. \qquad (25)$$

The above set of equations can be solved in order to determine the volumes of output of each sector in each region, given the targets in terms of $_{sr}c_i$'s. Interregional specification increases the number of variables and equations without changing the form of the system. The above inter-regional model can be extended to cover foreign transactions, technological changes, depreciation and replacement, and so on.

In practice the derivation of coefficients $_{sr}a_{ij}$ and $_{sr}b_{ij}$ may not be easy. Some attempts have been made to derive them indirectly. For instance, Moses[15] has suggested a method which consists of a set of trading coefficients along with the usual input-output coefficients. According to his method,

$$_{sr}x_{ij} = (_{sr}\mu_i) \, (_s a_{ij}) \, (_s x_j). \qquad (26)$$

Here $_{sr}\mu_i$ denotes the proportion of total import of good i in region s from region r, and

$$_s a_{ij} = \frac{_s x_{ij}}{_s x_j}, \qquad (27)$$

where $_s x_{ij}$ denotes the total input of good i in the production of good j and $_s x_j$, the total output of good j in region s. Consequently,

$$_{sr}a_{ij} = {}_{sr}\mu_i \, _s a_{ij} \qquad (28)$$
$$i, j = 1, 2, \ldots n$$
$$r, s = 1, 2, \ldots.$$

Similarly, we can express the amount of good i from region r used for capital formation as follows:

$$\sum_{s,j} \Delta_{sr}k_{ij} = \sum_{s,j} {}_{sr}\mu_i \, _s b_{ij} \, _s x_j, \qquad (29)$$

where $_{sr}\mu_i$ is the same as above and $_s b_{ij}$ is capital input-output ratios in region s. Consequently,

$$_{sr}b_{ij} = {}_{sr}\mu_i \, _s b_{ij}. \qquad (30)$$

Leontief[16] and Ghosh[17] have proposed gravity-type models for implementing these formulations statistically.

V. The Manne-Rudra Consistency Model

Alan S. Manne and Ashok Rudra have constructed a consistency model of what was expected to be India's Fourth Plan.[18] The general object of the model is to examine the effect on output levels and on imports of alternative assumptions regarding the growth of aggregate consumption and of investment. The authors have also examined their effect with respect to (i) the capital-output ratios assumed for agriculture and (ii) the degree of import substitution within the machine building industries.

The model used is of the conventional Leontief interindustry type, "with a few embellishments for the endogenous treatment of capital formation" to be discussed below. It is supposed that planners are free to set the 1970–71 domestic output targets for each branch of the economy. The model has 1960–61 as the base year. The relations of the model are as follows:

(i) current flow of sectors in 1970–71

$$\sum_j a_{ij} x_j + y_i = f_i + .17 z_i + .04 (x_i - x_i^0)$$

$$i = 1, \ldots . 30 \qquad (27)$$

(ii) fixed investment demand for four capital goods induced by output increase over the decade

$$\sum_j b_{ij} (x_j - x_j^0) = z_i \qquad i = 1, \ldots 4 \qquad (28)$$

(iii) foreign exchange balance, 1970–71

$$\sum m_i + \sum \overline{m}_i = \sum e_i + w \qquad (29)$$

The variables of the models fall into four categories:

(i) unknowns

x_j = annual rate of domestic production, process j, target year

y_i = annual import rate, item i, target year ($y_i = m_i + \overline{m}_i$)?

z_i = demand for investment good i induced by output increase, total for decade

w = annual rate of deficit on merchandise account, target year

m_i = endogenous merchandise imports

(ii) coefficients

a_{ij} = current account output (+) or input (−), item i, process j, target year

b_{ij} = capital coefficient for item i, process j, induced cumulated fixed investment per unit of annual output

$\acute{m}_{ij}$ = import of item i required per unit of process j, target year i≠j

$\acute{m}_{ii}$ = import of item i per unit of domestic output of item i

(iii) constants

x^o_j = annual rate of domestic production, process j, base year, for i≠j

(iv) knowns

f_i = final demand households, government, exports and exogenous fixed investments

$\bar{m}_i$ = exogenous merchandise imports

e_i = exogenous merchandise exports

In equation (27), $\sum_j a_{ij} x_j$ is the domestic output, net of interindustry demands. The coefficient value of .17 is a stock-flow conversion factor which will be described presently. The last term .04 ($x_i - x^o_i$) is the induced inventory investment, not applicable to service sectors. Inventory investment for the target year is approximated by supposing that each commodity-producing sector holds a three-month supply of its product, that is, has a ratio of inventory to gross output of .25. The coefficient of .04 is derived by multiplying the stock-flow conversion factor by the ratio of inventory to gross annual output, .17 x .25 = .04.

The import variables m_i may be eliminated from the above equations by noting that $m_i = \sum_j \acute{m}_{ij} x_j$. After this elimination is performed, we are left with 30 variables x_j, 4 variables z_i, and one variable W, that is, with exactly as many degrees of freedom as there are equations.

If the annual rate of investment is assumed to increase at the rate of r, then e^{rt} is the index of gross annual investment t years from the base period, and $\int_0^t e^{rt} dt$ becomes the index of gross capital formation. Investment in year t expressed as a proportion of total investment over the period of t years becomes $e^{rt} / \int_0^t e^{rt} dt = {}^r/1-e^{-rt}$, the target year's stock-flow conversion factor under the given growth rate assumption.

Assuming further that there is a time lag of θ years between investment and output, the stock-flow conversion factor is modified as follows:

$$\frac{\text{induced investment rate at time t}}{\text{cumulated investment induced by output increase}} = \frac{e^{rt}}{\int_{-\theta}^{t-\theta} e^{rt}dt} = \frac{r\ e^r}{1-e^{t\theta}}.$$

In the Manne-Rudra model, $t = 10$ years, θ is 2 years, and $r = 8.7$ percent. Hence the stock-flow conversion factor equals .17.

The stock-flow conversion factor is a device to ensure a smooth expansion of the flow of investment from the base to the target year. The device removes edge effects and makes a determinate solution possible.

For estimating the projections of coefficients for 1970–71, from the base year 1960–61, heavy reliance was placed upon the work summarized in the Perspective Planning Division (PPD).[19] Current account output or input coefficients a_{ij} were taken over directly from the 1960–61 transactions matrix, constructed by the PPD. But about a quarter of them were altered in the light of independent information from the PPD which affected chemical fertilizers, motor transport, petroleum products, electricity, and coal.

Capital coefficients, b_{ij}, are defined in terms of capital per unit of incremental annual output in each of the thirty domestic production sectors. The coefficients are measured in producers' prices for four sectors of origin: industrial and urban construction, rural construction, transport equipment, and other equipment.

Import coefficients, $\dot{m}_{ij}$, were not easy to estimate. They constitute best guesses as to minimum import requirements for 1970–71.

Exogenous exports are determined exogenously and are projected for 1970–71 at a growth rate of 5.5 percent per year. A minor volume of imports is tied to specific commodities as a result of bilateral clearing agreements. In order to allow for these agreements, the projection allows for some exogenous imports. The model places no *formal* constraint upon the deficit on merchandise account. However, the import coefficients $\dot{m}_{ij}$ and other parameters were adjusted during the course of the numerical experimentation, and they were set in such a way that the resulting trade deficit lies within tolerable limits from the viewpoint of India's ability to secure foreign loans and grants.

The Manne-Rudra consistency model is of the "open" type, in which the principal components of gross domestic expenditure are projected and translated into final demand for individual commodities exogenously and independently of the incomes generated through the process of production. This implies, as the authors observe, "that the Indian government has sufficient fiscal power so that it is unconstrained by the feedback link that operates in a market economy from the production process back to the distribution of incomes, savings and the generation of domestic expenditures."

The principal components of gross domestic expenditures are projected for 1970–71 on two sets of assumptions, one optimistic and the other pessimistic, the first with a compound annual growth rate of gross domestic expenditure at 6.6 percent, household consumption at 5.4 percent, government consumption 9.4 percent, and gross capital formation 9.8 percent, and the second with corresponding rates of 4.9 percent, 3.6 percent, 9.4 percent, and 7.8 percent, respectively.

Several alternative combinations of size and allocation of investment are considered. Though it will not be possible to enter into these details, some conclusions based on their benchmark case "partially endogenous" are given here. This is the case which combines an ambitious final demand program with the bulk of capital formation being calculated endogenously through multiplying each sector's output increase over the decade by its own capital-output ratio and a stock-flow conversion factor of 17 percent. In this case, the predetermined investment figure refers only to replacement plus housing, roads, education, research, and the like, sectors in which it was found hazardous to project investment requirements through capital-output ratios.

The exercise has shown that the current account transactions of the Indian economy are characterised by an almost block-angular structure. The bulk of current account transactions appears to take place within two virtually independent complexes, one based upon agriculture and the other upon mining, metals, machinery, and forestry products. The first of these supplies predominantly consumption goods and the second, investment goods that can substitute imports. A third and smaller sector produces items like fuel, power, transport, and chemicals, described as "universal intermediates." The authors point out that this block angularity may allow the planners to develop one complex independent of the other. In particular, a vigorous investment program may be undertaken with or without a corresponding expansion in agriculture. Some of the main results of the Manne-Rudra model are stated below.

(i)   An upward shift in agriculture's capital coefficient has a stimulating effect upon output targets within the mining, metals, and machinery sector, but the rest of the economy is barely affected.

(ii)   When the interindustry transactions are simplified into a block-angular structure, there occurs only a slight difference between the gross output levels. The following summary is obtained by adding up the sectoral results into totals for the three complexes:

	1970–71 gross output (Rs. crores)		Percentage differences
	without	with	
		block angularity	
Mining, metals, etc.	11,089	10,662	4
Food and fibre	16,596	16,422	1
Universal intermediates	5,103	5,009	2

The block angularity is obtained by equating the interblock coefficients a_{ij} to zero, but the capital coefficients b_{ij} are left unchanged. It goes without saying that if the interindustry transactions can be simplified into a block-angular structure, the process of data collection and numerical analysis is greatly facilitated.

However, for detailed sectoral balances for 1970–71, the block-angular simplification is not uniformly satisfactory. But, in most industries, it performs quite well.

(iii)   Rudra-Manne numerical experiments explore some implications of the program for replacing imports with domestic production of machinery. The results are interpreted as follows:

(a)   It makes a significant difference in the minimum trade deficit whether one is optimistic or pessimistic with respect to the machine import substitution.

(b)   Although success or failure in machine import substitution has a sizable effect upon the output requirements for metals, the program has a comparatively minor impact upon other domestic production sectors.

(c)   Even though it takes machinery to produce machinery, the import substitution has a comparatively minor impact upon other domestic sectors.

The Manne-Rudra model is one of the ambitious efforts which have been made in the application of input-output analysis to actual planning.

The authors have constructed their table on the basis of authentic and reliable sources of data. The table has been used in the formulation of several other consistency and optimality models[20] and has led to the construction of more detailed tables in India.

Appendix 4.A

Common Constant Target Rate of Growth of Consumption Components

Let $\underline{c}(t)$ denote the n-vector total consumption target for year t of the plan. Suppose that each component of the target grows at a common rate ψ, so that

$$\underline{c}(t) = \underline{c} (1 + \psi)^t, \tag{1}$$

where $\underline{c}$ is a given vector.

The balance equation in the absence of external transactions is

$$\underline{x}(t) = A\underline{x}(t) + \Delta k(t) + \underline{c}(t), \tag{2}$$

where A is the current input-output matrix, $\underline{x}(t)$ the vector of total sectoral outputs, and $\Delta\underline{k}(t)$ the vector of additions to sectoral capital stock.

$$\Delta\underline{k}(t) = B(\underline{x}(t+1) - \underline{x}(t)), \tag{3}$$

where B is the capital input-output matrix. Inserting (3) into (2), we have

$$\underline{x}(t) = A\underline{x}(t) + B(\underline{x}(t+1) - \underline{x}(t)) + \underline{c}(1+\psi)^t. \tag{4}$$

In the homogeneous part of (4), we try a solution $\underline{x}(t) = \underline{x}(1 + \lambda)^t$, where $\underline{x}$ is as yet an unspecified vector. This gives

$$(I - A + B\lambda)\underline{x} = 0. \tag{5}$$

Equation (5) will have nontrivial solutions only when $(I - A + B\lambda)$ is singular. If so, there will be n solutions for λ, λ_i $i = 1, \ldots, n$. Let us assume these are n distinct solutions for simplicity. Corresponding to each of these, there will be a vector $\underline{x}_i$ satisfying (5). Hence one of the solutions of the homogeneous part corresponding to the ith eigenvalue λ_i and ith eigenvector $\underline{x}_i$ is

$$\underline{x}(t) = a_i\underline{x_i}(1 + \lambda_i)^t, \tag{6}$$

where a_i is a constant. The general solution of the homogeneous part is, as stated in the preceding section,

$$\underline{x}(t) = \sum_{i=1}^{n} a_i\underline{x_i}(1 + \lambda_i)^t. \tag{7}$$

In (7) a's are arbitrary constants to be determined. On the other hand, the λ's and $\underline{x}$'s are structural constants to be given by the elements of matrices A and B.

To find the particular solution we try $\underline{x}(t) = \underline{q}(1 + \psi)^t$ in (4), where $\underline{q}$ is a time independent vector. This gives

$$\underline{q} = (I - A - B\psi)^{-1}\underline{c}. \tag{8}$$

The complete solution is the sum of the homogeneous and particular solutions. Thus

$$\underline{x}(t) = \sum_{i=1}^{n} a_i\underline{x_i}(1 + \lambda_i)^t + (I - A - B\psi)^{-1}\underline{c}\,(1 + \psi)^t. \tag{9}$$

A suitable way to determine the a_i's is through the terminal values of the components of $\underline{x}(t)$ for t = T, that is, $\underline{x}(T)$. However, the components of $\underline{x}(T)$ are determined only when the consumption levels in year T + 1 are given. Let us assume that the planners envisage the consumption vector to be $\underline{c}(T + 1)$ in year T + 1. As $\underline{c}(t + 1)$ may represent rates of growth of consumption components different from the ψ assumed for the plan period, the vector of capital formation in year T is then

$$\Delta\underline{k}(T) = B(I - A)^{-1}\,[\underline{c}(T + 1) - \underline{c}(T)].$$

Therefore,

$$\underline{x}(T) = A\underline{x}(T) + B(I - A)^{-1}\,[\underline{c}(T + 1) - \underline{c}(T)] + \underline{c}(T). \tag{10}$$

Using the components of $\underline{x}(T)$ in (9) for t = T, we can determine the values of a_i's.

Finally, we have to check whether the target consumption vectors $\underline{c}\,(t)$, t = 1, . . . T are feasible. This can be done by finding the solution vector $\underline{x}(0)$ for t = 0 in (9). If

$$\underline{x}(0) \leqslant \underline{x}_0,$$

then the consumption plan is feasible, where $\underline{x}_0$ is the vector of total sectoral outputs available at the end of year 0. We assume here that the availability of labor is not a limiting factor.

In this simplest of consistency planning models, all components of consumption target expand at a common constant rate during the plan. Hence the problem of some variables, that is, some sectoral outputs in some plan year becoming negative, does not arise.

All the roots λ's may not be real; some of them may be imaginary. In this case one or more couples of the roots will be conjugate complex. These will introduce an oscillatory element in the path of $\underline{x}(t)$ over time.

Appendix 4.B

Dynamic Inverse

One of the main characteristics of an input-output system is that it is additive. Two or more constellations of solution magnitudes derived for a certain year corresponding to vectors of final demand related to the same or different years in future can be directly added. This property of input-output analysis makes it very convenient to formulate a consistency planning model which allows freely chosen configuration of annual and terminal target vectors, and the introduction of alternative technology in successive plan years. Leontief has recently presented a systematic approach to this possibility in what he calls the dynamic inverse,[21] and we shall formulate a general consistency planning model based on this.

Unlike the preceding model, the annual consumption target vectors can now be chosen independently of the preceding plan years, and the nonnegative elements of a particular year's target vector need not have any fixed relationship among them. Let $\underline{c}(t) = [c_1(t), c_2(t), \ldots, c_n(t)]$ be the target in the plan year t, t = 1, ..., T and let $\underline{x}(t) = [x_1(t), x_2(t), \ldots, x_n(t)]$ denote the vector of sectoral outputs required in year t corresponding to $\underline{c}(t)$. A(t) denotes the n × n matrix of technical flow coefficients and B(t) the corresponding square matrix of capital coefficients. It is assumed as before that the capital goods produced in year t are installed and operated in the following year t + 1. Equation (4) can now be rewritten:

$$\underline{x}(t) - A(t)\underline{x}(t) - B(t)[\underline{x}(t+1) - \underline{x}(t)] = \underline{c}(t). \qquad (11)$$

This differs from (4) in that time subscripts are attached to both the flow and capital matrices of technology, introducing technological change in the dynamic system. One can use B(t+1) instead of B(t). Equation (11) can be rewritten as follows:

$$G(t) \, \underline{x}(t) - B(t) \, \underline{x}(t+1) = \underline{c}(t), \qquad (11a)$$

where $G(t) = [I - A(t) + B(t)]$. (11a) can be written in full as follows:

$$
\begin{bmatrix}
G(1) & -B(1) & & & & & & \\
& G(2) & -B(2) & & & & & \\
& & G(3) & -B(3) & & & & \\
& & & \cdot & \cdot & & & \\
& & & & \cdot & \cdot & & \\
& & & & & \cdot & \cdot & \\
& & & G(T\text{-}1) & -B(T\text{-}1) & & \\
& & & & G(T) & -B(T) & \\
& & & & & G(T\text{+}1) & -B(T\text{+}1)
\end{bmatrix}
\begin{bmatrix}
\underline{x}(1) \\
\underline{x}(2) \\
\underline{x}(3) \\
\cdot \\
\cdot \\
\cdot \\
\underline{x}(T\text{-}1) \\
\underline{x}(T) \\
\underline{x}(T\text{+}1)
\end{bmatrix}
=
\begin{bmatrix}
\underline{c}(1) \\
\underline{c}(2) \\
\underline{c}(3) \\
\cdot \\
\cdot \\
\cdot \\
\underline{c}(T\text{-}1) \\
\underline{c}(T) \\
\underline{c}(T\text{+}1)
\end{bmatrix}
\qquad (12)
$$

In (12) we have extended the system by one equation in order to be able to fix the value of $\underline{x}(T)$ in such a way as to avoid edge effects. As described above, $\underline{x}(T)$ is determined when $\underline{x}(T + 1)$ is fixed, but the latter depends on $\underline{c}(T + 1)$. Under the present assumptions of capital goods produced in year t being installed and operated in year t + 1, we need to go no further. Let us assume that the planners fix also the consumption target for one postplan year, namely, $\underline{c}(T + 1)$. Then, as above,

$$\Delta\underline{k}(T) = B(T) \, [I - A(t)]^{-1} \, [\underline{c}(T+1) - \underline{c}(T)] . \qquad (13)$$

$\Delta\underline{k}$ can also be derived by using the steady-state model of section VII, chapter two. Now:

$$\underline{x}(T) = A(T) \, \underline{x}(T) + \Delta\underline{k}(T) + \underline{c}(T) \qquad (14)$$

$$= [I - A(T)]^{-1} \, [\Delta\underline{k}(T) + \underline{c}(T)] . \qquad (14a)$$

The solution of system (12) yields the sequence of annual total sectoral outputs that will enable the economy to realize the annual target vectors $\underline{c}(t)$, $t = 1, \ldots, T$. Now that we have determined the value of $\underline{x}(T)$ exogeneously from the planners' postplan year consumption target, we delete the last equation from (12) and put $-B(T) = 0$ in the last but one row. Starting with this equation and substituting its solution in the preceding equation and thus proceeding upwards to the first, we arrive at (15) as the solution of (12).

In (15), $G(t) = [I - A(t) + B(t)]$, for $t = 1, \ldots, T - 1$, but $G(T) = [I - A(T)]$ and $x(T)$ is derived as in (14a). $R(t) = G^{-2}(t)B(t)$. In the absence of technological changes, time subscripts can be eliminated from (15), and it can be written as (15a), where $G = (I - A + B)$ and $R = G^{-1}B$.

The systems (15) and (15a) yield the total sectoral outputs in successive plan years which will realize the planned annual consumption vectors. The total sectoral output vector $\underline{x}(t)$ for any year t, $t = 1, \ldots, T$ can be easily obtained by premultiplying the column of consumption vectors by the corresponding tth row of the matrices of the dynamic inverse. For example, $\underline{x}(1)$ can be obtained by premultiplying the column of consumption targets by the first row of the matrices in (15) or (15a), and $\underline{x}(2)$ by premultiplying by the second row, and so on. Thus for each plan year we derive the vector of total sectoral outputs which is required by the consumption target of that and all the following plan years.

[(15) appears on page 146]

$$
\begin{bmatrix}
\underline{x}(1) \\
\underline{x}(2) \\
\underline{x}(3) \\
\cdot \\
\cdot \\
\cdot \\
\underline{x}(T-2) \\
\underline{x}(T-1) \\
\underline{x}(T)
\end{bmatrix}
=
\begin{bmatrix}
G^{-1} & RG^{-1} & R^2G^{-1} & \cdots & R^{T-2}G^{-1} & R^{T-1}(I-A)^{-1} \\
 & G^{-1} & R\,G^{-1} & \cdots & R^{T-3}G^{-1} & R^{T-2}(I-A)^{-1} \\
 & & G^{-1} & \cdots & R^{T-4}G^{-1} & R^{T-3}(I-A)^{-1} \\
 & & & & & \\
 & & & G^{-1} & RG^{-1} & R^2(I-A)^{-1} \\
 & & & & G^{-1} & R\,(I-A)^{-1} \\
 & & & & & (I-A)^{-1}
\end{bmatrix}
\begin{bmatrix}
\underline{c}(1) \\
\underline{c}(2) \\
\underline{c}(3) \\
\cdot \\
\cdot \\
\cdot \\
\underline{c}(T-2) \\
\underline{c}(T-1) \\
\underline{c}(T) + \Delta\underline{k}(T)
\end{bmatrix}
\qquad (15a)
$$

[(15a) precedes (15), see page 145]

$$
\begin{bmatrix}
\underline{x}(1) \\
\underline{x}(2) \\
\underline{x}(3) \\
\vdots \\
\underline{x}(T-2) \\
\underline{x}(T-1) \\
\underline{x}(T)
\end{bmatrix}
=
\begin{bmatrix}
G^{-1}(1) & R(1)G^{-1}(2) & R(1)R(2)G^{-1}(3) & \cdots & R(1)R(2)\ldots R(T-2)G^{-1}(T-1) & R(1)R(2)\ldots R(T-2)R(T-1)G^{-1}(T) \\
 & G^{-1}(2) & R(2)G^{-1}(3) \cdots & & R(2)\ldots R(T-2)G^{-1}(T-1) & R(2)\ldots R(T-2)R(T-1)G^{-1}(T) \\
 & & G^{-1}(3) \cdots & & R(3)\ldots R(T-2)G^{-1}(T-1) & R(3)\ldots R(T-2)R(T-1)G^{-1}(T) \\
 & & & & & \\
 & & G^{-1}(T-2) & & R(T-2)G^{-1}(T-1) & R(T-2)R(T-1)G^{-1}(T) \\
 & & & & G^{-1}(T-1) & R(T-1)G^{-1}(T) \\
 & & & & & G^{-1}(T)
\end{bmatrix}
\begin{bmatrix}
\underline{c}(1) \\
\underline{c}(2) \\
\underline{c}(3) \\
\vdots \\
\underline{c}(T-2) \\
\underline{c}(T-1) \\
\underline{c}(T)+\Delta\underline{k}(T)
\end{bmatrix}
$$

(15)

Feasibility of the plan can be checked as before by finding the vector $\underline{x}(0)$ from the model and comparing it with the vector of actual output $\underline{x}_0$ in year 0.

From (11a)

$$\underline{x}(0) = G^{-1}(0)B(0)\underline{x}(1) + G^{-1}(0)\underline{c}(0)$$

$$= G^{-1}(0)B(0)\underline{x}(1) + G^{-1}(0)\underline{c}_0,$$

where $\underline{c}(0) = \underline{c}_0$ is the vector of actual consumption in year 0. Now the plan will be feasible if

$$\underline{x}(0) \leqslant \underline{x}_0. \tag{16}$$

If (16) does not hold, then the plan will not be feasible. In this case the consistency planning would require the consumption target vectors to be modified. For characteristics of the solution, references can be made to Leontief.[22]

Appendix 4.C

Consistency Model with Foreign Trade

We shall now extend the analysis of the preceding section to account for total sectoral exports and imports.

The balance equation now is

$$\underline{x}(t) = A\underline{x}(t) + B(\underline{x}(t+1) - \underline{x}(t)) + \underline{c}(t) + \underline{e}(t) - \underline{m}(t). \tag{1}$$

In equation (1), $\underline{e}(t)$ is the vector of export and $\underline{m}(t)$ that of imports in period t. Suppose for the sake of simplicity that the components of consumption grow at a common constant rate ψ, so that the target consumption vector in plan year t, $\underline{c}(t) = \underline{c}(1+\psi)^t$, where $\underline{c}$ is a given vector independent of time. We further assume that the imports in a sector form a constant proportion of that sector, so that

$$\underline{m}(t) = \hat{M}\underline{x}(t),$$

where $\hat{M}$ is a diagonal matrix with elements on the diagonal representing the ratio of imports to total outputs of the corresponding sectors.

Finally, we assume that the sectoral exports are expected to grow at a common constant rate ε, so that $\underline{e}(t) = \underline{e}(1 + \varepsilon)^t$ where $\underline{e}$ is a given time-independent vector. Putting the value of $\underline{c}(t)$, $\underline{m}(t)$, and $\underline{e}(t)$ in (1), we get

$$\underline{x}(t) = A\underline{x}(t) + B[\underline{x}(t+1) - \underline{x}(t)] = \underline{c}(1+\psi)^t + \underline{e}(1+\varepsilon)^t - M\underline{x}(t). \quad (3)$$

To find the solution of the homogeneous part first, we try a solution, $\underline{x}(t) = \underline{x}(1+\lambda)^t$, where $\underline{x}$ is as yet an unspecified time-independent vector, to get

$$(I - A + M - B\lambda)\underline{x} = 0. \quad\quad (4)$$

As before, (4) will have a nontrivial solution only when $[I - A + M - B\lambda]$ is singular. If so, there will be n solutions of λ, such that corresponding to the ith row characteristic root λ_i is a characteristic vector $\underline{x}_j$. Hence the form of the solution corresponding to the ith root is

$$\underline{x}(t) = a_i \underline{x}_j (1 + \lambda_i)^t, \quad\quad (5)$$

and the general solution of the homogeneous part is

$$\underline{x}(t) = \sum_{i=1}^{n} a_i \underline{x}_i (1 + \lambda_i)^t. \quad\quad (6)$$

For the particular solution we try

$$\underline{x}(t) = \underline{q}_\psi (1 + \psi)^t + \underline{q}_\varepsilon (1 + \varepsilon)^t, \quad\quad (7)$$

where $\underline{q}_\psi$ and $\underline{q}_\varepsilon$ are constant vectors to be determined. Substituting equation (7) in (3), we get

$$[(B^{-1}(I+\hat{M}-A) - \psi B)\underline{q}_\psi - \underline{c}](1+\psi)^t$$
$$- [(B^{-1}(I+\hat{M}-A) - \varepsilon B)\underline{q}_\varepsilon - \underline{e}](1+\varepsilon)^t = 0. \quad\quad (8)$$

In order that the above holds for all t, the coefficients of $(1 + \psi)^t$ and $(1 + \varepsilon)^t$ must be identically zero, so that $q_\psi = [B^{-1} (I + \hat{M} - A) - \psi B]^{-1}\underline{c}$ and $q_\varepsilon = [B^{-1} (I + M - A) - \varepsilon B]^{-1}$ e. $[B^{-1} (I + M - A) - \psi B]^{-1}$ and $[B^{-1} (I + M - A) - \varepsilon B]^{-1}$ will exist only when $\psi \neq \lambda_i$ and $\varepsilon \neq \lambda_i, i = 1, \ldots, n$. The complete solution is now

$$\underline{x}(t) = \sum_{i=1}^{n} a_i \underline{x}_i (1 + \lambda_i)^t + [B^{-1} (I + \hat{M} - A) - \psi B]^{-1} \underline{c}(1 + \psi)^t$$
$$+ [B^{-1} (I + \hat{M} - A) - \varepsilon B]^{-1} \underline{e}(1 + \varepsilon)^t. \quad (9)$$

In order to formulate the planning model without edge effects and to prevent capital depletion in the terminal plan year, we assume as above that the planners envisage the provision of consumption given by the vector $\underline{c}(T + 1)$ and of exports by the vector $\underline{e}(T + 1)$ in the first postplan year, $T + 1$, and that imports form the same proportion of sectoral outputs, as before,

$$\underline{x}(T + 1) = A\underline{x}(T + 1) + \underline{c}(T + 1) + \underline{e}(T + 1) - \hat{M}\underline{x}(T + 1)$$

or $\qquad x(T + 1) = (I - A + M)^{-1} [\underline{c}(T + 1) + \underline{e}(T + 1)].$

Therefore,

$$\Delta \underline{k}(T) = B[\underline{x}(T + 1) - \underline{x}(T)],$$

and so

$$\underline{x}(T) = A\underline{x}(T) + B[\underline{x}(T + 1) - \underline{x}(T)] + \underline{c}(1 + \psi)^T + \underline{e}(1 + \varepsilon)^T - \hat{M}\underline{x}(T)$$
$$= (I - A + B + \hat{M})^{-1} [B(I - A + \hat{M})^{-1} (\underline{c}(T + 1) + \underline{e}(T + 1))$$
$$+ \underline{c}(I + \psi)^T + \underline{e}(I + \varepsilon)^T]. \quad (10)$$

Using the n values of the components of $\underline{x}(T)$, we determine the n values a_i, $i = 1, \ldots, n$.

Feasibility of the consistency model can be checked by putting $t = 0$ in (9) and comparing $\underline{x}(0)$ with $\underline{x}_0$, the vector of total sectoral outputs available in period 0. If $\underline{x}_0 \geqslant \underline{x}(0)$, the plan is feasible; otherwise, it is not. In the latter case either the consumption or the export targets will have to be revised.

Appendix 4.D

Uniform Gestation Lags in Investment Planning

In order to be able to find a convenient analytical solution, we shall assume (i) that there is a uniform gestation lag of g periods; (ii) that the investment of inputs is uniformly spread over the gestation periods; and (iii) that components of consumption given as target increase at a common constant rate ψ.

In view of the first two assumptions, one gth part of the inputs invested in period t will go to produce additional capacity for production in the beginning of period $t + 1$, another gth part will go to create additional completed capacity at the beginning of period $t + 2$, and so on, until the last gth part will go to create additional completed capacity for production in $(t + g)$th period. Assuming a constant capital coefficient matrix, the investment in period t is related to the production of additional outputs by the following equation:

$$\underline{i}(t) = \frac{B}{g} [\underline{x}(t+1) - \underline{x}(t)] + \frac{B}{g} [\underline{x}(t+2) - \underline{x}(t+1)] + \ldots$$

$$+ \frac{B}{g} [\underline{x}(t+g) - \underline{x}(t+g-1)]$$

$$= \frac{B}{g} [\underline{x}(t+g) - \underline{x}(t)] . \tag{1}$$

In order to simplify the analysis, we shall assume here a closed economy. Under this assumption, the balance equation can be written as follows:

$$\underline{x}(t) = A\underline{x}(t) + \frac{B}{g} [\underline{x}(t+g) - \underline{x}(t)] + \underline{c}(1+\psi)^t. \tag{2}$$

For the solution of the homogeneous part of equation (1), we try $\underline{x}(t) = \underline{x}\lambda^t$, where $\underline{x}$ is an as yet unspecified vector independent of t.
This gives

$$[gB^{-1}(I - A + \frac{B}{g}) - \lambda^g]\underline{x} = 0. \tag{3}$$

Equation (3) gives n solutions of λ^g, say λ_i^g, $i = 1, \ldots, n$, to each of which corresponds a vector $\underline{x}_i$. For each solution λ_i^g, we have

$$\underline{x}_i(t) = \sum_{j=1}^{g} a_{ij}\underline{x}_i\lambda^t_{ij} \qquad i = 1, \ldots, n. \tag{4}$$

The general solution will be the sum of solutions corresponding to individual solutions of equations (4), so that

$$\underline{x}(t) = \sum_{i=1}^{n} \sum_{j=1}^{g} a_{ij}\underline{x}_i \lambda_{ij}^t. \tag{5}$$

For the particular solution we try $\underline{x}(t) = Q(1 + \psi)^t$

$$Q = [I - A + \frac{B}{g} - \frac{B}{g}(1 + \psi)^g]^{-1} \underline{c}. \tag{6}$$

Hence the particular solution is

$$\underline{x}(t) = [I - A + \frac{B}{g} - \frac{B}{g}(1 + \psi)^g]^{-1} \underline{c}(1 + \psi)^t. \tag{7}$$

The complete solution, therefore, is

$$\underline{x}(t) = \sum_{i=1}^{n} \sum_{j=1}^{g} a_{ij}x_i \lambda_{ij}^t + [I - A + \frac{B}{g} - \frac{B}{g}(1 + \psi)^g]^{-1} \underline{c}(1+\psi)^t. \tag{8}$$

The gn unknown a_{ij}'s can be determined by the g n–vectors x(T) x(T + 1), ... x(T + g – 1). These g n–vectors can be obtained by the consumption vectors envisaged in the 2g postplan years.

We have shown above how to derive one terminal vector $\underline{x}(T)$ under the assumption that output invested in year t begins to produce in years t + 1. In order to illustrate a longer gestation lag, a simple example of gestation lag of 2 years, that is, g = 2, would suffice. Let the total consumption vectors in years T + 1, T + 2, T + 3, T + 4, be $\underline{c}(T + 1)$, $\underline{c}(T + 2)$, $\underline{c}(T + 3)$, and $\underline{c}(T + 4)$, respectively. Then

$$\underline{x}(T + 3) = A\underline{x}(T + 3) + \frac{B}{2}[\underline{c}(T+4) - \underline{c}(T+3)] + \underline{c}(T+3) \tag{9}$$

$$\underline{x}(T + 2) = A\underline{x}(T + 2) + \frac{B}{2}[\underline{x}(T+3) - \underline{x}(T+2)] + \frac{B}{2}[\underline{c}(T+4) - \underline{c}(T+3)]$$

$$+ \underline{c}(T+2)$$

$$\underline{x}(T + 1) = A\underline{x}(T+1) + \frac{B}{2}[\underline{x}(T+2)-x(T+1)] + \frac{B}{2}[\underline{x}(T+3)-\underline{x}(T+2)$$

$$+ \underline{c}(T+1) \hspace{4cm} (\text{9 cont'd})$$

$$\underline{x}(T) = A\underline{x}(T) + \frac{B}{2}[\underline{x}(T+1) - \underline{x}(T)] + \frac{B}{2}[\underline{x}(T+2)-\underline{x}(T+1)] + \underline{c}(T).$$

The two n-vectors $\underline{x}(T)$ and $\underline{x}(T + 1)$ when placed in (8) will give the gn values of $a_{ij}, i = 1, \ldots, g$, for $g = 2$.

The feasibility and convergence aspects can be handled as above.

Appendix 4.E

Heterogenous Lags with Technological Changes

In the above two sections we have considered homogeneous lags, the investment inputs being uniformly spread over the gestation period. In reality, the investment inputs are not equally divided among the gestation years, nor is the length of the gestation period identical in all sectors.

Heterogeneous lags can be introduced in the consistency planning model by using time-variant structural matrices and allowing a gestation period of more than one year. For the sake of simplicity of demonstration, we shall assume here a gestation period of two years. The method can be easily extended to lags of three or more years. The balance equation with these specifications can be written as follows:

$$\underline{x}(t) = A(t)\underline{x}(t) + {}^1B(t)(\underline{x}(t+1) - (\underline{x}(t)) + {}^2B(t)(\underline{x}(t+2)-\underline{x}(t+1))+c(t)$$

$$= G^{-1} (t)\underline{c}(t) + R(t)\underline{x}(t+1) + S(t)\underline{x}(t+2),$$

where $G^{-1}(t) = [I-A(t)+{}^1B(t)]$; $R(t) = G^{-1}(t) [{}^1B(t)-{}^2B(t)]$;

$$S(t) = G^{-1} (t) {}^2B(t).$$

Let the plan be of T years and let the consumption vectors for each plan year be given as target. Under the assumption of a two-year gestation lag, the total outputs produced in year T can be determined only when the total sectoral outputs in years $T + 1$ and $T + 2$ are known. Similarly the total sectoral outputs in year $T - 1$ can be determined only when the total sectoral outputs in year T and $T + 1$ are known. The sectoral outputs in the postplan years $T + 1$ and $T + 2$ would have to come from information envisaged to be made available for postplan years. Using the procedure stated above, $\underline{x}(T+1)$ and $\underline{x}(T+2)$ can be estimated either on the basis of some steady-state analysis or on some simple assumptions such as that the planners want to allocate for investment in year T to allow for the production of given volumes of consumption in years $T+1$ and $T+2$ but are not concerned with investment in these years. Under these assumptions, the relevant values of $\underline{x}(T+1)$ and $\underline{x}(T+2)$ are given by

$$\underline{x}(T+1) = A(T+1)\,\underline{x}(T+1) + \underline{c}(T+1)$$

$$= [I - A(T+1)]^{-1}\,\underline{c}(T+1) \qquad (2)$$

and, similarly, $\underline{x}(T+2) = [I - A(T+2)]^{-1}\,\underline{c}(T+2)$.

From (1) and (2), we can now write the allocations in the final plan year T as follows:

$$\underline{x}(T) = G^{-1}(T)\,\underline{c}(T) + R(T)\,H(1)\,\underline{c}(T+1) + S(T)H(2)\underline{c}(T+2), \qquad (3)$$

where $H(1) = [I - A(T+1)]^{-1}$ and $H(2) = [I - A(T+2)]^{-1}$

The balance equation for plan year T−1 is

$$x(T-1) = G^{-1}(T-1)\,\underline{c}(T-1) + R(T-1)\underline{x}(T) + S(T-1)\,\underline{x}(T+1) \qquad (4)$$

$$= G^{-1}(T-1)\,\underline{c}(T-1) + R(T-1)\,[G^{-1}(T)\underline{c}(T)+R(T)H(1)\underline{c}(T+1)$$

$$+ S(T)H(2)\underline{c}(T+2)] + S(T-1)H(1)\underline{c}(T+1)$$

$$= G^{-1}(T-1)\underline{c}(T-1) + R(T-1)G^{-1}(T)\underline{c}(T)+[R(T-1)R(T)$$

$$+ S(T-1)]\,H(1)\underline{c}(T+1)+R(T-1)S(T)H(2)\underline{c}(T+2).$$

Iterating backward we can work out the sectoral outputs and their allocations for each year of the plan.

The feasibility of the above plan can be checked with reference to $\underline{x}_o$, the vector of total sectoral outputs in the preplan year o. The plan is feasible if

$$\underline{x}_o \geqslant \underline{x}(o) = G^{-1}(o)\underline{c}(o) + R(o)\underline{x}(1) + S(o)\underline{x}(2). \qquad (5)$$

The problem of gestation lags has been discussed by Tinbergen and Bos in *Mathematical Models of Economic Growth*[23] and some numerical methods of estimation have been suggested.

NOTES

1. Abram Bergson, *The Economics of Soviet Planning* (New Haven: Yale University Press, 1964).

2. Ibid.

3. J. M. Montias, *Central Planning in Poland,* Appendix A, "Planning by Successive Approximations Consistency Problems" (New Haven: Yale University Press, 1962).

4. N. P. Fedorenko, "The Role of Economics-Mathematical Methods in the Planning and Management of the Economy of the Soviet Socialist Republics," *Journal of Development Planning,* no. 1 (1969).

5. Michael Kaser, *Soviet Economics* (London: World University Library, 1970).

6. W. W. Leontief, "Quantitative Input-Output Relations in the Economic System of the United States," *Review of Economics and Statistics* 18 (August 1936); and *The Structure of the American Economy, 1919-1939* (London: Oxford University Press, 1951).

7. H. B. Chenery and P. G. Clark, *Interindustry Economics* (New York: Wiley, 1967).

8. This was probably first perceived and formally proved by Samuelson; see Paul A. Samuelson, "Abstracts of a Theorem Concerning Substitutability in Open Leontief Models," in T. C. Koopmans (ed.), *Activity Analysis of Production and Allocation* (New York: Wiley, 1951).

9. R. Bellman, *Introduction to Matrix Analysis* (New York: McGraw-Hill, 1960).

10. H. B. Chenery and J. B. Clark, *Interindustry Economics.*

11. F. V. Waugh, "Inversion of the Leontief Matrix by Power Series," *Econometrica* 18 (1950).

12. H. B. Chenery and J. B. Clark, *Interindustry Economics.*

13. A. Ghosh, "Input-Output Analysis with Substantial Independent Groups of Industries," *Econometrica* 28 (January 1960).

14. This is in effect Tinbergen's semiinput-output method; see Jan Tinbergen, *Development Planning* (World University Library, 1967).

15. L. N. Moses, "A General Equilibrium Model of Production, Interregional Trade, and Location of Industry," *Review of Economics and Statistics* 42 (November 1960).

16. W. W. Leontief and Alan Strout, "Multiregional Input-Output Analysis," in T. Barna (ed.), *Structural Interdependence and Economic Development* (New York: St. Martin's Press, 1963).

17. A. Ghosh, *Planning, Programming and Input-Output Models* (Cambridge: Cambridge University Press, 1968).

18. Alan S. Manne and Ashok Rudra, "A Consistency Model of India's Fourth Plan," *Sankhya* 27, series B (1965).

19. Perspective Planning Division, *Notes on Perspectives of Development, India: 1960-61 to 1975-76* (New Delhi: Planning Commission, 1964).

20. Joel Bergson and Alan S. Manne, "An Almost Consistent Model for India's Fourth and Fifth Plans," in Irma Adelman and Erik Thorbecke

(eds.), *The Theory and Design of Economic Development* (Baltimore: John Hopkins Press, 1966); Alan S. Manne and Thomas E. Weisskopf, "A Dynamic Multisectoral Model for India, 1967-75," in A. P. Carter and A. Brody (eds.), *Applications of Input-Output Analysis* (Amsterdam: North Holland, 1970).

21. W. W. Leontief, "The Dynamic Inverse," in A. P. Carter and A. Brody (eds.), *Contributions to Input-Output Analysis* (New York: American Elsever, 1970).

22. Ibid.

23. H. C. Bos and J. Tinbergen, *Mathematical Models of Economic Growth* (New Haven: Yale University Press, 1962).

CHAPTER FIVE

Optimality Planning

I. Economic Planning and Mathematical Programming

1. *Optimization*

Optimization is the process that seeks the maximum or minimum of an objective function with or without given constraints and derives the conditions therefor. It stands to reason that the problem of optimization must have been faced from the very beginning of human existence. The word "optimum" was coined by Leibniz as far back as 1710 in his *Theodicy.*[1] However, major breakthroughs for constrained optimization have occurred with the advent of what is now known as mathematical programming initiated by the discoveries of Kantorovich and Dantzig.

2. *Mathematical Programming*

Mathematical programming now refers to almost all techniques and algorithms which are connected with the process of constrained optimization. Programming may be static when optimization is carried out for a single period or it may be dynamic, involving several interdependent periods. Further, a program is linear when all the relations and constraints are expressed in linear form and nonlinear when some or all of these are expressed in nonlinear form. Furthermore, a program is either deterministic or probabilistic. In the first case, all the variables and relations are assumed to be known with certainty; in the second case, some of them are assumed to be subject to random variations. There are some other distinctive characteristics; for example, some programs require that the solution of some of the variables take on specific values, or that the optimization has to be carried out at more than one level.

3.   *Optimal Planning and Mathematical Programming*

An optimal plan is drawn up with the purpose of maximizing a function of target variables with the initially given resources and the existing and prospective economic structure. The function to be maximized represents in some sense what is assumed to be national preference. The initially given resources include natural and human resources, produced capital goods, infrastructure and acquired skills, and imported capital and other goods. Economic structure is represented by the production possibilities in form of a production function or a matrix of technologies and banking, financial, and trading institutions.

The problems and difficulties involved in quantifying the resources, specifying the national preference, and expressing the economic structure have been described earlier. Given the degree of success with which these have been handled, the framework of an optimal plan can be stated in the following way: Find the values of target variables which maximize the preference function using the initially given resources and operating through the available economic structure. More formally, the above can be restated as follows:

$$\text{Maximize} \quad z = z(x_1, x_2, \ldots x_n), \tag{1}$$

$$\text{subject to} \quad g_i(x_1, \ldots x_n) \leqslant b_i \tag{2}$$

$$x_j \geqslant 0 \quad i = 1, \ldots m \tag{3}$$

$$j = 1, \ldots n.$$

The preference function which has to be maximized is z. It is a function of the variables with which the representatives of the citizens and the planners are concerned. The left-hand side of (2) represents the economic structure and the right-hand side the amounts of resources. It says that the formulation of the plan should be such that it requires at most the initially given amounts of resources, no more. The inequalities (3) state the obvious fact that the variables cannot be negative.

The above framework of an optimal plan is exactly that of a mathematical program. In the latter, (1) is generally called the objective function; (2) is the set of constraints; and (3) is sometimes called the set of restraints. Indeed, the correspondence between optimal planning and mathematical programming is so great that not infrequently the terms "planning" and "programming" are used interchangeably.

4.   *Plan of the Chapter*

In section II, we describe linear programming and its solution, since it is the most widely used technique in the formulation of planning models so far. Included in this section are brief discussions of shadow prices and sensitivity analysis. In section III, some special cases of linear programming which are useful in planning and have been applied are briefly discussed. In section IV, nonlinear programming is introduced, and a simple method of solving a special type of nonlinear program with separable variables is given. Kuhn-Tucker conditions, which are generally employed in the solution of nonlinear programs, are given in appendix 5.A, and a method of solving a quadratic program is given in appendix 5.B. Section V introduces the dynamic optimality planning and gives some representation of dynamic linear planning. The methods of control theory such as variational calculus, Bellman's dynamic programming, and maximum principles are briefly described in appendices 5.C, 5.D, and 5.E. Appendix 5.F discusses very simple applications of these methods in deriving optimal rate of savings.

II. Linear Programming

1.   *Concepts and Definitions*

When all the relations and functions of a mathematical program are linear, it is called a linear program. Linear programming is the most widely used branch of mathematical programming because many physical and social phenomena can be more conveniently and confidently expressed in linear rather than in any other form. Moreover, that complete and effective techniques have been developed to solve linear programs is not the case for other programs. Furthermore, nonlinear forms can often be approximated by linear forms, leading to solutions of nonlinear programs through the techniques of linear programming.

Kantorovitch[2] in 1939 was perhaps the first to formulate the linear programming model, though without finding an efficient method of solution. It was left to George Dantzig[3] in 1947 to discover an efficient computational technique, known as the simplex method. The method is so widely used that we give only a simple description here.

2. Linear Program and Its Solution

A simple linear program involving four target variables and three resources can be expressed as follows:

$$\text{Maximize} \quad z = w_1 x_1 + w_2 x_2 + w_3 x_3 + w_4 x_4 \qquad (4)$$

$$\text{subject to} \quad a_{11} x_1 + a_{12} x_2 + a_{13} x_3 + a_{14} x_4 \leqslant b_1 \qquad (5)$$

$$a_{21} x_1 + a_{22} x_2 + a_{23} x_3 + a_{24} x_4 \leqslant b_2$$

$$a_{31} x_1 + a_{32} x_2 + a_{33} x_3 + a_{34} x_4 \leqslant b_3$$

$$x_1 \geqslant 0, x_2 \geqslant 0, x_3 \geqslant 0, x_4 \geqslant 0. \qquad (6)$$

In the above, x's are the target variables, w's are the weights attached to them by the planners, a_{ij}'s are input coefficients denoting the amount of ith resource required per unit of jth target variable, and b's are the initially given amounts of resources. The model can be extended to any number of target variables and resources. Any values of target variables which satisfy (5) and (6) give a feasible solution, but we want a solution which maximizes (4). For this, the first step is to convert the inequalities in (5) to equalities by introducing slack variables equal to the difference between the two sides of the inequalities. This can then be written as follows:

$$a_{11} x_1 + a_{12} x_2 + a_{13} x_3 + a_{14} x_4 + x_5 = b_1$$

$$a_{21} x_1 + a_{22} x_2 + a_{23} x_3 + a_{24} x_4 + x_6 = b_2 \qquad (7)$$

$$a_{31} x_1 + a_{32} x_2 + a_{33} x_3 + a_{34} x_4 + x_7 = b_3.$$

In (7), x_5, x_6, and x_7 can be nothing but the resources 1, 2, and 3, respectively.

When there are three resources, the values of only three variables can be set at such levels that all the resources are fully exhausted. Moreover, the per unit resource requirements of the fourth variable can be derived by multiplying the per unit resource requirements of the three variables by appropriate numbers and adding them. Therefore, for the optimal solution, we should consider only three variables such that per unit resource requirements of any of these cannot be derived from the other two in the way just mentioned. However, it may be that solution of (7) for any three such variables, equating the other variables to zero yields a negative value of one or more variables, which will contradict (6). The solution of (7) for a set of three variables such that per unit resource requirement for any of these cannot be derived from those of the other two and that the solution values of the variables is non-negative is called the *basic feasible* solution, and the variables in the set are said to form a basis. One obvious feasible basis is formed by x_5, x_6, and x_7, and, in most practical cases, it is convenient to start with this basis. Since it is intended here to show the procedure of solution, we assume that variables x_1, x_2, and x_3 form a feasible basis. Then,

$$a_{11}x_1 + a_{12}x_2 + a_{13}x_3 = b_1$$

$$a_{21}x_1 + a_{22}x_2 + a_{23}x_3 = b_2 \tag{8}$$

$$a_{31}x_1 + a_{32}x_2 + a_{33}x_3 = b_3.$$

The imputed values of the resources for this basis are such that the unit cost of each variable in the basis equals the weight or the price attached to it in the objective function. Therefore,

$$c_1 a_{11} + c_2 a_{21} + c_3 a_{31} = w_1$$

$$c_1 a_{12} + c_2 a_{22} + c_3 a_{32} = w_2 \tag{9}$$

$$c_1 a_{13} + c_2 a_{23} + c_3 a_{33} = w_3.$$

The solution values of c's in (9) give the imputed values of resources when variables x_1, x_2, and x_3 form the feasible basis. The per unit costs of nonbasis variables at these prices are as follows:

$$u_4 = c_1 a_{14} + c_2 a_{24} + c_3 a_{34}$$

$$u_5 = c_1 a_{15} + c_2 a_{25} + c_3 a_{35} \tag{10}$$

$$u_6 = c_1 a_{16} + c_2 a_{26} + c_3 a_{36}$$

$$u_7 = c_1 a_{17} + c_2 a_{27} + c_3 a_{37}.$$

Now, the profitability of the nonbasis variables can be derived by deducting their per unit cost from the weight or price attached to them in the objective function. Thus

$$z_4 = w_4 - u_4$$

$$z_5 = w_5 - u_5 \qquad (11)$$

$$z_6 = w_6 - u_6$$

$$z_7 = w_7 - u_7.$$

In the above, w_5, w_6, and w_7 are zero since they are the weights or prices attached to the slack variables which do not appear in the objective function.

If any z's are positive, it means that the value of the objective function can be raised by introducing the corresponding variable in the basis. If more than one nonbasis variable have positive z's, it is advisable to introduce the variable corresponding to the highest profitability. Suppose that $z_4 > 0$ and we wish to introduce variable x_4 in the basis. This can be done by excluding one of the variables already in the basis in such a way that the new basis containing variable x_4 is feasible. From our preceding discussion we can write

$$d_{14} \begin{bmatrix} a_{11} \\ a_{21} \\ a_{31} \end{bmatrix} + d_{24} \begin{bmatrix} a_{12} \\ a_{22} \\ a_{32} \end{bmatrix} + d_{34} \begin{bmatrix} a_{13} \\ a_{23} \\ a_{33} \end{bmatrix} = \begin{bmatrix} a_{14} \\ a_{24} \\ a_{34} \end{bmatrix}. \qquad (12)$$

Suppose now that variable x_1 is to be removed from the basis; then (12) can be written as follows:

$$\begin{bmatrix} a_{11} \\ a_{21} \\ a_{31} \end{bmatrix} = \frac{1}{d_{14}} \begin{bmatrix} a_{14} \\ a_{24} \\ a_{34} \end{bmatrix} - \frac{d_{24}}{d_{14}} \begin{bmatrix} a_{12} \\ a_{22} \\ a_{32} \end{bmatrix} - \frac{d_{34}}{d_{14}} \begin{bmatrix} a_{13} \\ a_{23} \\ a_{33} \end{bmatrix} \qquad (13)$$

Substituting from (13) in (8), we write

$$\frac{a_{14}}{d_{14}}(x_1) + a_{12}(x_2 - x_1 \frac{d_{24}}{d_{14}}) + a_{13}(x_3 - x_1 \frac{d_{34}}{d_{14}}) = b_1$$

$$\frac{a_{24}}{d_{14}}(x_1) + a_{22}(x_2 - x_1 \frac{d_{24}}{d_{14}}) + a_{23}(x_3 - x_1 \frac{d_{34}}{d_{14}}) = b_2 \qquad (14)$$

$$\frac{a_{34}}{d_{14}}(x_1) + a_{23}(x_2 - x_1 \frac{d_{24}}{d_{14}}) + a_{33}(x_3 - x_1 \frac{d_{34}}{d_{14}}) = b_3.$$

We note that $\frac{a_{14}}{d_{14}} = a_{11}$, $\frac{a_{24}}{d_{14}} = a_{21}$, and $\frac{a_{34}}{d_{14}} = a_{31}$. Thus the coefficients of the variables written in parentheses in (14) are the same as those in (8). The system of equations in (8) form a feasible basis only when the values in the parentheses are positive.

$$x_1 \geqslant 0, x_2 - x_1 \frac{d_{24}}{d_{14}} \geqslant 0, x_3 - x_1 \frac{d_{34}}{d_{14}} \geqslant 0,$$

or

$$x_1 \geqslant 0, \frac{x_2}{d_{24}} \geqslant \frac{x_1}{d_{14}}, \frac{x_3}{d_{34}} \geqslant \frac{x_1}{d_{14}}. \qquad (15)$$

Since x_1 is positive, the following must hold:

$$\frac{x_1}{d_{14}} = \min \left\{ \frac{x_1}{d_{14}}, \frac{x_2}{d_{24}}, \frac{x_3}{d_{34}} \right\}.$$

Hence, in general, variable x_k can be excluded from the basis and a nonbasis variable x_j can be introduced to form a new feasible basis when

$$\frac{x_k}{d_{kj}} = \min_s \left\{ \frac{x_s}{d_{sj}} \right\}, \text{ s indexing basis activities.} \qquad (16)$$

The above procedure has to be repeated until a feasible basis is reached when the profitability of none of the nonbasis variables is positive. Then the basis is optimal, since there is no way to improve the value of the preference function by altering the basis.

The steps in solving a linear planning model by the simplex method can now be summarized:

(i)   Find an initial feasible basis, solve for the values of the variables, and compute the imputed values c's of resources corresponding to this basis.

(ii)   Compute the profitability of nonbasis variables z_j's,
where $z_j = w_j - \sum\limits_{i=1}^{m} c_i a_{ij}$.

Include jth nonbasis variable into the basis whose z_j is
positive and preferably whose positive z_j is highest.

(iii)   Exclude kth variable from the basis for which

$$\frac{x_k}{d_{kj}} = \min_{s} \left| \frac{x_s}{d_{sj}} \right|,$$ s indexing the basis variables, and d_{kj}

and d_{sj} are the numbers with which the resource
requirements of kth and sth variables are multiplied and
summed up to arrive at the resource requirements of the
jth variable.

(iv)   This inclusion and exclusion principle has to be repeated
until we arrive at the basis such that $z_j \leqslant 0$ for all the
variables in the nonbasis.

At this stage the optimum basis has been found and the optimum
value of the preference function can be calculated.

3.   *Duality and Shadow Prices*

An economic problem has two facets; if it is expressed in real terms,
it has a counterpart in value terms, and vice versa. An economic plan
similarly can be expressed in physical terms with a counterpart in value or
financial terms, and vice versa. Mathematical programs have the same
characteristics; there is a dual to any primal program. Production function
and cost function provide a good example of duality in economics and also
in mathematical programming.

The linear program of the preceding subsection which we can take as
primal is as follows:

$$\text{Maximize } z = \sum_{j=1}^{4} w_j x_j, \tag{17}$$

$$\text{subject to } \sum_{j=1}^{4} a_{ij} x_j \leqslant b_i \qquad i = 1,2,3, \tag{18}$$

$$x_j \geqslant 0. \tag{19}$$

The dual of the above program is as follows:

$$\text{Minimize } Z = \sum_{i=1}^{3} \pi_i b_i, \tag{20}$$

subject to $\quad \displaystyle\sum_{i=1}^{3} a_{ij}\,\pi_i \geqslant w_j \qquad j=1,2,3,4 \qquad\qquad (21)$

$$\pi_i \geqslant 0. \qquad\qquad (22)$$

In a sense the primal program is a production model and typifies a physical plan, and the dual is a cost model and is related to financial planning or planning through pricing. In the dual the π's are the variables expressing the prices of resources, such that the total cost of resources $\displaystyle\sum_{i=1}^{3} \pi_i b_i$ is minimized but without making the unit cost of any of the outputs less than their given values w_j's. Here these associated prices have also to be non-negative.

In order to show some interesting properties, multiply (18) by π_i and sum over i's and multiply (21) by x_j and sum over j's to get

$$\sum_j w_j x_j \leqslant \sum_{i,j} \pi_i a_{ij} x_j \leqslant \sum_i \pi_i b_i. \qquad\qquad (23)$$

Suppose now that x_j^o (j=1,2,3,4) and π_i^o (i=1,2,3) are basic feasible solutions to the primal and dual programs, respectively, such that

$$\sum_j w_j x_j^o = \sum_{i,j} \pi_i^o a_{ij} x_j^o = \sum_i \pi_i^o b_i. \qquad\qquad (24)$$

If (24) is true, then, considering (23),

$$\sum_j w_j x_j \leqslant \sum_j w_j x_j^o, \qquad\qquad (25)$$

and thus x_j^o (j=1,2, ... 4) is optimal, since there cannot be any other x_j's which will make the value of $\displaystyle\sum_j w_j x_j$ higher. Similarly, if (24) holds, then, considering (23) again,

$$\sum_i \pi_i^o b_i \leqslant \sum_i \pi_i b_i, \qquad\qquad (26)$$

and thus π_i^o (i=1,2,3) is optimal, since there cannot be any other π_i's which can make the value of $\Sigma \pi_i b_i$ lower. Hence the optimal values of the primal and dual are equal. Conversely, if the values of some basic feasible solutions of the primal and the dual are equal, then they are optimal. The optimal value of the ith resource π_i^o (i=1,2,3) is called the shadow price of this resource. The shadow prices can be derived from solving the dual program. Or once the primal program has been solved and the optimal values of the variables are known, the values of shadow prices can be obtained by replacing the inequalities (21) by equalities for all j's for which x_j^o is positive, that is, by solving

$$\sum_i a_{ij} \pi_i = w_j \qquad j = 1, \ldots 4. \qquad (27)$$

It can be seen that, when an optimal plan is formulated in physical terms, that is, according to the primal program above, the values of the shadow prices of the resources are the solution values of the dual program, and, if the optimal plan is contemplated through fixing the prices of resources at their shadow prices, the magnitudes of the target variable x_j's are the solution values of the primal program.

In an economy where an optimal plan is to be in operation, the shadow prices of resources are equal to their marginal productivities. This is because $Z^o = z^o = \sum_i \pi_i^o b_i$. Therefore,

$$\frac{\partial z^o}{\partial b_i} = \pi_i^o \qquad i = 1,2,3. \qquad (28)$$

As regards the signs of π_i^o's, they are determined by the nature of the programming problem. The above primal program maximizes the objective function, under the constraints that the resource requirements must be less than their availability, and the restraints that all the variables be positive. Under these conditions, if the amount of any of the resources is increased by however little, the value of the objective function can only increase; it cannot decrease. Hence

$$\frac{\partial z^o}{\partial b_i} = \pi_i^o \geqslant 0 \qquad i = 1,2,3. \qquad (29)$$

If the constraints of the primal program are changed such that the inequalities are reversed, the objective function and the restraints remaining the same, then an increase in any of the resources will reduce the region in which the values of variables can move. This can only result in a reduction in the objective function and in no way in an increase. Hence

$$\frac{\partial Z^o}{\partial b_i} = \pi_i^o \leqslant 0 \qquad i = 1,2,3 \qquad (30)$$

when inequalities in the constraints of the primal program are reversed.

When the constraints are in the form of equalities, all of any resource would be used up in any feasible program. Then it is not possible to determine whether the domain of maximization will be reduced or increased, and thus an increase in b_i may result in either an increase or decrease in z^o. Therefore,

$$\frac{\partial Z^o}{\partial b_i} = \pi_i^o > \text{ or } = \text{ or } < 0,$$

that is, π_i^o is unrestricted in sign if $\sum_{j=1}^{4} a_{ij}x_j = b_i$ $i=1,2,3$.

The signs of shadow prices are reversed when an objective function is minimized instead of being maximized, and vice versa. Table 5.1 gives a classification of linear programs with corresponding duals and the shadow prices.

Table 5.1

Equation Systems of Linear Programs and Their Duals

Primal	objective	$\sum_j w_j x_j$	max	min	max	min	max	min
	constraints	$\sum_j a_{iy}x_j$ $i=1,2,\ldots$	$\leqslant b_i$	$\leqslant b_i$	$\geqslant b_i$	$\geqslant b_i$	$\leqslant b_i$	$= b_i$
	restraints	x_j $j=1,2,\ldots$	$\geqslant 0$	$\geqslant 0$	$\geqslant 0$	$\geqslant 0$	unrestricted	$\geqslant 0$
Dual	objective	$\sum_i \pi_i b_i$	min	max	min	max	min	max
	constraints	$\sum_i a_{ij}b_i$ $j=1,2,\ldots$	$\geqslant w_j$	$\lesseqgtr w_j$	$\geqslant w_j$	$\geqslant w_j$	$= w_j$	$\geqslant w_j$
	restraints	π_i $i=1,2,\ldots$	$\geqslant 0$	$\leqslant 0$	$\leqslant 0$	$\leqslant 0$	$\geqslant 0$	unrestricted

The following relationship holds between the primal and the dual:

(i) If the primal is a maximizing problem, then the dual is a minimizing problem.

(ii)   The constraint constants of the primal problem are the weights in the objective function of the dual.

(iii)   The weights of the variables in the objective function of the primal problem are the constraints constants of the dual.

(iv)   The variables in the dual are the shadow prices of the variables in the primal.

(v)   If the inequalities of the constraints and restraints are in the same direction in one of the programs, then they are in the opposite directions in its dual.

(vi)   The dual of the dual is the primal program.

Duality aspects and shadow prices are helpful in the formulation and evaluation of optimal plans. Since the primal and the dual have the same optimal solutions, and the optimal values of the variables of the one are implied in and can be derived from the solution of the other, it does not matter in principle which of these is used in the formulation of an optimal plan. In a frictionless society, the two will yield identical results. However, the structure of some economies like those of the socialist countries of the Soviet type is such that physical planning may be more appropriate. In these countries, almost all the economic activities are carried out by the state and its agencies and enterprises. Each agency and enterprise has to follow the commands of a higher agency or authority. In such a country, once the physical magnitudes have been decided by the central authority, whatever the degree of consultation with and participation by the lower agencies, they have to be realized by the agencies and enterprises according to their assignment of the physical magnitudes which can be more conveniently and directly derived from solving the primal program (17), (18), and (19).

In mixed or private enterprise economies, only a fraction of the total economic activities is controlled by the state. The rest is undertaken and managed by private entrepreneurs who do not have to follow the state directives related to the level of their operation and the size of their output. Their activities can only be influenced through indirect fiscal means and maneuvering of prices. For optimal planning in such countries, the dual program (20), (21), and (22) may be more relevant, where shadow prices of resources can be used for guidance in monetary-fiscal policies.

We have seen that shadow prices are equilibrium prices compatible with the optimal utilization of resources. In underdeveloped countries, the prevailing prices differ greatly from such equilibrium prices. This is due to structural disequilibria caused by market imperfections, immobilities, rigidities, and institutional and social factors, resulting into higher prices of factors like unskilled labor, which are in abundant supply, and lower prices of capital and foreign exchange, which are scarce. It is appropriate, therefore, that in these countries shadow prices of factors be used in the choice of projects and in the plan formulation in general.

Shadow prices play a strategic role in the process of formulating a decentralized plan and in the solution of the related decomposed program. The decomposition principle and its usefulness in decentralized planning will be discussed in a following section.

Shadow prices can be effectively used in evaluating the optimality of national plans. If the shadow price of a resource is nearly the same in each region and administrative unit, then the plan is likely to be optimal.

4.   *Sensitivity Analysis*

Sensitivity analysis is the procedure of analyzing the changes in the optimal values of the objective function and those of the variables due to changes in the parameters of a program. It is useful in formulation and evaluation of a plan in important respects. First, if a plan is formulated in such a way that it is very sensitive to small changes in its parameters, then a slight disturbance in the materialization of the relevant parameters may result in a much larger shortfall in the realization of the plan. Therefore, attempts may be made to reformulate the plan to make it less vulnerable. Second, sensitivity analysis may show that a relatively small change in some of the parameters such as a moderate increase in the availability of some resource or the introduction of a new technique leads to a sizable increase in the value of the target or preference function. Thus efforts may be made to introduce these changes. Third, sensitivity analysis may be useful in evaluating the optimality of a plan when the values of the parameters are not exactly and accurately known. In this case a range of plausible values of parameters may be considered. If the plan is shown to be optimal within the range of these parameters, then it may be optimal; otherwise, not.

The three sets of parameters in an optimal plan formulation are the weights attached to the target variables, the amounts of available resources, and the technical coefficients. When the change in any parameters are such that the same target variables appear in the optimal selection as before, the recalculation of the magnitudes of the variables, their shadow prices, and the value of the plan (that is, the value of the objective function) can be done without solving any further linear programs. In fact, a change in the amounts of resources available, which does not cause a change in the inclusion of variables in the optimal set, does not change the values of the shadow prices. This is because the values of the shadow prices depend on the relative weights of the target variables and their technical coefficients, not on the amounts of resources, so long as the optimal basis does not change.

On the whole, sensitivity analysis provides valuable insight into the working of a planning model, shows up flaws and discrepancies if any, and indicates alternative ways of reformulating the model.

III. Some Special Cases of Linear Programs

The general linear program can be modified and extended, as has been extensively done, to suit various special aspects of economic planning. The three most important cases are (i) the transportation problem, (ii) integer programming, and (iii) the decomposition principle. A brief outline of each of these is given below.

1. *The Transportation Problem*

The form of linear programming which is known as the transportation problem has the distinction of being conceived and worked out first.[4] In the original problem of this type some good has to be transported from points of origin to points of destination in such a way that the total cost of transportation is minimized. Let x_{ij} denote the amount of good to be transported from origin i to destination j, and c_{ij} the corresponding unit cost of transportation. Let a_i denote the amount of good available at origin i to be transported to different destinations, and b_j the amount required at destination j from various origins. The problem can now be formulated as follows:

$$\text{Minimize } z = \sum_{i,j} c_{ij} x_{ij}, \tag{31}$$

$$\text{subject to} \quad \sum_j x_{ij} = a_i \tag{32}$$

$$\sum_i x_{ij} = b_j \tag{33}$$

$$x_{ij} \geqslant 0 \tag{34}$$

$$i = 1, \ldots, m$$
$$j = 1, \ldots, n.$$

In the above program there are $m+n$ constraints. However, since $\sum\limits_{i} a_i$ $= \sum\limits_{j} b_j$, there are only $m+n-1$ constraints which are mutually exclusive. Hence the basis consists of $m+n-1$ variables only. The program can be solved by the straightforward application of the simplex method. However, because of the special characteristics of the program in the sense that the coefficients are unity, the simplex criteria of exclusion and inclusion of variables are as follows:

(i)   Introduce a variable x_{ij} in the basis for which

$$z_{ij} - c_{ij} > 0. \tag{35}$$

Here z_{ij} and c_{ij} replace z_j and w_j, since in the transportation problem the variables are double-indexed, and we are concerned with a minimizing problem.

(ii)   Exclude the variable x_{sk} from the basis for which

$$x_{sk} = \min \{x_{st}\}, \text{ st indexing the basis variables.} \tag{36}$$

The optimal solution is reached when there is no variable in the nonbasis for which (ii) is true. A simple method for computing $z_{ij} - c_{ij}$ was advanced by Dantzig.[5] Let $c_{ir}, c_{qr}, \ldots c_{st} \ldots, c_{ws}, c_{wj}$ be the $m+n-1$ unit costs of transportation corresponding to the variables in any basis. Then set the following:

$$
\begin{aligned}
c_{ir} &= u_i + v_r \\
c_{qr} &= u_q + v_r \\
\cdots &\quad \cdots \\
c_{st} &= u_s + v_t \\
\cdots &\quad \cdots \\
c_{ws} &= u_w + v_s \\
c_{wj} &= u_w + v_j.
\end{aligned} \tag{37}
$$

In (37) there are $(m+n-1)$ equations in $m+n$ variables u's and v's. Putting any one of these u's or v's equal to an arbitrary value, say o, all the remaining u's and v's can be solved in terms of c's. It can be shown that

$$z_{ij} = u_i + v_j, \tag{38}$$

and, consequently, the values of the simplex criteria $z_{ij} - c_{ij}$ can be computed very easily.

The structure of the transportation problem can be transformed into a simple regional planning model, the aim of which is to minimize the cost of producing national commodities by optimal distribution of their production among regions. Let there be l_1 national sectors, $1, 2, \ldots$ $\ldots l_1$, and l_2 regional sectors, $l_1 + 1, l_1 + 2, \ldots, l_1 + l_2$. Given the income y_r to be created in each region r, the amount of commodity i required in region r is given by

$$x_{ir}^d = q_{ir}y_r \quad i=1, \ldots, l_1, l_1 + 1, \ldots, l_1 + l_2, \tag{39}$$

where q_{ir} is the amount of commodity i demanded per dollar of income in region r.

If the demand of each region for each commodity is to be fully met, then the amount of ith commodity to be produced in the economy is given by

$$x_i = \sum_{r=1}^{R} x_{ir}^d = \sum_{r} q_{ir}y_r. \tag{40}$$

The amount of regional commodities required by each region is by definition to be produced in the region itself. The income created in region r in producing the amounts of regional commodities is given by

$$\sum_{i=l_1 + 1}^{l_1 + l_2} \xi_{ir}q_{ir}y_r, \tag{41}$$

where ξ_{ir} is the income created per unit of commodity i produced in region r.

The income to be created in each region after deducting the income created in producing the amounts of regional commodities is given by

$$\breve{y}_r = y_r - \sum_{i=l_1 + 1}^{l_1 + l_2} \xi_{ir}q_{ir}y_r. \tag{42}$$

Let c_{ir} denote the cost of production per unit of commodity i in region r.

Now the simple optimal regional planning model can be stated as follows:

$$\text{Minimize} \sum_{i=1}^{l_1} \sum_{r=1}^{R} c_{ir} x_{ir},$$

$$\text{subject to} \sum_{r=1}^{R} x_{ir} = x_i \qquad i=1, \ldots, l_1, \qquad (43)$$

$$\text{and} \sum_{i=1}^{l_1} \xi_{ir} x_{ir} = \check{y}_r \qquad r=1, \ldots, R$$

$$x_{ir} \geqslant 0.$$

The above model is in large measure similar to the transportation problem. It can be made exactly identical with the transportation problem with some further assumptions. First, suppose that the income created per unit of output of each commodity in each region is the same, so that $\xi_{ir} = \xi_i$ and that each output is measured in such units that income generated in the production per unit of each commodity is the same, and let this be unity. Then (43) can be written as follows:

$$\text{Minimize} \sum_{i=1}^{l_1} \sum_{r=1}^{R} c_{ir} x_{ir},$$

$$\text{subject to} \sum_{r=1}^{R} x_{ir} = x_i \qquad i=1, \ldots l_1 \qquad (44)$$

$$\sum_{r=1}^{l_1} x_{ir} = \check{y}_r \qquad r=1, \ldots R$$

$$x_{ir} \geqslant 0.$$

The model can be made somewhat more realistic by imposing capacity limitations on regional production. It can be reformulated to deal with an employment problem rather than income distribution.[6] The above illustration is advantageous in the search for optimal location of industries among different regions, ensuring a desired income redistribution.

2.   *Integer Programming*

Linear programming is called integer programming when the solution values of the variables are required to be integers, pure integer programming when all the variables are to be integers, and mixed when only some of them have to be integers. Several methods have been developed to handle such programming; illustrated here is the first and best known method for pure integer programming.[7]

Consider a simple linear program with three variables and two resources. Let the constraints of the program be

$$a_{11}x_1 + a_{12}x_2 + a_{13}x_3 = b_1$$

$$a_{21}x_1 + a_{22}x_2 + a_{23}x_3 = b_2. \tag{45}$$

Let us suppose that the variables x_1 and x_2 form a basis and express the basis variables in terms of the nonbasis variables, using Cramer's rule

$$x_1 = \alpha_{10} - \alpha_{13}x_3 \tag{46}$$

$$x_2 = \alpha_{20} - \alpha_{23}x_3, \tag{46a}$$

where $\alpha_{10} = \dfrac{b_1 a_{22} - b_2 a_{12}}{a_{11}a_{22} - a_{12}a_{21}}$; $\alpha_{13} = \dfrac{a_{22}a_{13} - a_{12}a_{23}}{a_{11}a_{22} - a_{12}a_{21}}$,

and similarly for α_{20} and α_{23}.

If α_{10} and α_{20} are nonintegers, then, in the optimal solution, when x_3 is zero, x_1 and x_2 will be nonintegers. To arrive at an integer solution, divide $\alpha_{10}, \alpha_{20}, \alpha_{13}$, and α_{23} into two parts each, one the greatest integer (not necessarily positive) and the other a positive fraction. Thus

$$\alpha_{10} = \iota_{10} + \phi_{10}, \alpha_{20} = \iota_{20} + \phi_{20} \tag{47}$$

$$\alpha_{13} = \iota_{13} + \phi_{13}, \alpha_{23} = \iota_{23} + \phi_{23}. $$

Here ι's are integers unrestricted in sign, and ϕ's are positive fractions. Using (47) in (46) and (46a), we have

$$x_1 - \iota_{10} + \iota_{13}x_3 = \phi_{10} - \phi_{13}x_3 \tag{48}$$

$$x_2 - \iota_{20} + \iota_{23}x_3 = \phi_{20} - \phi_{23}x_3. \tag{48a}$$

If the constraint (46) is replaced by the left-hand side of (48) equated to zero, that is, by $x_1 - \iota_{10} + \iota_{13}x_3 = 0$, x_1 will have an integer value in the solution of (46). But this is derived by deducting the right-hand side of (48) from (46). Thus to ensure an integer value for x_1, the right-hand side of (48) can be sliced away from (46). This can be done by introducing an additional constraint with, say, an additional variable x_4, which equals the negative of the right side of (48),

$$x_4 = - \phi_{10} + \phi_{13}x_3. \tag{49}$$

The system of constraints (45) is now

$$a_{11}x_1 + a_{12}x_2 + a_{13}x_3 \quad = b_1$$

$$a_{21}x_1 + a_{22}x_2 + a_{23}x_3 \quad = b_2 \tag{50}$$

$$- \phi_{13}x_3 + x_4 = -\phi_{10}.$$

Putting $x_3 = 0$, we have a basic solution in three variables x_1, x_2, and x_4. But since $\phi_{10} > 0$, $x_4 < 0$. Hence the basis is infeasible. The simplex criterion can then be used to eliminate x_4 from the basis and to find another feasible basis. The method introduces one variable at a time for each variable assuming a nonintegral value in the optimal solution. This increases the number of constraints each time by one and augments the basis by one, which may reduce the value of the objective function.

Techniques of integer programming may be helpful in planning where size of plants, economies of scale, and discontinuities in production are crucial considerations. Capacities of different sizes of plants can be introduced as integer values, by changing units of measurement if necessary, in order to help select optimal sizes of plants and equipment.

3.   *The Decomposition Principle*

The decomposition principle has become an important tool in economic planning and promises to be widely used. The principle is illustrated here with the following simple program, containing 4 variables and 6 categories of resources:

Maximize $w_1x_1 + w_2x_2 + w_3x_3 + w_4x_4$,

subject to $a_{11}x_1 + a_{12}x_2 + a_{13}x_3 + a_{14}x_4 \leqslant b_1$ \hfill (51)

$$a_{21}x_1 + a_{22}x_2 + a_{23}x_3 + a_{24}x_4 \leqslant b_2 \qquad \text{(51 cont'd)}$$

$$a_{31}x_1 + a_{32}x_2 \qquad \qquad \leqslant b_3$$

$$a_{41}x_1 + a_{42}x_2 \qquad \qquad \leqslant b_4$$

$$a_{53}x_3 + a_{54}x_4 \leqslant b_5$$

$$a_{63}x_3 + a_{64}x_4 \leqslant b_6$$

$$x_1 \geqslant 0, x_2 \geqslant 0, x_3 \geqslant 0, x_4 \geqslant 0.$$

The above program is a simple linear program with x_3 and x_4 zeros in the third and fourth inequality constraints, and x_1 and x_2 zeros in the fifth and sixth constraints. The program can be solved by straightforward application of the simplex method. However, when the number of variables and resources is larger, there is great computational advantage in using the decomposition principle. The main advantage of the decomposition principle in economic planning, however, is the procedure which allows decentralization in decision making.

Since the first two rows of the program contain all the variables, the next two rows the first two variables, and the last two rows the last two variables, the program in this case can be decomposed into three parts, the one involving the first two rows called the restricted master program, and the two containing two variables each of the remaining four called the subprograms.

We note that any variable x can be approximated by a grid $0 < x^o < x^1 < \ldots < x^T$, where x^T is the highest value that the variable can ever take. Thus

$$x = v_o x^o + v_1 x^1 + \ldots + v_T x^T, \sum_i v_i = 1, \qquad (52)$$

where all v's are zero except those associated with the two adjacent x's, say x^i and x^j, between which the variable x lies. For example, if $x = 36$ and grid points are 0,10,25,30,40,56,69,80, then all v's are zero except v_3 and v_4, which take on the values .6 and .4 respectively.

Using grid points, the restricted master program can be written as follows:

$$\text{Maximize } \sum_{t=0}^{T} (w_1 x_1{}^t + w_2 x_2^t + w_3 x_3^t + w_4 x_4^t)\, v_t,$$

$$\text{subject to } \sum_{t=o}^{T} (a_{11}x_1^t + a_{12}x_2^t + a_{13}x_3^t + a_{14}x_4^t)\, v_t \leqslant b_1 \tag{53}$$

$$\sum_{t=0}^{T} (a_{21}x_1^t + a_{22}x_2^t + a_{23}x_3^t + a_{24}x_4^t)\, v_t \leqslant b_2$$

$$\sum_{t=0}^{T} v_t = 1$$

$$v_t \geqslant 0.$$

The above is a standard linear program in variables v's. Any feasible solution yields a point

$$x_j = \sum_{t=0}^{T} x_j^t v_t, \quad j = 1,2,3,4. \tag{54}$$

The dual of the above program is as follows:

Minimize π_3,

$$\text{subject to } \sum_{j=1}^{4} a_{1j}x_j^t \pi_1 + \sum_{j=1}^{4} a_{2j}x_j^t \pi_2 + \pi_3 \geqslant \sum_{j=1}^{4} w_j x_j. \tag{55}$$

Now assume that v^k is optimal for the restricted program, so that $x_j^k = \sum_{t=0}^{T} x_j^t v_t^k$ is the optimal solution for the original restricted program, and let π^k be the optimal solution of the dual program; then it is easy to see that if

$$\sum_{j=1}^{2} a_{1j}x_j \pi_1^k + \sum_{j=3}^{4} a_{2j}x_j \pi_2^k + \pi_3^k \geqslant \sum_{j=1}^{4} w_j x_j \tag{56}$$

for all x_j which satisfy

$$\left.\begin{array}{l} \sum\limits_{j=1}^{2} a_{3j}x_j \leqslant b_3 \\[2em] \sum\limits_{j=1}^{2} a_{4j}x_j \leqslant b_4 \end{array}\right\} \text{ and } \left.\begin{array}{l} \sum\limits_{j=3}^{4} a_{5j}x_j \leqslant b_5 \\[2em] \sum\limits_{j=4}^{5} a_{6j}x_j \leqslant b_6 \end{array}\right\} \qquad (57)$$

then x_j^k, j=1,2,3,4 is truly optimal. But if there exists an x_j^{T+1} satisfying the constraints of the subprograms just stated which violates (56), then adding this point as a new grid point in the restricted master program may result in an improved solution. The procedure is to be repeated until an acceptable degree of convergence has been achieved. It can be shown that such a convergence always takes place.[8]

The decomposition principle and its several algorithms can be highly adaptive to problems of national planning, particularly when it is undertaken through a coordination of activities at several sublevels. These sublevels may be administrative, such as ministries, or spatial, such as regions, or a mixture of both, such as states or republics. The advantage of the application of the decomposition principle is that the sublevels need not furnish fully detailed information to the center, and the center needs to send only the shadow prices of its resources to the sublevels. This facilitates the task of planning in practice to a great extent.

The optimization of the plan itself takes place simultaneously at the center and at the sublevels. To start with, the indicators in the form of shadow prices of central resources are handed down from the center to the sublevels which are utilized in the optimization of the sublevel plans, and the solution values of the target variables are sent up to the center for optimization in the second round. Thus a gradual convergence of the center and the sublevel plans takes place, and a plan which is optimal at both the center and the sublevels is formulated.

The above sketch is related to two levels only, but it can be extended to multilevel plans. For discussions and application of the decomposition principle to two-level or multilevel planning, reference may be made to contributions by Kornai and others.[9]

IV. Nonlinear Planning

1. *Nonlinearity in Planning*

Planning models containing linear relations only are often good approximations to reality. The existence of solutions and the convenience with which these can be obtained help explain their extensive usage.

All the same, it is readily recognized that most of the relations involved in planning are not exactly linear. To assume a linear form for the target or preference function of the plan is very restrictive since it implies constant marginal utilities. It would be more realistic to assume a form which implies diminishing marginal utilities, such as logarithmic, exponential, or quadratic. Of these, the last allows more interaction between variables and appears more promising.

Constraints of plans are generally the production possibilities. If the productive activity of a sector is characterized by varying returns to scale, the corresponding constraint will not be linear. However, the constraint can still be kept linear by introducing additional constraints corresponding to different scales of production in that sector and using integer programming.

As an empirical fact, only the Leontief input-output table has been constructed for different countries, with a linear relationship between inputs and outputs. In a comprehensive planning model, therefore, the constraints have to be generally linear.

A program with a quadratic objective function and linear constraints is called a quadratic program. A plan with a quadratic preference function and linear constraints can be called a quadratic plan. There are several ways of solving a quadratic program; in appendix 5.B we briefly outline one of these which essentially uses the linear programming technique.

Any nonlinear program with separable variables can be turned into a linear program. We show this here. Nonlinear programs with nonseparable variables usually require Kuhn-Tucker conditions for their solutions. We derive these conditions in appendix 5.A and discuss a relatively simple, that is, quadratic, nonlinear program in appendix 5.B.

2. Separable Variables

In formulating a nonlinear planning model, it is often convenient to construct a preference function with separable variables. If the constraints are also nonlinear, they may be expressed in terms of separable variables. Such a planning model can be solved by using the linear programming technique. A program or plan with separable variables is that in which functions and relations are such that the variables are not coupled together. A simple example with two variables and two resources can be expressed as follows:

Maximize $f_1(x_1) + f_2(x_2),$ (58)

subject to $g_{11}(x_1) + g_{12}(x_2) \leqslant b_1$

$g_{21}(x_1) + g_{22}(x_2) \leqslant b_2$ (59)

$x_1 \geqslant 0, x_2 \geqslant 0.$

In the above program the two variables x_1 and x_2 are completely separable. In some other programs they can be made separable by some transformation if they are not so to begin with. Consider $f_1(x_1)$ the first function of the preference function. Let the range of x_1 start from zero and extend up to $\overline{x}_1$. Let the interval be divided in r_1 parts not necessarily equal by grid points $0, x_1^1, x_1^2 \ldots, x_1^{r_1} = \overline{x}_1$. The corresponding values of $f_1(x_1)$ at these grid points are $f_1(0), f_1(x_1^1), f_1(x_1^2), \ldots f_1(x_1^{r_1})$. Any point x_1 between two consecutive grid points x_1^k and x_1^{k+1} can be expressed as follows:

$x_1 = \lambda_1^k x_1^k + \lambda_1^{k+1} x_1^{k+1}$

$\lambda_1^k + \lambda_1^{k+1} = 1$ (60)

$\lambda_1^k, \lambda_1^{k+1} \geqslant 0.$

The approximate value of $f_1(x_1)$, $\overline{f}_1(x_1)$, at x_1 is given by

$$\overline{f}_1(x_1) = f_1(x_1^k) + \frac{f_1(x_1^{k+1}) + f_1(x_1^k)}{x_1^{k+1} - x_1^k} (x_1 - x_1^k).$$ (61)

Substituting (60) into (61), we get

$$\overline{f}_1(x_1) = \lambda_1^k f_1(x_1^k) + \lambda_1^{k+1} f_1(x_1^{k+1})$$ (62)

$\lambda_1^k + \lambda_1^{k+1} = 1, \lambda_1^k \geqslant 0, \lambda_1^{k+1} \geqslant 0.$

From the above, any x_1 and the approximative function $\overline{f}_1(x_1)$ can be written as follows:

$$x_1 = \sum_{k=0}^{r_1} \lambda_1^k x_1^k$$

$$\bar{f}_1(x_1) = \sum_{k=0}^{r_1} \lambda_1^k f_1(x_1^k) \tag{63}$$

$$\lambda_1^k + \lambda_1^{k+1} = 1$$

$$\lambda_1^k \geqslant 0, k = 1, \ldots, r_1,$$

where all λ_1^k's are zero except at most two adjacent ones defining a particular x_1. We can similarly express $f_2(x_2)$ and $g_{ij}(x_j)$'s of the constraints. The nonlinear program (58), (59) can now be written as follows:

$$\text{Maximize} \quad z = \sum_{k=0}^{r_1} \lambda_1^k f_1(x_1^k) + \sum_{k=0}^{r_2} \lambda_2^k f_2(x_2^k) \tag{64}$$

$$\text{subject to} \quad \sum_{k=0}^{r_1} \lambda_1^k g_{11}(x_1^k) + \sum_{k=0}^{r_2} \lambda_2^k g_{12}(x_2^k) \leqslant b_1$$

$$\sum_{k=0}^{r_1} \lambda_1^k g_{21}(x_1^k) + \sum_{k=0}^{r_2} \lambda_2^k g_{22}(x_2^k) \leqslant b_2 \tag{67}$$

$$\sum_{k=0}^{r_1} \lambda_1^k = 1, \sum_{k=0}^{r_2} \lambda_2^k = 1$$

$$\lambda_1^k \geqslant 0, \lambda_2^k \geqslant 0 \text{ for all } k,$$

and not more than two adjacent λ_j^k, $j = 1,2$ are nonzero for each j.

The above program is a straightforward linear program in variables λ_j^k's. The larger the number of subdivisions in which the range of x_j, $j = 1,2$ is divided, the closer will be the values of approximative solutions to the optimal solution.

V. Dynamic Optimality Planning

1. *Introduction*

Since medium-term plans cover five to ten years, their optimal formulation requires a dynamic approach. This involves the selection of target variables, the specification of the functional relationship in which these variables are to be maximized or minimized and the way in which this relationship changes over time, the description of the constraints at each point of time, and the determination of the initial and/or terminal conditions. There are various ways of formulating a dynamic planning model depending on the way in which the above mentioned elements are specified. A T-year plan with two target variables and two resources may be formulated in the following way:

$$\text{Maximize} \quad \sum_{t=1}^{T} f(c_1(t), c_2(t), t), \tag{68}$$

$$\text{subject to} \quad g_1(x_1(t), x_2(t), \ t) \leqslant b_1(t)$$

$$g_2(x_1(t), x_2(t), t) \leqslant b_2(t) \tag{69}$$

$$\text{and} \quad b_1(1) = \underline{b_1}, b_2(1) = \underline{b_2}$$

$$h(b_1(T), b_2(T)) = 0 \tag{70}$$

$$c_1(t) \geqslant 0, c_2(t) \geqslant 0, x_1(t) \geqslant 0, x_2(t) \geqslant 0 \tag{71}$$

$$t = 1, \ldots, T.$$

In (68), $c_1(t)$ and $c_2(t)$ are the volumes of consumption of the two goods in period t, and f is the utility or preference function. The target of the plan is to maximize the sum of consumption utilities over the plan period.

If there is no inflow or outflow of resources from the system, then

$$b_1(t) = b_1(t-1) + x_1(t) - c_1(t),$$

$$b_2(t) = b_2(t-1) + x_2(t) - c_2(t), \quad t=2,3,\ldots, \tag{72}$$

where the resources b_1 and b_2 are expressed net of depreciation. The constraints (69) then state as before that in any period the utilization of resources cannot exceed their availability.

The initial resources $\underline{b}_1(1)$ and $\underline{b}_2(1)$ are given in (70). The terminal resources are the outcome of decision making by the planners. They may want the relative sizes of the two resources to be such as to be appropriate for the postplan years. This will depend on the consumption preferences of the community and the technological change and progress in the postplan years.

An alternative formulation of a dynamic plan would be the following:

$$\text{Maximize} \quad h(b_1(T), b_2(T)), \tag{73}$$

$$\text{subject to} \quad g_1^t(x_1(t), x_2(t)) \leqslant b_1(t) \tag{74}$$

$$g_2^t(x_1(t), x_2(t)) \leqslant b_2(t)$$

$$\underline{c}_1(t) \leqslant c_1(t) = x_1(t) - \Delta b_1(t)$$

$$\underline{c}_2(t) \leqslant c_2(t) = x_2(t) - \Delta b_2(t) \tag{75}$$

$$b_1(1) = \underline{b}_1, b_2(1) = \underline{b}_2 \tag{76}$$

$$x_1(t) \geqslant 0, x_2(t) \geqslant 0 \tag{77}$$

$$t = 1, \ldots, T.$$

In the above formulation, the target is the maximization of preference function of terminal resources. The constraints (74) are the same as in the first version. The inequalities (75) correspond to the equalities (72). Here, a minimum level of consumption of each item for each period is given, so that the consumption of the items cannot fall below them. The initial conditions (76) are the same as before. For practical purposes, perhaps this alternative formulation may be more useful, since it ensures the minimum consumption level in each period. The efficiency of the first formulation depends on how accurately the consumption preferences have been estimated.

2.   *Methods of Solving Dynamic Plans*

In recent decades several methods for solving a dynamic planning model of the above type have been developed. All of these can be grouped under the umbrella of control theory, since they are methods of solving dynamic constrained optimization problems. These can be classified into three categories: variational calculus, dynamic programming or the principle of optimality, and the maximum principle. A simple dynamic planning model may be solved by any of these methods, though there may be some advantage in applying one or the other method to less simple models. We briefly describe these three techniques in appendices 5.C, 5.D, and 5.E, respectively. Some very simple applications of control theory in deriving optimal rate of savings are described in appendix 5.F.

Linear programming can be treated as a special case of nonlinear programming, which is easier to solve. Similarly, dynamic linear programming can be treated as a special case of control theory, a case which is surer and easier to be solved by the same methods as used for static linear program. Also, a dynamic linear plan is easier to formulate, even though it may be more difficult to take into account certain basic considerations such as diminishing marginal preferences, technological progress, and so forth.

3. Dynamic Linear Planning

A simple dynamic linear plan with two variables and two resources can be formulated as follows:

$$\text{Maximize} \quad \sum_{t=1}^{T} [w_1^t c_1(t) + w_2^t c_2(t)], \tag{78}$$

$$\text{subject to} \quad a_{11}^t x_1(t) + a_{12}^t x_2(t) - b_1(t) \leqslant 0 \tag{79}$$

$$a_{21}^t x_1(t) + a_{22}^t x_2(t) - b_2(t) \leqslant 0$$

$$u_1 b_1(T) + u_2 b_2(T) = 0$$

and $\tag{80}$

$$b_1(1) = \underline{b}_1, b_2(1) = \underline{b}_2$$

$$c_1(t), c_2(t) \geqslant 0; x_1(t), x_2(t) \geqslant 0 \tag{81}$$

$$t = 1, \dots, T,$$

where $c_1(t) = x_1(t) - \Delta b_1(t) = x_1(t) + b_1(t+1) + b_1(t)$

$$c_2(t) = x_2(t) - \Delta b_1(t) = x_2(t) + b_2(t+1) + b_2(t). \tag{82}$$

The above is a linear program spread over T years. There are at least T times as many parameters, constraints, and variables as in a corresponding static linear program. It should be possible to solve a plan of the above type in the same way as a static plan, after some transformations. The preference function (78) has to be transformed by substituting for $c(t)$ from (82), so that (78) now becomes the following:

$$\text{Maximize } \sum_{t=1}^{T} [w_1^t(x_1(t) - b_1(t+1) + b_1(t)) + w_2^t(x_2(t) - b_2(t+1) + b_2(t))] . \tag{83}$$

In the planning model above, all x's and b's are variable except $b_1(1)$ and $b_2(1)$.

The above model can be simplified if we assume that w_j's and a_{ij}'s remain constant over the plan period.

The alternative way of formulating the linear model is as follows:

$$\text{Maximize } \quad u_1 b_1(T) + u_2 b_2(T) \tag{84}$$

subject to

$$a_{11}x_1(t) + a_{21}x_2(t) - b_1(t) \leqslant 0$$

$$a_{21}x_1(t) + a_{22}x_2(t) - b_2(t) \leqslant 0 \tag{85}$$

$$-x_1(t) - b_1(t) + b_1(t+1) + \underline{c_1(t)} = 0$$

$$-x_2(t) - b_2(t) + b_2(t+1) + \underline{c_2(t)} = 0 \tag{86}$$

$$t = 1, \ldots, T$$

$$b_1(1) = \underline{b_1}, b_2(2) = \underline{b_2}. \tag{87}$$

In the above program $\underline{c_1(t)}$ and $\underline{c_2(t)}$, $t = 1, \ldots, T$ are the given minimum levels of consumption of the two items in period t. Empirical dynamic planning models constructed so far have been mostly linear. A good example of such a model is a recent study by Eckaus and Parikh.[10]

Appendix 5.A

Kuhn-Tucker Conditions

Kuhn-Tucker conditions[11] are almost as central to the solution of nonlinear programs as the simplex criteria for that of linear programs. These conditions must be satisfied at the optimum solution points of most nonlinear programs, and the criteria for recognizing when a local optimum has been achieved are derived directly from them. Since these conditions are so widely applicable in the solution of nonlinear plans and shall be used in the solution of the quadratic plan below, we give a simple treatment of them.

A general nonlinear program with two variables and two constraints can be written as follows:

$$\text{Maximize} \quad f(x_1, x_2), \tag{1}$$

$$\text{subject to} \quad g_1(x_1, x_2) \leqslant b_1 \tag{2}$$

$$g_2(x_1, x_2) \leqslant b_2$$

$$x_1 \geqslant 0, x_2 \geqslant 0.$$

Just as in a linear program, we turn the inequalities in (2) into equalities by introducing slack variables,

$$g_1(x_1, x_2) + q_1 = b_1$$
$$\tag{3}$$
$$g_2(x_1, x_2) + q_2 = b_2.$$

Now we form the Lagrange function,

$$L = f(x_1, x_2) + \lambda_1 [b_1 - g_1(x_1, x_2) - q_1] + \lambda_2 [b_2 - g_2(x_1, x_2) - q_2], \tag{4}$$

where λ_1 and λ_2 are the Lagrange multipliers. L is a function of x_1, x_2, λ_1, λ_2, q_1, and q_2. Let the values of these variables which maximize L be denoted by $x_1^*, x_2^*, \lambda_1^*, \lambda_2^*, q_1^*$, and q_2^*, respectively. It follows that

$$L^* = L(x_1^*, x_2^*, \lambda_1^*, \lambda_2^*, q_1^*, q_2^*) \geqslant L(x_1^* + h\Delta x_1, x_2^*, \lambda_1^*, \lambda_2^*, q_1^*, q_2^*), \tag{5}$$

where h is an arbitrary, small positive number. Expanding the right-hand side of (5) in Taylor's series, we have $L^* \geq L^* + h\frac{\partial L}{\partial x_1} \Delta x_1 + \frac{1}{2!}h^2(\Delta x_1)^2 \cdot \frac{\partial^2 L}{\partial x_1^2}$ + terms involving higher powers of h. Deleting terms with 2 or higher

(5a)

powers of h, we have,

$$\frac{\partial L}{\partial x_1} \Delta x_1 \leq 0. \tag{6}$$

Since $x_1 \geq 0$, $x_1^* = 0$ or $x_1^* > 0$. If $x_1^* = 0$, then $\Delta x_1 > 0$; then from (6) it follows that

$$\frac{\partial L}{\partial x_1} < 0, \quad \text{when } x_1^* = 0. \tag{7}$$

But if $x_1^* > 0$, then Δx_1 can be either greater than zero or less than zero; then from (6) it follows that

$$\frac{\partial L}{\partial x_1} = 0, \quad \text{when } x_1^* > 0. \tag{8}$$

Combining (7) and (8) we have

$$\frac{\partial L}{\partial x_1} \leq 0, \text{ and } x_1 \frac{\partial L}{\partial x_1} = 0. \tag{9}$$

Similarly, for x_2,

$$\frac{\partial L}{\partial x_2} \leq 0, \text{ and } x_2 \frac{\partial L}{\partial x_2} = 0. \tag{10}$$

Differentiating partially with respect to λ_1 and λ_2,

$$\frac{\partial L}{\partial \lambda_1} = 0, \quad \frac{\partial L}{\partial \lambda_2} = 0. \tag{11}$$

Again, q_1 and q_2 are nonnegative; therefore,

$$\frac{\partial L}{\partial q_1} \leq 0, \quad \frac{\partial L}{\partial q_2} \leq 0, \text{ and } q_1\frac{\partial L}{\partial q_1} = q_2\frac{\partial L}{\partial q_2} = 0. \tag{12}$$

Replacing the slack variables q_1 and q_2 by $b_1 - g_1(x_1, x_2)$ and

$b_2 - g_2(x_1, x_2)$, respectively, yields the Kuhn-Tucker conditions,

$$\frac{\partial f(x_1, x_2)}{\partial x_1} - \lambda_1 \frac{\partial g_1(x_1, x_2)}{\partial x_1} \leqslant 0 \tag{13}$$

$$\frac{\partial f(x_1, x_2)}{\partial x_2} - \lambda_2 \frac{\partial g_1(x_1, x_2)}{\partial x_2} \leqslant 0$$

$$x_1 \geqslant 0, \quad x_2 \geqslant 0 \tag{14}$$

$$b_1 - g_1(x_1, x_2) \geqslant 0 \tag{15}$$

$$b_2 - g_2(x_1, x_2) \geqslant 0$$

$$\lambda_1(b_1 - g_2(x_1, x_2)) = 0 \tag{16}$$

$$\lambda_2(b_2 - g_2(x_1, x_2)) = 0$$

$$\lambda_1 \geqslant 0, \quad \lambda_2 \geqslant 0. \tag{17}$$

Any sets of values of x's and λ's which satisfy the above conditions in a nonlinear program (1) and (2) are optimal, that is, yield the locally optimal solutions.

Appendix 5.B

Quadratic Planning

In order to illustrate one of the uses of Kuhn-Tucker conditions, we discuss here the method of solving a quadratic planning model. This is the type of model which seems most appropriate for nonlinear planning in the near future.[12] A quadratic plan with two target variables and two resources can be expressed as follows:

$$\text{Maximize } z = w_1 x_1^2 + w_{12} x_1 x_2 + w_2 x_2^2, \tag{1}$$

$$\text{subject to} \quad a_{11} x_1 + a_{12} x_2 \leqslant b_1$$

$$a_{21} x_1 + a_{22} x_2 \leqslant b_2 \tag{2}$$

$$x_1 \geqslant 0, x_2 \geqslant 0.$$

First we turn the inequalities (2) into equalities by introducing slack variables,

$$a_{11}x_1 + a_{12}x_2 + q_1^2 = b_1$$

$$a_{21}x_1 + a_{22}x_2 + q_2^2 = b_2 \tag{3}$$

$$x_1 + r_1^2 = 0, \; x_2 + r_2^2 = 0.$$

The slack variables are squared to stress their nonnegativity and as a help in the following treatment.

Forming the Lagrange function, we have

$$L = w_1 x_1^2 + w_{12}x_1 x_2 + w_2 x_2^2 + \lambda_1(b_1 - a_{11}x_1 - a_{12}x_2 - q_1^2)$$

$$+ \lambda_2(b_2 - a_{21}x_1 - a_{22}x_2 - q_2^2) + \mu_1(-x_1 + r_1^2) + \mu_2(-x_2 + r_2^2). \tag{4}$$

Differentiating (4) partially and equating to zero, we have,

$$2w_1 x_1 + w_{12}x_2 - \lambda_1 a_{11} - \lambda_2 a_{21} - \mu_1 \qquad\qquad = 0 \tag{5}$$

$$w_{12}x_1 + 2w_2 x_2 - \lambda_1 a_{12} - \lambda_2 a_{22} \qquad - \mu_2 \qquad = 0 \tag{6}$$

$$a_{11}x_1 + a_{12}x_2 \qquad\qquad\qquad + q_1^2 \quad = b_1 \tag{7}$$

$$a_{21}x_1 + a_{22}x_2 \qquad\qquad\qquad + q_2^2 \quad = b_2 \tag{8}$$

$$\lambda_1 q_1 \qquad = 0 \tag{9}$$

$$\lambda_2 q_2 \qquad = 0 \tag{10}$$

$$-x_1 \qquad\qquad\qquad\qquad + r_1^2 \quad = 0 \tag{11}$$

$$-x_2 \qquad\qquad\qquad\qquad + r_2^2 \quad = 0 \tag{12}$$

$$\mu_1 r_1 \qquad = 0 \tag{13}$$

$$\mu_2 r_2 \quad = 0 \tag{14}$$

Combining (7) and (9) and (8) and (10), we can write

$$a_{11}x_1 + a_{12}x_2 + y_1 = b_1 \tag{15}$$

$$a_{21}x_1 + a_{22}x_2 + y_2 = b_2 \tag{16}$$

$$\lambda_1 y_1 = 0 \tag{17}$$

$$\lambda_2 y_2 = 0, \tag{18}$$

where $y_1 = q_1{}^2$ and $y_2 = q_2{}^2$.

Combining (11) and (13) and (12) and (14), we can write

$$\mu_1 x_1 = 0 \tag{19}$$

$$\mu_2 x_2 = 0. \tag{20}$$

The quadratic planning problem can be solved by using the simplex method described above. The technique is to introduce two artificial non-negative variables v_1 and v_2 corresponding to the variables x_1 and x_2 and expressing the problem as a minimizing one:

$$\text{Minimize} \quad v_1 + v_2, \tag{21}$$

subject to
$$2w_1 x_1 + w_{12} x_2 - \lambda_1 a_{11} - \lambda_2 a_{21} - \mu_1 + v_1 \quad\quad = 0$$

$$w_{12} x_1 + 2w_2 x_2 - \lambda_1 a_{12} - \lambda_2 a_{22} \quad - \mu_2 \quad + v_2 = 0$$

$$a_{11} x_1 + a_{12} x_2 \quad\quad\quad\quad\quad\quad\quad\quad + y_1 = b_1 \tag{22}$$

$$a_{21} x_1 + a_{22} x_2 \quad\quad\quad\quad\quad\quad\quad\quad + y_2 = b_2$$

and the complementary slackness conditions

$$\lambda_1 y_1 = 0, \quad \lambda_2 y_2 = 0$$

$$\mu_1 x_1 = 0, \quad \mu_2 x_2 = 0 \tag{23}$$

$$x_1, x_2 \geqslant 0, \quad y_1, y_2 \geqslant 0; \quad \lambda_1, \lambda_2 \geqslant 0; \quad \mu_1, \mu_2 \geqslant 0.$$

Except for the two sets of conditions in (23), the above is a usual linear program. These two conditions can be introduced by checking that, if y_1

is introduced, then λ_1 is either not in the basis or is driven out, and similarly for y_2, λ_2, x's, and μ's.

Appendix 5.C

Dynamic Planning via Variational Calculus

The classical approach to constrained dynamic optimization is calculus of variations. The variational problem in two variables can be expressed as follows:

$$\text{Maximize} \quad \int_1^T f(x_1, x_2; u_1, u_2; t)dt \tag{1}$$
$$u_1(t), u_2(t)$$
$$\text{subject to} \quad x_1(1) = \underline{x}_1^1, x_2(1) = \underline{x}_2^1 \tag{2}$$

$$x_1(T) = \underline{x}_1^T \quad x_2(T) = \underline{x}_2^T$$

In the language of control theory, x_1 and x_2 are the state variables, and u_1 and u_2 are the control (instrument or policy) variables. In variational calculus, the control variables are simply the time rates of change of the state variables: $u_1 = \dot{x}_1$, $u_2 = \dot{x}_2$. In the problem above, the initial and terminal values of the state variables are fixed. In general, they may be expressed in a functional form,

$$h^1(x_1(1), x_2(1)) = 0$$
$$\tag{3}$$
$$h^T(x_1(T), x_2(T)) = 0.$$

In planning, the initial values of the state variables are fixed; hence one may have a condition of type (3) only for the terminal period.

The solution of the problem (1)–(2) is given by

$$\frac{\partial f}{\partial x_1} - \frac{d}{dt}\left(\frac{\partial f}{\partial \dot{x}_2}\right) = 0$$
$$\tag{4}$$
$$\frac{\partial f}{\partial x_2} - \frac{d}{dt}\left(\frac{\partial f}{\partial \dot{x}_2}\right) = 0$$

and the conditions (2). Equation (4) is a set of two differential equations of second order which can be solved with the four initial and terminal conditions (2).

When the terminal conditions are given as in (3), the solution includes transversality conditions. The second equation containing the terminal values of the state variables can be written as $x_2(T) = \varphi(x_1(T))$. The transversality conditions can be shown to be

$$\left[\frac{\partial f}{\partial \dot{x}_1} + \frac{\partial f}{\partial \dot{x}_2} \frac{\partial \varphi}{\partial x_1} \right]_{t=T} = 0. \qquad (5)$$

The above condition and the equation $x_2(T) = \varphi(x_1(T))$ in general determine two arbitrary constants in the general solution of the system of Euler's equation, the two remaining arbitrary constants being determined by the initial conditions.

The dynamic optimality model (1)–(2)–(3) of section V can be transformed so as to make the variational calculus technique applicable if the inequalities in constraints (2) are turned into equalities. Some extensions of variational calculus can take into account inequalities, too, but they will not be touched upon here. Under the assumptions of equality for each t, $x_1(t)$ and $x_2(t)$ can be expressed as functions of $b_1(t)$ and $b_2(t)$,

$$x_1(t) = \psi_1(b_1(t), b_2(t)), \quad t = 1, \ldots, T$$

$$\qquad (6)$$

$$x_2(t) = \psi_2(b_1(t), b_2(t)).$$

Further,

$$c_1(t) = x_1(t) - \Delta b_1(t) = x_1(t) - \dot{b}_1(t)$$

$$\qquad (7)$$

$$c_2(t) = x_2(t) - \Delta b_2(t) = x_2(t) - \dot{b}_2(t).$$

Using (6) and (7) in the target function (1) of section V, and assuming continuous time variation, we have the standard integral of the variational calculus:

$$\text{Maximize} \quad \int_1^T F(b_1(t), b_2(t); \dot{b}_1(t), \dot{b}_2(t), t) dt, \qquad (8)$$

$$\text{subject to} \quad b_1(1) = \underline{b}_1, b_2(t) = \underline{b}_2 \qquad (9)$$

$$h(b_1(T), b_2(T)).$$

Appendix 5.D

The Optimality Principle and Dynamic Planning

Bellman's dynamic programming,[13] using the optimality principle, can be expressed in terms of continuous processes as the variational problem of appendix 5.C. However, in some cases, when analytical solutions of programs expressed as such are not easy to find, they can be expressed in terms of discrete processes to find numerical solutions. We shall, therefore, illustrate Bellman's dynamic programming with discrete processes.

A stationary, discrete, and deterministic process can be written as follows:

$$x_1(t+1) = F_1 [x_1(t), x_2(t), u_1(t), u_2(t)]$$

$$x_2(t+1) = F_2 [x_1(t), x_2(t), u_1(t), u_2(t)].$$
(1)

This expresses that the process transforms the state variables $x_1(t)$ and $x_2(t)$ and the policy variables $u_1(t)$ and $u_2(t)$ at stage t to the state variables at stage t+1, namely, $x_1(t+1)$, $x_2(t+1)$. We assume that, at the initial stage 1, the system is specified by state variables $x_1(1) = p_1$ and $x_2(1) = p_2$. Now if we choose the value of the policy variables $u_1(1)$, $u_2(1)$ at stage 1, then the state at stage 2 is uniquely determined, given the transformation functions F_1, F_2. Again depending on the choice of the policy variables $u_1(2)$, $u_2(2)$ at stage 2, the state variables at stage 3 are determined, and so on. Thus, in order to determine the future states of the system, we do not require any knowledge of the past history of the system. This fact of independence of the past is basic to the principle of optimality.

Dynamic programming is concerned with processes in which $u_1(t)$ and $u_2(t)$ are chosen so as to maximize a prescribed scalar function of the state and decision variables. The values of the state and decision variables may be subject to various constraints such as lower and upper bounds. Occasionally, the constraints may combine both the state and decision variables, for example,

$$0 \leqslant u_i(t) \leqslant x_i(t) \qquad i = 1,2.$$
(2)

Each stage can be imputed a return H, so that

$$H(t) = H[x_1(t), x_2(t); u_1(t), u_2(t)], \tag{3}$$

where H is a scalar function of x's and u's. The total return, R from the T stages, depends on the returns from each stage according to a functional relationship. Thus

$$R = R[H(1), H(2), \ldots, H(t)]. \tag{4}$$

Stemming from the fact of independence of the past, the principle of optimality states that "An optimal policy has the property that, whatever the initial decisions are, the remaining decisions must constitute an optimal policy with regard to the state resulting from the first decision."

The principle of optimality is applicable whenever the return function satisfies the following:

$$R[H(1), \ldots, H(T)] = R[H(1), R[H(2), \ldots, H(T)]]. \tag{5}$$

The most common return function which satisfies the above condition is

$$R = \sum_{t=1}^{T} H(T). \tag{6}$$

Let us denote the optimal return function by $f_T(p_1, p_2)$ and define it as the value of R, using the optimal policy over the T stages starting from the state $x_1(1) = p_1$ and $x_2(1) = p_2$, so that

$$f_T(p_1, p_2) = \max_{u_1(1), \ldots u_1(T); u_2(1), \ldots, u_2(T)} \sum_{t=1}^{T} H(t), \tag{7}$$

subject to any restrictions.

After the first decision $(u_1(1), u_2(1))$, starting in state $x_1(1) = p_1$ and $x_2(1) = p_2$, the state at stage 2 becomes

$$x_1(2) = F_1[p_1, p_2; u_1(1), u_2(1)]$$

$$x_2(2) = F_2[p_1, p_2; u_1(1), u_2(1)], \tag{8}$$

and there are T-1 stages to go. The return function from the last T-1 stages starting from $(x_1(2), x_2(2))$ is $f_{T-1}[x_1(2), x_2(2)]$, and the return function from the first stage is $H(1) = H[p_1, p_2; u_1(1), u_2(1)]$. So the total return, using optimal policy over the last T-1 stages, is

$$R = H[p_1, p_2; u_1(1), u_2(1)] + \max_{(u_1(2), u_2(2)), \ldots (u_1(T), u_2(T))} \sum_{t=2}^{T} H(t)$$

$$= H[p_1, p_2; u_1(1), u_2(1)] + f_{T-1}[x_1(2), x_2(2)]. \tag{9}$$

When the total return is maximized with respect to all decisions, including those of the first stage, the optimal return over the T stages is

$$f_T(p_1, p_2) = \max_{u_1(1), u_2(1)} \{ H[p_1, p_2; u_1(1); u_2(1)] + f_{T-1}[F_1[p_1, p_2; u_1(1), u_2(1)],$$

$$F_2[p_1, p_2; u_1(1), u_2(1)]] \}. \tag{10}$$

Equation (10) is the basic functional equation of Bellman's dynamic programming. In order to solve the finite stage processes, we need to know the optimal return function for some one stage. The required return function for the initial stage is always at hand, since $f_1(p_1, p_2)$ is either a known function, or we can derive it from

$f_1(p_1, p_2) = \max\limits_{u_1(1), u_2(1)} \{ H[p_1, p_2; u_1(1), u_2(1)] \}$. Putting $T = 2$ and using $f_1(p_1, p_2)$, in equation (10), we can derive $f_2(p_1, p_2)$ and similarly find $f_3(p_1, p_2), \ldots, f_T(p_1, p_2)$. At each stage, the procedure will yield the optimal values of policies $u_1(t)$ and $u_2(t)$, $t = 1, 2, \ldots T$.

The planning model (1)–(2)–(3) of section V can be expressed in a manner suitable for the application of the dynamic programming technique outlined above. Using equations (6) and (7) of appendix 5.C, $c_1(t)$ and $c_2(t)$ can be written as functions of $b_1(t)$, $b_2(t)$ and $\dot{b}_1(t)$, $\dot{b}_2(t)$. Using summation instead of integration we can write, ignoring the time variable, the following:

$$\text{Maximize } \sum_{t=1}^{T} [F(b_1(t), b_2(t); u_1(t), u_2(t))]$$

$$0 \leqslant u_1(t) \leqslant \dot{b}_1(t)$$

$$0 \leqslant u_2(t) \leqslant \dot{b}_2(t).$$

Since $b_1(1)$ and $b_2(1)$ are known, the recursive process can be started from stage 1 and be linked up with the terminal conditions at stage T.

Besides the possibility of numerical solutions allowed by Bellman's dynamic programming, it is much more general than the classical variational calculus. In the latter, the movers of the system are the time variations of the state variables, and only these. This is very restrictive, although quite suitable for physical planning models in which optimal additions to capital stock are the main causal factors. This explains the early application of this technique in finding the optimal rate of savings which follows from the optimal allocation of resources, and is not a separate problem.

Appendix 5.E

The Maximum Principle

The Pontryagin maximum[14] principle is the culmination and generalization of the variational calculus, the optimality principle, and the Kuhn-Tucker conditions. It gives the conditions for the optimality of a dynamic system. The fundamental problem of the maximum principle is stated as follows.

Consider a system with two variables $x_1(t)$, $x_2(t)$ and the set of admissible control variables $u = u(t) \epsilon U$. The problem then can be stated: Among all the admissible controls, find one for which the functional

$$J = \int_1^T f^0 [x_1(t), x_2(t); u(t)] \, dt \tag{1}$$

takes on the least possible value, such that the solution $x_1(t)$, $x_2(t)$ of the equations giving the law of motion of the object,

$$\frac{dx_1}{dt} = f^1 [x_1(t), x_2(t); u(t)]$$

$$\frac{dx_2}{dt} = f^2 [x_1(t), x_2(t); u(t)] \tag{2}$$

is defined for all t, $1 \leqslant t \leqslant T$, and it satisfies the initial and the final conditions

$$x_1(1) = x_1^{\,1}, x_2(1) = x_2^{\,1},$$

$$x_1(T) = x_1^{\,T}, x_2(T) = x_2^{\,T}. \tag{3}$$

Equations (1) and (2) can be adjoined; thus

$$\frac{dx_i}{dt} = f^i(x_1, x_2; u) \tag{4}$$

$$i = 0, 1, 2,$$

where $x_0 = J$.

Let us consider the problem in a three-dimensional phase space. The initial point will now be denoted by $(0, x_1{}^0, x_2{}^0)$ and the terminal point by $(x_0, x_1{}^T, x_2{}^T)$. Now the problem can be restated in an alternative way: Among all admissible controls, find one in the three-dimensional phase space satisfying equation (2), such that its initial position is $(0, x_1{}^0, x_2{}^0)$ and the terminal position $(x_0, x_1{}^T, x_2{}^T)$, where the last two of the terminal positions x_1^T and x_2^T are given, but the first, x_0, is required to be as small as possible.

In order to formulate the theorem in a way which yields the solution of the fundamental problem, Pontryagin and his associates consider another system of equations in the auxiliary (supplementary) variables ψ_0, ψ_1, ψ_2,

$$\frac{d\psi_i}{dt} = - \sum_{j=0}^{2} \frac{\partial f^j(x_1, x_2; u)}{\partial x_i} \psi_j \quad i = 0, 1, 2. \tag{5}$$

If we choose an admissible control $u(t)$, $0 \leqslant t \leqslant T$ and have the initial position of the corresponding phase trajectory coincide with $(0, x_1{}^0, x_2{}^0)$, then equations (2) determine $x_i(t)$, $i = 0, 1, 2$, in the three-dimensional phase-space, and then equations (5) take the form of

$$\frac{d\psi_i}{dt} = - \sum_{j=0}^{2} \frac{\partial f^j(x_1(t), x_2(t); u(t))}{\partial x_i} \psi_j \quad i = 0, 1, 2. \tag{6}$$

System (6) is linear and homogeneous in ψ_i's, $u(t)$ and $x(t)$'s already determined. Hence for any initial condition it yields the unique solution ψ_0, ψ_1, ψ_2, and it is defined on the entire interval for which $x_1(t), x_2(t)$, and $u(t)$ are defined.

Systems (2) and (5) can be combined into one entry by forming the Hamiltonian H of $x_1, x_2, \psi_0, \psi_1, \psi_2$, and u.

$$H = H(\psi_0, \psi_1, \psi_2, x_1, x_2, u) = \sum_{j=0}^{2} \psi_j f^j(x_1, x_2, u). \tag{7}$$

It can be immediately seen that systems (2) and (5) can be written from Hamiltonian (7):

$$\frac{dx_i}{dt} = \frac{\partial H}{\partial \psi} \qquad i = 0,1,2,3 \tag{8}$$

$$\frac{d\psi_i}{dt} = -\frac{\partial H}{\partial x_i} \qquad i = 0,1,2,3. \tag{9}$$

It is readily seen that for fixed (constant) values of ψ_0, ψ_1, ψ_2 and x_1, and x_2, the Hamiltonian H becomes a function of the parameter $u \epsilon U$. Pontryagin and his associates have proved that for an admissible control $u(t)$, $0 \leqslant t \leqslant T$, and the corresponding phase trajectory satisfying system (6), with an initial phase position $(0, x_1^{\,o}, x_2^{\,o})$, and passing through a terminal phase position $(x_0, x_1^{\,T}, x_2^{\,T})$, a necessary condition that the first component of the terminal phase position take on an optimal (least) value is the following: that there exist a set of functions $\psi_0(t)$, $\psi_1(t)$, $\psi_2(t)$, such that the function $H(\psi_0(t)$, $\psi_1(t)$, $\psi_2(t)$; $x_1(t)$, $x_2(t)$, $u)$ of the variable $u \epsilon U$ attains its maximum at the point $u = u(t)$ for every t. They further showed that at the terminal point of time, T, $\psi_0(T) \leqslant 0$, and that the maximum value of the Hamiltonian, that is, $\sup\limits_{u \epsilon U} H(\psi_0(T), \psi_1(T),$ $\psi_2(T)$; $x_1(T)$, $x_2(T)$; $u(T)) = 0$.

Furthermore, it turns out that if the functions $\psi_0(t)$, $\psi_1(t)$, $\psi_2(t)$, and $x_1(t)$, $x_2(t)$ satisfy (8) and (9) and the optimality condition just above, the time function, $\psi_0(t)$ and $\sup\limits_{u \epsilon U} H(\psi_0(t)$, $\psi_1(t)$, $\psi_2(t)$; $x_1(t)$, $x_2(t)$; $u(t))$ are constant.

Thus the conditions at the terminal phase point, namely, $\psi_0(t) \leqslant 0$ and $\sup\limits_{u \epsilon U} H(\psi_0(t)$, $\psi_1(t)$, $\psi_2(t)$; $x_1(t)$, $x_2(t)$; $u(t))=0$ can be satisfied at any point t, $0 \leqslant t \leqslant T$ and not just at $t = T$.

The maximum principle theory essentially finds the necessary condition for determining the optimal control and optimal phase trajectory, which, translated in the language of planning, are the optimal values of policy variables and the optimal path of the movement of the target variables. It is observed that the dynamic problem of optimization over an interval of time is reduced to instantaneous optimization at each point of time within the interval. Also, the theory provides the necessary conditions for the end points, which again turn out to be applicable at each point of the interval. These end point conditions are similar to Kuhn-Tucker conditions.

Appendix 5.F

Optimum Rate of Savings

1.   INTRODUCTION

In an intertemporal optimal planning model, the question of optimal rate of savings necessarily arises. For this problem is crucially linked with the allocation of resources among sectors and over time, the consumption profile, and the choice of techniques.

In recent years there has been a spate of research on optimum rate of savings. This is partly due to the growing concern with growth and development the world over, but quite considerably the amount of research concentrated on this problem is also due to the inroad made by mathematical methods of research and some recent discoveries and development of optimizing methods by mathematicians. These methods are of universal application to all types of dynamic optimizing problems, including those of economics. We have already discussed some of these methods in earlier sections of this chapter.

Most of the researchers on the problem of optimum rate of savings are repetitive in economic content.[15] They differ in a large number of cases in the method of solution and the application of mathematical techniques. We present here first a simple model of optimum savings which uses Bellman's principle of optimality and has as the terminal condition the "golden-age" path popularized by Phelps.[16]

2.   OPTIMUM SAVINGS ALONG PHELPS' GOLDEN-AGE PATH

In this approach, instead of Ramsey's Bliss level,[17] the terminal condition is taken to be the maximization of total consumption under golden-age assumptions. "A golden-age path is a growth path on which literally every variable changes over time (if at all) at a constant proportionate rate."[18] Accordingly, let labor and capital grow at a constant rate λ, so that

$$L(t) = L_o \, e^{\lambda t}$$

$$K(t) = K_o \, e^{\lambda t} = L_o \, e^{\lambda t} k, \tag{1}$$

where $k = K/L = K(o)/L(o)$ and o denotes the initial period and t subsequent time subscripts. Further, a linear homogeneous production is assumed, so that

$$F = F(L(o) e^{\lambda t}, L(o)e^{\lambda t}k)$$

$$= L(o)e^{\lambda t} f(k), \text{ denoting } F(1, k) = f(k).$$

(2)

Moreover, since we have for investment

$$I = \dot{K} = \lambda L(o) e^{\lambda t}k, \tag{3}$$

we derive total consumption

$$C = F - I = L(o)e^{\lambda t}[f(k) - \lambda k]. \tag{4}$$

Treating k as variable, and differentiating C with respect to k and equating to zero, we get the consumption maximizing the golden-age path. It is given when

$$f'(k) = \lambda. \tag{5}$$

Let the value of k derived from this solution be $\hat{k}$. Then the maximum sustainable per capita consumption (dividing equation (4) by $L = L_o e^{\lambda t}$) is

$$\hat{c} = f(\hat{k}) - \lambda\hat{k}. \tag{6}$$

Let u denote the utility function. The problem of an optimal rate of saving is then reduced to minimizing the difference between the utilities of maximum sustainable per capita consumption and current consumption under the income constraint, that is,

$$\text{Maximize} \quad \int_o^\infty [u(c(t) - u(\hat{c})] \, dt, \tag{7}$$

$$\text{subject to} \quad c(t) + \dot{k}(t) = F(k(t)),$$

$$k(o), \text{ capital per worker at the}$$
$$\text{beginning of period o.}$$

The solution to the above problem can be derived in several ways, using variational calculus, Bellman's optimality principle, or Pontryagin's maximal principle, all in their most elementary levels. We employ first Bellman's optimality principle for illustration.

In order to formulate the problem according to Bellman's usual dynamic programming, we consider discrete time intervals. We assume that time is divided into periods of equal length equal to Δ. In the initial time interval Δ, we have k_0 amount of capital per worker. The problem is to adopt such a policy which maximizes the welfare emanating from k_0. In our simple model, the only policy we have is regarding the decision as to the rate of saving or consumption. We have a maximum per worker consumption equal to $\hat{u}$ given by the golden-age assumption. As the welfare of the worker depends on his consumption, the problem is reduced to minimizing the difference between the maximum sustainable utility level and the utility derived in each time interval over the whole time horizon. This is the same as maximizing the difference between the current utility from consumption and the maximum sustainable utility from consumption over time. Our return function then is approximated by

$$R = \sum_{o}^{\infty} \Delta(u(c(t) - \hat{u}). \tag{8}$$

Let us denote[19] the optimal return function by $w(k(0))$, so that

$$w(k(o)) = \max_{\text{over all } c\text{'s}} \sum_{o}^{\infty} \Delta(u(c(t)) - \hat{u}). \tag{9}$$

Equation (9) is of the additive form so that Bellman's dynamic programming can be applied. According to the principle of optimality, which implies the independence of the past, once the decision in the initial period has been taken, the remaining decisions must be optimal with regard to the state resulting from the first decision. Let us suppose that in the initial period $c(o)$ was decided to be consumed. Then the investment per worker in period o is

$$i(o) = \Delta(f(k_o) - c(0)). \tag{10}$$

Therefore, capital at the beginning of period 1 is

$$k(o) + \Delta(f(k(o)) - c(o)). \tag{11}$$

Using the principle of optimality we can now write[20]

$$w(k(o)) = \max_{c(o)} \{ \Delta(u(c(o)) - \hat{u}) + w(k(o) +$$

$$\Delta(f(k(o)) - c(o)) \}. \tag{12}$$

Using Taylor's expansion in the second element on the right-hand side of equation (12), we have

$$w(k(o)) = \max_{c(o)} \{ \Delta(u(c(o)) - \hat{u}) + w(k(o)) + w'k(o)\Delta[f(k(o)) - c(o)] \}. \tag{13}$$

      Maximizing the quantity within the braces with respect to c(o), we have

$$u'(c(o)) = w'(k(o)). \tag{14}$$

Using equation (14) in (13), we have[21]

$$w(k(o)) = \Delta(u(c(o)) - \hat{u}) + w(k(o)) + u'(c(o)) \Delta[f(k(o)) - c(o)]. \tag{15}$$

Now cancelling out w(k(o)) from both sides and dividing through by Δ, we have the celebrated Ramsey equation,[22]

$$\dot{k}(o) = f(k(o)) - c(o) = \frac{\hat{u} - u(c(o))}{\dot{u}(c(o))}. \tag{16}$$

3. OPTIMUM SAVINGS USING THE MAXIMUM PRINCIPLE

      We have illustrated the derivation of optimum savings with a simple model using the Bellman's principle of optimality. Here we shall illustrate the same, using Pontryagin's maximum principle. As in the preceding case, we will consider a one sectoral model for the sake of simplicity. Further, instead of using the golden-age concept for fixing the terminal condition, we shall consider a finite time horizon, the terminal period being T. The aim of the model would be to find the time shape of rate of savings, so that the sum of per capita consumption from the initial period o to the terminal period T is maximized such that the per capital capital in the terminal period k(T) is greater than or equal to a certain given level k_T starting from the initial per capita level $k(o) = k_o$.

Let $y(t)$, $k(t)$, $c(t)$, and $\dot{k}(t)$ represent, respectively, the per capita output $Y(t)/N(t)$, capital $K(t)/N(t)$, consumption $C(t)/N(t)$, and investment $\dot{K}(t)/N(t)$. Let the per capita output be represented as a function of per capita capital, as in the preceding subsection, so that $y(t) = f(k(t))$. Further, $\dot{k}(t) = d/dt\,(K(t)/N(t)) = \dot{K}(t)/N(t) - K(t)/N(t)\,\dot{N}(t)/N(t) = \dot{k}(t) - nk(t) = s(t)y(t) - nk(t)$. Here $Y(t)$, $K(t)$, $C(t)$ represent total output, capital, and consumption, respectively, and n is the exogenously given rate of growth of labor, and $s(t)$ is the time function of rate of savings. Obviously, $s(t)$ must lie between zero and unity, so that $0 \leqslant s(t) \leqslant 1$.

The savings optimizing problem of the simplest type then can be stated as follows:

$$\text{Minimize} \quad \int_{o}^{T} - c(t)dt, \tag{17}$$

$$\text{subject to} \quad \dot{k}(t) = s(t)\,y(t) - nk(t) \tag{17a}$$

$$0 \leqslant s(t) \leqslant 1 \tag{17b}$$

$$k(o) = k_o \text{ and } k(T) = k_T. \tag{17c}$$

In the above equation, $y(t) = f(k(t))$ and $c(t) = (1 - s(t))y(t)$. In the above model, there is one state variable $k(t)$ and one control variable $s(t)$. The initial value of the state variable is given; the lower limit of the terminal value is also given, but, as the model aims at maximizing the aggregate of per capita consumption, the terminal value of k will not exceed k_T; hence $k(T) = k_T$ instead of $k(T) \geqslant k_T$. The control variable is constrained between o and 1. We shall assume it to be piecewise continuous. The state variable is also subject to the constraint that its time derivative is a function of itself and the control variable. This is the essential equation linking the state and control variables at any point t.

We rewrite (17) as follows:

$$k^o = \int_{o}^{T} - (1 - s(t))\,f(k(t))\,dt. \tag{18}$$

Therefore,

$$\frac{dk^o}{dt} = - (1 - s(t))f(k(t). \tag{19}$$

And, from (17a),

$$\frac{dk}{dt} = s(t) \, f(k(t)) - nk(t). \tag{20}$$

We now form the Hamiltonian, using the auxiliary variables $\psi^\circ(t)$ and $\psi(t)$:

$$H = \psi^\circ \{-(1-s) \, f(k)\} + \psi \, \{sf(k) - nk\}, \tag{21}$$

so that,

$$\frac{d\psi^\circ(t)}{dt} = -\frac{\partial H}{\partial k^\circ} \tag{22}$$

$$\frac{d\psi(t)}{dt} = -\frac{\partial H}{\partial k}, \tag{23}$$

and, as before,

$$\frac{dk^\circ}{dt} = \frac{\partial H}{\partial \psi^\circ} \tag{24}$$

and

$$\frac{dk}{dt} = \frac{\partial H}{\partial \psi}. \tag{25}$$

Let us now restate the maximum principle. Let $M(x,\psi) = \max H(x, \psi \, u)$.
u admissible
In order that $s(t)$, $k^\circ(t)$, and $k(t)$ be optimal, it is necessary that there exist nonzero continuous functions $\psi^\circ(t)$ and $\psi(t)$, such that (i) for every t, $0 \leqslant t \leqslant T$, the function $H(\psi^\circ(t), \psi(t), s)$ of admissible variables s, $0 \leqslant s \leqslant 1$, attains its maximum at the point $s = s(t)$:

$$H(\psi^\circ(t), \psi(t), k(t), s(t)), = M(\psi^\circ(t), \psi(t), k(t)) \tag{26}$$

(it makes no essential difference whether the substitutions $x = x(t)$, $\psi = \psi(t)$ are performed *before* or *after* the maximization); and (ii) at the terminal point T, the relations

$$\psi^\circ(T) \leqslant 0, \quad M(\psi^\circ(T), \ \psi(T), \ k(T)) = 0 \tag{27}$$

are satisfied. Furthermore, if $\psi^\circ(t)$, $\psi(t)$, $k^\circ(t)$ and $k(t)$, and $s(t)$ satisfy equations (22) to (26), the time functions $\psi^\circ(t)$ and $M(\psi^\circ(t), \psi(t) k(t))$ are constant. This means that (27) can be verified at any time t, $0 \leqslant t \leqslant T$, and not just at T.

Consider the value of $\psi^\circ(t)$. Part two of the above theorem states that $\psi^\circ(T) \leqslant 0$ and $\psi^\circ(t)$ is constant for all t, $0 \leqslant t \leqslant T$. Hence $\dot{\psi}^\circ = 0$, and $\psi^\circ(t)$ for all t including T is a negative constant. Let this be -1; hence $\psi^\circ(t) = -1$ for all t, including T.[23]

The Hamiltonian, as a function of t, now is

$$H = (1 - s(t) f(k(t)) + \psi(t) \{s(t) f(k(t)) - nk(t)\}. \tag{28}$$

According to Pontryagin's principle, the Hamiltonian function must be maximum with respect to s, with the values of $k(t)$ and $\psi(t)$ considered fixed. This means that

$s(t)$, $0 \leqslant s(t) \leqslant 1$, must maximize

$$\{1 - s + \psi(t) s\} \ f(k(t)) - \ \psi(t) nk(t), \tag{29}$$

and, from (25),

$$\frac{dk}{dt} = s(t) f(k(t)) - nk(t), \tag{30}$$

and, from (23),

$$\frac{d\psi}{dt} = + n\psi(t) - \{1 - s(t) + \psi(t) \ s(t)\} \ f'(k(t)), \tag{31}$$

with the initial condition

$$k(o) = k_o \text{ and } k(T) = k_T. \tag{32}$$

Now (30) will be maximized with respect to $s(t)$, $0 \leqslant s(t) \leqslant 1$, when $\{1 - s(t) + \psi(t) s(t)\}$ is maximized for $0 \leqslant s \leqslant 1$. (33)

From this it follows that

$$s(t) = 1, \text{ when } \psi(t) > 1; \tag{34}$$

$$0 \leqslant s(t) \leqslant 1, \text{ when } \psi(t) = 1;$$

(34 cont'd)

$$s(t) = 0, \text{ when } \psi(t) < 1.$$

In order to study the shapes of the solution functions, we attempt phase-plane analysis, which can be done, as our simple system is autonomous. In order to do so, we have to determine the direction of the movement of the variables k and ψ in different regions of the (k, ψ) plane. In other words, we have to study the signs of $\dot{k}$ and $\dot{\psi}$. If $\dot{k} > 0, \dot{\psi} > 0$, the curve in the (k, ψ) plane will move upward and to the right; if $\dot{k} < 0, \dot{\psi} < 0$, the curve will move downward and to the left; if $\dot{k} < 0, \dot{\psi} > 0$, the curve will move upward and to the left; and if $\dot{k} > 0, \dot{\psi} < 0$, the curve will move downward and to the right. In order to demarcate the regions in the plane with respect to these signs and to indicate lines where the signs change, we perform the following operations.

The sign of the time derivative of a variable will change along the curve obtained by equating it to zero. Here these curves are given by $\dot{\psi} = 0$ and $\dot{k} = 0$. Thus from (31) we have

$$\dot{\psi} = n\psi - \{1 - s + \psi s\} f'(k) = 0, \tag{35}$$

and, making use of (34), we have the following:

$$f'(k) = n, \quad \text{for } \psi \geqslant 1; \tag{36}$$

$$f'(k) = n\psi, \quad \text{for } \psi \leqslant 1. \tag{37}$$

The demarcating line for the sign of ψ is given by (36) and (37). It is vertical for $\psi > 1$, at k = k* given by (36) since ψ does not appear in (36). For $\psi < 1$, the line will bend down towards the right, as shown in Figure 5.1, because $f'(k) > 0$ and $f''(k) < 0$ by assumption.

Next from (30), we have

$$\dot{k} = sf(k) - nk = 0. \tag{38}$$

Again using (34), we have

$$f(k) = nk, \quad \text{for } \psi > 1; \tag{39}$$

$$k = 0, \quad \text{for } \psi < 1. \tag{40}$$

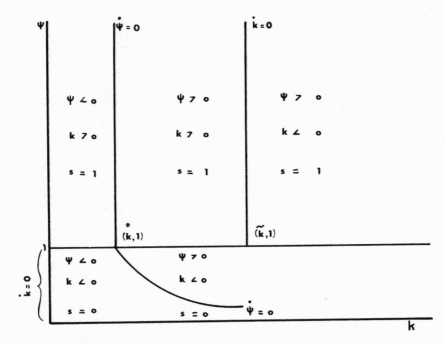

Fig. 5.1. Partition of Phaseplane according to Signs of Changes in State and Auxiliary Variables

For $\psi = 1$, the curve is undefined; s in (38) may assume any value between 0 and 1. The demarcating line for the sign of $\dot{k}$ is given by (39) and (40). For $\psi < 1$, it is a vertical line at $k = 0$; for $\psi > 1$, it is a vertical line at $k = \tilde{k}$ given by (39).

In Figure 5.1 the signs of $\dot{\psi}$ and $\dot{k}$ in different regions of the plane (k, ψ) are shown. They can be easily derived from equations (35) and (38). For example, from (35), when $\psi \geqslant 1$, $\dot{\psi} > 0$ for $k > k^*$ and $\dot{\psi} < 0$ for $k < k^*$, and when $\psi \leqslant 1$, $\dot{\psi} > 0$ for any (k, ψ) lying to right of line, $\dot{\psi} = 0$ and $\dot{\psi} < 0$ for any (k, ψ) to the left of $\dot{\psi} = 0$. Similarly, the signs of $\dot{k}$ can be determined from (38).

The phase diagrams in Figure 5.2 are easy to draw after the signs of $\dot{\psi}$ and $\dot{k}$ have been noted. As the system is autonomous, any point on any of the curves can be assigned a particular time index, and then the rest of the time sequence will be determined on that curve. Thus, if we assign t = 0 to a point on one of the curves, corresponding to $k(o) = k_o$ on individual curves, we have to check which of these curves has the value $k(T) = k_T$ at point of time T. The curve which fulfills these conditions is the optimal solution curve. From Figure 5.2 typical cases, as shown in Figure 5.3, arise.

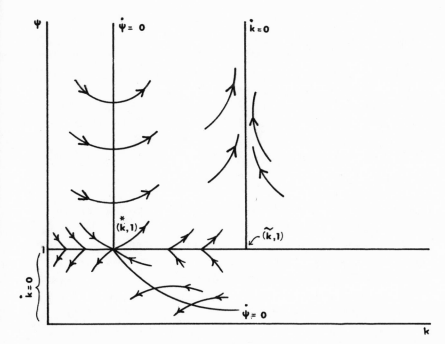

Fig. 5.2. Movement of Trajectories

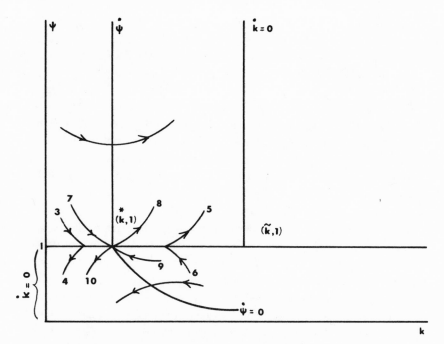

Fig. 5.3. Distinct Trajectories

We are not considering the movement of k around $\dot{k} = 0$. $\bar{k}$ is the Solow's stable equilibrium level of k.[24] $\bar{k}$ is positive for $\psi \geqslant 1$. It is zero for $\psi \leqslant 1$. The reason for this omission is that if k_o and k_T are on two curves moving upwards asymptotically from right and left towards $\dot{k} = 0$ (see Figure 5.2), k will become stable at $\bar{k}$ and stop short of moving towards k_T. Moreover, we shall not consider cases where k_o and k_T lie on a trajectory wholly on one side of $\dot{\psi} = 0$ and $\psi = 1$, for this case is less interesting; the optimal value of k will move smoothly from k_o to k_T. We shall consider cases where k_o and k_T lie on opposite sides of either $\dot{\psi} = 0$ or $\psi = 1$.

Out of the cases shown in Figure 5.3, trajectories 1 and 2 do not meet $\psi = 1$. They cross $\dot{\psi} = 0$ and are continuous. Trajectory 1 crosses $\dot{\psi} = 0$ above the straight line $\psi = 1$, and its direction is from left to right. Trajectory 2 has a direction from right to left, corresponding to the uninteresting case of "optimal decrease" of k from k_o to k_T.

Let us consider now the trajectories labeled 3 and 4. Suppose that the line $k = k_o$ crosses trajectory 3 at $t = 0$ and $k = k_T$ crosses trajectory 4 *at time T*. Then k will move from k_o to its highest value on $\psi = 1$ and then will decrease to k_T. If $k = k_o$ crosses trajectory 6 at $t = 0$ and $k = k_T$ crosses trajectory 5 *at time T,* k will move from k_o to its lowest point on $\psi = 1$ and then increase to k_T. In both cases there is a kink in the movement of k at $\psi = 1$, but the value of k does not cease to move at these kinks. The reason is that $\dot{\psi} \neq 0$ at these turning points in the movement of k ($\dot{\psi}$ is analogous to momentum in physical sciences). The two movements are depicted in Figures 5.4 and 5.5.

We now call attention to a peculiar phenomenon in the interpretation of the phase diagram. Any curve lying entirely above $\psi = 1$ corresponds to $s = 1$. The differential equation (39) for k does not involve q; hence, after k_o, T, and k_T are prescribed, the points of the trajectories indexed t=T all lie on a vertical line, say, $k = \check{k}_T$. Similarly, all curves lying below $\psi = 1$ correspond to $s = 0$, equation (39) does not involve q, and, similarly, all points indexed t=T lie on a vertical line, say, $k = \hat{k}_T$.

Let us analyze further only the first of these two cases, the analysis of the second case being similar. If $k_T > \check{k}_T$, the savings-goal is unattainable (see Figure 5.6). If $k_T < \check{k}_T$, then the goal is attainable, and the optimal trajectory is as follows: follow trajectory 7, pause for a while at the point $(k^*, 1)$, and then resume motion on trajectory 8.

If $k_T = \check{k}_T$, the situation is highly degenerate. *All* trajectories of type 1 or 7,8 correspond to the same program of capital accumulation ($s = 1$), so that the shadow-price ψ is unimportant so long as it is greater than 1, that is, sufficiently high to insure $s = 1$.

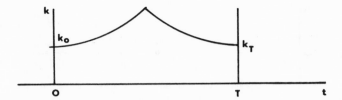

Fig. 5.4. Low Initial and Terminal Values of State Variable

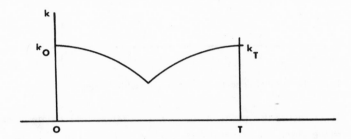

Fig. 5.5. High Initial and Terminal Values of State Variable

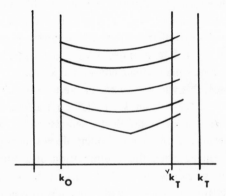

Fig. 5.6. Degenerate Situation

(All these problems can be attributed to an unrealistic choice of the integral to be optimized. If one had maximized utility of consumption rather than total consumption, the maximum of H would never be attained at $s = 1$, but always at $s = 0$ or $0 < s < 1$, and there would be no region of the phase-plane with $s = 1$. Since our purpose here is to illuminate a mathematical method rather than to solve a real-life problem, we tolerate these "degenerate" solutions.)

Let us now consider trajectories 7, 8, 9, and 10, all of which meet $\psi = 1$ where $\dot{\psi} = 0$. This means that momentum of k at these points is zero.

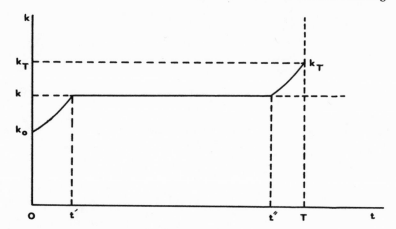

Fig. 5.7. Optimal Trajectory according to Golden Rule

If k reaches this point, it may cease to move until a time when it has to move along another trajectory, to reach k_T at time T located at it. For example, if $\check{k}_T > k_T > k^* > k_o$, then k will move down to the right on trajectory 7 and increase to k^* at $\psi = 1$ and $\dot{\psi} = 0$, at point of time t'. Depending on the length of T, k will remain at level k^* until time t'', when it starts moving along trajectory 8 to reach k_T at time T. The case of trajectories 7 and 10 is similar to that of trajectories 3 and 4, and that of trajectories 8 and 9 to that of trajectories 5 and 6, with the difference that, in the first cases, k may remain constant at k^* for some duration and, in the second cases, this will not be so. In the uninteresting case of $k_o > k^* > k_T$, k will decrease from k_o to k^* on trajectory 9, stay there, depending on the length of T, and finally decrease to k_T on trajectory 10.

All the movements of the phase-point along trajectories which pass through $(k^*, 1)$ can be given the interpretation of a "turnpike theory." Figure 5.4 depicts the case when $k_o < k^* < k_T$. As shown in the preceding subsection, k^* is the value of k which maximizes consumption at the golden-age path. If it is feasible for the economy with initial $k(o)=k_o$ to achieve the target k_T at T, and $0 < t' < t'' < T$, then we will have a turnpike, as shown in Figure 5.7. Starting from k_o, k will move along the optimal trajectory leading to k^* at t' and remain at this level until t'', when a trajectory from k_T at $t = T$ will reach k^* at t'' (indexing backwards in time along trajectory 8); $s = 1$ from $t = 0$ to $t = t'$ and from $t = t''$ to $t = T$; $s = nk^*/f(k^*)$ for $t' \leqslant t \leqslant t''$.

Extremely implausible values of s for $0 \leqslant t \leqslant t'$ and $t'' \leqslant t \leqslant T$ are due to the form of the integral. If, instead, we had used a utility function

ω, $\omega' > 0$, $\omega'' < 0$, these situations could be avoided. One way of making the example more realistic may be to narrow down the admissible values for the control variable s. This may be done by putting an upper bound on s, such as $0 \leqslant s \leqslant .25$ or $0 \leqslant s \leqslant .30$.

In the above illustration the utility function used is of the simplest type, $\omega(c) = c$. In order to make the application of Pontryagin's principle more visible, let us consider a utility function $\omega(c) = c^v$. Then the Hamiltonian is, from (28),

$$H = \{(1 - s) f(k)\}^v + \psi \{s f(k) - nk\}. \tag{41}$$

From (25) again,

$$\frac{dk}{dt} = s(t) f(k(t)) - nk(t), \tag{42}$$

and, from (23),

$$\frac{d\psi}{dt} = v \{(1 - s(t)) f(k(t))\}^{v-1} s(t) f'(k(t))$$

$$+ \psi(t) \{s(t) f'(k(t)) - n\}. \tag{43}$$

According to part one of Pontryagin's maximum principle, we have to see that a function $\psi(t)$ exists such that the Hamiltonian H is maximized with respect to s at each point of time t. Assuming for the sake of simplicity and exposition that the values of s for which H is maximized are interior to the admissible region, that is, $0 < s < 1$, s(t) which maximizes H is given by

$$\frac{\partial H}{\partial s} = -v \{(1 - s(t) f(k(t))\}^{v-1} f(k(t)) + \psi(t) f(k(t)) = 0. \tag{44}$$

From (44), s(t) can be expressed in terms of, or as a function of, k(t) and $\psi(t)$,

$$s(t) = s(k(t), \psi(t))$$
$$\text{or} \quad s = 1 - \frac{1}{f(k)} \left(\frac{\psi}{v}\right)^{\frac{1}{v-1}}. \tag{45}$$

Substituting for s(t) from (45) in (42) and (43), we get two differential equations of the first order in k and ψ. They can in general be solved for k and ψ. For complete solution we need two additional conditions. These could be taken as $k(o) = k_o$ and $k(T) = k_T$. We can then, in general, determine with these end conditions the functions $\psi(t)$ and k(t). Substituting back these functions in (45), we find the optimal control function s(t).

4.   OPTIMUM SAVINGS WITH VARIATIONAL CALCULUS

In order to show that simple problems of the above type can better be tackled by the classical methods of variational calculus, let us restate the problem:

Maximize the functional,

$$\int_o^T \omega(c(t))\, dt, \tag{46}$$

where $$c(t) = f(k(t)) - \dot{k}(t) \tag{47}$$

$$k(o) = k_o \text{ and } k(T) = k_T. \tag{48}$$

According to the Euler equation, the necessary condition for the mazimization of the functional ω is given by

$$\omega_k - \frac{d}{dt}\, \omega_{\dot{k}} = 0, \tag{49}$$

or, in full,

$$\omega_k - \omega_{\dot{k}t} - \omega_{\dot{k}k}\dot{k} - \omega_{\dot{k}\dot{k}}\, \frac{d\dot{k}}{dt} = 0. \tag{50}$$

Note that our functional (46) does not contain t as an explicit argument. Hence $\omega_{\dot{k}t} = 0$ and (50) is reduced to

$$\omega_k - \omega_{k\dot{k}}\dot{k} - \omega_{\dot{k}\dot{k}}\, \frac{d\dot{k}}{dt} = 0. \tag{51}$$

Multiplying both sides of the above equation by $\dot{k}$, we can transform it into an exact derivative,[25] $d(\omega - \dot{k}\omega_{\dot{k}})/dt$. As a consequence, we have the following first integral:

$$\omega - \dot{k}\omega_{\dot{k}} = C_1, \tag{52}$$

where C_1 is a constant of integration. Equation (52) is a differential equation of first order in k, and the solution will involve another integration constant, say, C_2. The values of C_1 and C_2 can be determined by initial and terminal conditions, $k(o) = k_o$ and $K(T) = k_T$.

As a concrete example, let $\omega(c(t)) = (c(t))^v$, and $f(k(t))=bk(t)$. Now $\omega(c(t)) = [bk(t) - k(t)]^v$. In this case, instead of using equation (52), we can work with equation (49) directly to get

$$vb\ \{bk(t) - \dot{k}(t)\}^{v-1} + \frac{d}{dt}\ [\ v\{bk(t) - \dot{k}(t)\}^{v-1}] = 0,$$

$$\text{or } (v-1)\ \ddot{k}(t) - \{b(v-2)\}\ \dot{k}(t) - b^2 k(t) = 0. \tag{53}$$

The above is a linear homogeneous equation of second order. Trying a solution $k = e^{\lambda t}$, we get

$$(v-1)\ \lambda^2 - \{b(v-2)\}\ \lambda - b^2 = 0. \tag{54}$$

The two roots of (47) are $\lambda_1 = (bv - 1)/(v - 1)$ and $\lambda_2 = 1/(1-v)$. Hence the general solution of (46) is

$$k = C_1\ e^{\frac{bv-1}{v-1}} + C_2\ e^{\frac{1}{1-v}}. \tag{55}$$

The integration constants C_1 and C_2 can be obtained from initial conditions $k(o) = k_o$ and $K(T) = k_T$.

For further extensions of this line of approach, reference may be made to contributions by Goodwin,[26] Chakravarty,[27] and others.

NOTES

1. G. W. Leibniz, *Theodicy, Essays on the Goodness of God, the Freedom of Man and the Origin of Evil,* quoted in D. J. Wilde and C. S. Beighter, *Foundations of Optimization* (New York: Prentice Hall, 1967), p. 4.

2. L. V. Kantorovitch, "Mathematical Methods in the Organization and Planning of Production" (Publication of the Leningrad University, 1939), translated in *Management Science* 6 (July 1960).

3. George B. Dantzig, "Programming of Interdependent Activities," *Econometrica* 17 (July-October 1949).

4. The transportation problem was originally formulated and solved by F. L. Hitchcock, "The Distribution of a Product from Several Sources to Numerous Localities," *Journal of Mathematical Physics* 20 (1941). Similar ideas were also developed by L. V. Kantorovich, "Mathematical Methods . . . . "

5. George B. Dantzig, *Linear Programming and Extensions* (Princeton: Princeton University Press, 1963).

6. L. B. M. Mennes, Jan Tinbergen, and J. G. Wardenburg, *The Element of Space in Development Planning* (Amsterdam: North Holland, 1969).

7. R. E. Gomory, "Outline of an Algorithm for Integer Solutions to Linear Programs," *Bulletin of the American Mathematical Society* 64 (1958).

8. J. Kornai and T. Liptak, "Two-Level Planning," *Econometrica* 33 (January 1965); G. B. Dantzig and Philip Wolfe, "Decomposition Principle for Linear Programs," *Operations Research* 8 (January-February 1960).

9. Ibid.

10. R. S. Eckaus and K. S. Parikh, *Planning for Growth* (Cambridge, Mass.: MIT Press, 1968).

11. H. W. Kuhn and A. W. Tucker, "Nonlinear Programming," in Jerzy Neyman (ed.), *Proceedings of the Second Berkeley Symposium on Mathematical Statistics and Probability* (Berkeley and Los Angeles: University of California Press, 1950).

12. Philip Wolfe, "The Simplex Method for Quadratic Programming," *Econometrica* 27 (July 1959).

13. Richard E. Bellman, *Dynamic Programming* (Princeton: Princeton University Press, 1957).

14. L. S. Pontryagin, G. V. Boltyanskii, R. V. Gamkrelidge, and E. F. Mischenko, *The Mathematical Theory of Optimal Processes* (New York: Wiley, 1962).

15. For a fairly exhaustive bibliography of the articles and contributions, see K. Shell (ed.), *Essays on the Theory of Optimal Economic Growth* (Cambridge, Mass.: MIT Press, 1967).

16. E. S. Phelps, *Golden Rules of Economic Growth* (New York: Norton, 1966).

17. F. P. Ramsey, "A Mathematical Theory of Saving," *Economic Journal* 38 (December 1928). The Bliss level of utility $\hat{u}$ is the upper bound on instantaneous utility which is achieved at a point where either the utility of consumption ceases to increase or the output of capital ceases to increase, or both, that is, $u(c) \leqslant u(\hat{c}) = \hat{u}$ for all $c > \hat{c}$ or $F(K) \leqslant F(\hat{K}) = \hat{F}$ for all $K > \hat{K}$. Ramsey treated $\hat{u}$ and $\hat{F}$ as constants.

18. E. S. Phelps, *Golden Rules*.

19. In appendix 5.D we have denoted the optimal return function by f(p). We change the notation here to avoid confusion with the production function.

20. It is to be noted that it is possible to write the second element on the right-hand side of equation (12) because the summation runs up to infinity.

21. We have here essentially the same procedure as used by Phelps, *Golden Rules.*

22. If $f(k) = k^{.25}$, $\lambda = .025$, u c$^{.5}$, then $\dot{k} = .7578$ and the optimal rate of saving $\dot{k}/f(k) = .34$.

23. This can be formally shown to be the case, as has been done by Liang-Tseng Fan and Chiu-sen Wang, *The Discrete Maximum Principle* (New York: Wiley, 1964).

24. R. M. Solow, "A Contribution to the Theory of Economic Growth," *Quarterly Journal of Economics* 70 (February 1956).

25. This can be easily checked; see L. E. Elsgole, *Calculus of Variations* (Reading, Mass.:, Pergamon Press, 1962), p. 36.

26. R. M. Goodwin, "The Optimal Growth Path for an Under-developed Economy," *Economic Journal* 71 (December 1961).

27. S. Chakravarty, *Capital and Development Planning* (Cambridge, Mass.: MIT Press, 1969).

CHAPTER SIX

Implementation

I. Introduction

1. *Definition of Plan Implementation*

In the preceding chapters, methods of feasibility, consistency, and optimality planning have been studied mostly from the physical point of view. So far we have not considered how these magnitudes might be achieved, the subject matter of this chapter. By implementation we mean the determination of economic policies and measures required to achieve the physical magnitudes of the plan.

The derivation of such physical magnitudes rests on relatively universal laws of production, irrespective of sociopolitical structure or specific economic framework. On the contrary, there is enormous disparity among policies and measures which have to be used to implement a plan.

2. *Procedure of Implementation*

Despite such disparity due to sociopolitical and economic conditions prevailing in different countries, their determination can be seen to follow a logical structure. To start with, one has to take stock of instruments and policies that are expected to affect directly or indirectly the targets and other magnitudes of the plan. Then a choice should be made of policies and measures that are permissible or practicable in the country under consideration. The next task is to formulate an implementation model linking the policies with the variables whose physical magnitudes have to be achieved. Solving this model, the sets of values of policy variables which can achieve the physical magnitudes should be derived. From these, finally, that set which is most desirable to introduce has to be determined. In fact, the problem can be expressed as a programming problem and solved as such.

3. *Choice of Policies*

The problem can be tackled by attaching weights to policies according to their relative desirability. These weights can be derived by interviewing politicians and responsible persons. Then a linear function of policies which is to be maximized in order to achieve the physical magnitudes may be constructed. Nonlinear or quadratic preference functions related to policies may also be constructed on the lines shown in chapter two.

The policies and measures may have upper and lower bounds within which they can be used. These limits can also be fixed by eliciting information from knowledgeable and responsible persons, and on the basis of past trends.

An alternative way may be to find the different sets of policies which can lead to the realization of target magnitudes and then present these sets to responsible persons who can choose the set which they like best. In this procedure the task of assigning weights to individual policies is replaced by the choice by politicians of the optimal or most desirable set from the feasible and consistent sets which can be derived without formal application of mathematical programming. We shall outline this procedure before discussing programming approaches.

II. A Feasible and Consistent Set of Policies

1. *Introductory Remarks*

The methods discussed in the preceding three chapters yield the magnitudes of the plan variables. In consistency planning, the magnitudes of the target variables are already given, and the solution of the model gives other magnitudes, including the total sectoral outputs and their allocation. In optimality planning the targets may be total sectoral outputs or inputs, or some components thereof, which are expressed in form of a function. The solution of the model gives the absolute magnitudes of the target variables, and other magnitudes can be derived through consistency analysis.

The first step in formulating an implementation model is to spot all the factors and elements which affect the size of the target variables and to select the ones which have significant influence. Some of these factors and elements represent variables which are data not controlled by the planners such as the supply of unskilled labor or world market prices, and legal, political, or natural circumstances. Some other elements may represent variables which are not explicitly relevant to the plan magnitudes under consideration but which are necessary to interlink the variables of the model. These variables may be called irrelevant variables. For example, when we have plan magnitudes as consumption and investment, we may have to include national income in setting up the equations of the model.

The remaining factors and elements represent variables which directly and indirectly affect the target variables and which can be controlled by the planners. These variables are called instrument, policy, or control variables. The usual examples of instruments are various types of taxes, public expenditure, government borrowing and lending, interest rate, exchange rate, administered price, and so forth.[1] The purpose of the implementation model is to find a set or sets of values of instrument variables which can achieve targets. An implementation model consists of a system of equations containing the target variables, the data, the irrelevant variables, and the instrument variables.[2]

2.   *Setting Up a Consistency Model*

The implementation of the plan is determined by the structural relations among the variables. Such relations may be grouped into behavioral, definitional, and technical equations. Demand and supply equations describe the behavior of consumers and producers. Definitional equations are illustrated by the identity "total value sold = sum of individual quantities sold multiplied by their respective prices." Technical equations are such as the one existing between the volume of output and the quantities of productive agents used, or the relation between the quantity of money and income.

Assuming here for simplicity that the relations are all linear, a system of structural equations can be written in the following general form:

$$\sum_j a_{ij}x_j + \sum_k \beta_{ik}y_k + \sum_l \gamma_{il} z_l = u_i. \quad \begin{array}{l} i = 1, \ldots, I \\ j = 1, \ldots, J \\ k = 1, \ldots, K \\ l = 1, \ldots, L \end{array} \quad (1)$$

In this system let the x_j's represent the irrelevant variables, y_k's the target variables, and z_l's the instrument variables; u_i's represent the sum of all terms containing data.

The values of the target variables, which have already been derived from consistency or optimality planning, are fixed. The values of the irrelevant variables may be of no immediate concern. However, the instrument variables can assume values within a certain range specified by practical considerations. For example, tax rates and interest rates can vary only within a certain range. The instrument variables may therefore be subject to boundary considerations

$$\underline{z}_l \leqslant z_l \geqslant \bar{z}_l \qquad\qquad l = 1, \ldots, L, \qquad (2)$$

where $\underline{z}_l$ and $\bar{z}_l$ are the lower and upper bounds giving the range of permissible variation of the instrument variable z_l.

The implementation model can now be written as follows:

Find the values of z_l, $l = 1, \ldots, L$ to achieve y_k, $k = 1, \ldots, K$, subject to (1) and (2). $\hspace{4cm}$ (3)

In a well-defined model, the number of equations will be equal to the number of noninstrument variables, namely, the irrelevant and target variables, so that $I = J+K$. Now if the number of targets is equal to the number of instruments, that is, $K=L$, then $I = J+L$. Thus the number of unknown variables in the system will be equal to the number of equations, and the model can be solved for all the unknowns, that is, the irrelevant and instrument variables. In this case, when the relations are linear, there may be a unique solution, and there may be only one set of policies which will achieve the targets, provided the boundary conditions are not violated.

The number of instrument variables may, however, be different from the number of target variables. If the number of instrument variables is more than the number of target variables, then there may be more than one set of solutions. In fact, if the instrument variables are continuously variable, there may be an infinite number of solutions. The planners may classify the solutions into a fairly limited number of sets of solutions and may present them to the responsible politicians to choose. In practice, however, many of the sets of solutions may be too outlandish and may be rejected offhand by the planners themselves.

When the number of targets is more than the number of instrument variables, then the number of equations will exceed the number of unknowns. This means that no set of values of instrument variables can realize all the targets. In other words, the number of instruments is inadequate, the model is incapable of realizing the targets or the plan magnitudes, and the implementation problem is infeasible.

In a special case, however, the targets can be achieved even when the number of instruments is fewer than the number of targets. If we eliminate the irrelevant and instrument variables from the system of equations (1), we are left with I-J-L equations in terms of the target variables y_k's and the data u_i's. If the values of the target variables or the plan magnitudes are such that these I-J-L equations are satisfied, then the implementation problem is still soluble. This in fact means that values of only L target variables are independent, and the values of the remaining K-L target variables can be expressed in terms of other L target variables. Thus the numbers of independent targets and instruments become equal. If these target conditions do not hold, then the only way to solve the implementation problem is either to drop or modify some of the plan magnitudes or to introduce some more instrument variables in the model.

3.   *Some Simple Illustrations*

First, we take a simple, one-sectoral example to illustrate the above procedure and observations. Let us suppose that we have two fixed targets to be achieved in the coming year, a certain level of consumption c, and a certain level of investment i. Since we have two targets, we select two instruments and avoid the problem of too many or too few instruments as compared with targets. Let these instruments be direct tax rate t and interest rate r. Now we must go about establishing a relationship between these targets and instruments. The first relationship that comes to mind is that, in a closed economy, income must equal consumption plus investment. This (demand) balance equation or identity can be written as

$$y = c + i. \tag{4}$$

In (4) c and i are target variables, and y an irrelevant variable which needs to be introduced to enable us to link the target and instrument variables in a system of equations. Equation (4) shows how income is spent. The next logical step is to consider how it accrues or is earned. One simple division is between income earned as wages and nonwage income, and we write

$$y = w + v. \tag{5}$$

In (5) we introduce two more irrelevant variables w and v, representing wage and nonwage incomes. This is also a (supply) balance equation or identity.

Wage and nonwage incomes, in turn, depend on total productive activity or output. Hence we must relate these to total output. We introduce a linear relationship between wage and nonwage incomes and total output,

$$w = w'x \tag{6}$$

$$v = v'x. \tag{7}$$

In (6) and (7) we introduce one more irrelevant variable, total output x, and two technical coefficients, w' and v', giving the proportion between wage and nonwage incomes to total output.

Total output, of course, depends on the production function and the factors of production utilized. In order to retain linearity and simplicity, we shall assume a linear relationship between output and the amount of labor or capital, or both, given in the beginning of the year. Hence

$$x = aL$$

or $$= bK \tag{8}$$

or $$= aL + \beta K.$$

In (8), a technical equation, L and K are data, and a, b, a, and β are given parameters or coefficients.

Now we consider the consumption function. We assume a linear function between consumption and disposable wage and nonwage income,

$$c = c_o + c' (y - ty) = c_o + c'(1-t)y. \tag{9}$$

In (9) we have introduced one of the instruments, the direct tax rate, and linked it with consumption. Here c_o may be taken as data; c' is constant marginal propensity to consume. This is a behavioral equation.

Finally, we introduce the investment function, which is assumed to be linear to keep the system linear,

$$i = i_o + i'v - qr. \tag{10}$$

Here i_o is the amount of autonomous investment which may be taken as data, i' as a given coefficient. In (10) we introduce the other instrument r, which is multiplied by a number q. Investment changes inversely with r.

This completes the system of equations for the simple implementation model. It contains two target variables c and i, two instrument variables t and r, four irrelevant variables y, x, w, and v, and the data L or K or L and K. We should have as many equations as the number of target and irrelevant variables. We have listed seven equations; the first two are balance equations, the next three technical equations, and the last two behavioral. However, one of the equations (5), (6), and (7) is dependent on the other two. Hence, in all, there are only six independent equations, equal to the number of target and irrelevant variables.

After having set up the model, the next step is to eliminate the irrelevant variables and solve for t and r. After this, the implementation problem can be written as follows:

Find the values of t and r such that

c and i equal their target values ĉ and î , subject to

$$t = \frac{c_0 + c(c' - 1) + c'i}{c + i} \qquad (11)$$

$$r = \frac{i_0 + i'(c + i - w'bK)}{q} \qquad (12)$$

and lower and upper bound restraints on t and r. In the above we have used the production function $x = bK$ of (8).   (13)

Replacing c and i by ĉ and î in (11) and (12), if we find values of t and r which lie within admissible range given by (13), then we get the values of the two instrument variables which solve the implementation problem.

A Two-Sectoral Closed Structure. In order to give another very simple illustration of implementation, we consider a two-sectoral input-output model, as shown in Table 6.1, where we represent the magnitudes in physical terms. We have two sectors, and the total output of each of these sectors is distributed over intermediate deliveries, consumption, and investment. In this illustrative model we do no include exports and imports. Thus the final demand consists of consumption and investment volumes only.

Let us ramify the physical input-output table by associating prices with the physical magnitudes and including other costs of production and expenditure of values received. This is shown in Table 6.2.

Table 6.1

Two-Sectoral Input-Output Model

Delivering Sectors	Receiving Sectors (1)	(2)	Consumption	Investment	Row Sum
(1)	x_{11}	x_{12}	c_1	i_1	x_1
(2)	x_{21}	x_{22}	c_2	i_2	x_2

Table 6.2

Two-Sectoral Model with Prices and Financial Flows

Delivering Sectors	Receiving Sectors (1)	(2)	Consumption	Investment	Row Sum
(1)	$p_1 x_{11}$	$p_1 x_{12}$	$p_1 c_1$	$p_1 i_1$	$p_1 x_1$
(2)	$p_2 x_{21}$	$p_2 x_{22}$	$p_2 c_2$	$p_2 i_2$	$p_2 x_2$
Other Costs					
Wages	W_1	W_2	$-W_c$	$-W_i$	0
Interest	R_1	R_2	$-R_c$	$-R_i$	0
Taxes	T_1	T_2	$-T_c$	$-T_i$	0
Profits and Surplus	S_1	S_2	$-S_c$	$-S_i$	0
Column Sum	$p_1 x_1$	$p_2 x_2$	0	0	$p_1 x_1 + p_2 x_2$

In Table 6.2, W_1 and W_2 are the wages that will accrue in sectors 1 and 2; out of this, W_c represents the amount spent on consumption, and W_i on investment; similarly, for interest income, taxes, and profits.

It is now supposed that the consumption volumes c_1 and c_2 and investment volumes i_1 and i_2 are given as targets. They might have been arrived at directly from questioning the political leaders or by optimizing some preference function based on interview data. It is further assumed that these magnitudes are tested to be feasible, consistent, and possibly optimal through feasibility, consistency, or optimality planning.

The implementation problem is to find the values of instrument variables which lead to the realization of the magnitude of the targets. The policy instruments included in Table 6.2 are $p_1, p_2, T_1, T_2, T_c, T_i$, and R. It is reasonable that only one of the sets of (p_1, p_2) or (W_1, W_2) be treated as instruments. Taxes and public expenditure are usual policy measures. T_1, T_2, and T_c and T_i in Table 6.2 are basic instrument variables. In the table, R, the interest rate, does not appear. It is assumed that the authorities fix only one interest rate and that interest costs or earnings R_1 and R_2 correspond to that interest. Hence R_1 and R_2 do not represent two instrument variables but only one. In the event that the authorities resort to differential credit policy, R_1 and R_2 may be treated as two separate instrument variables.

All these instrument variables are subject to constraints. Prices cannot be fixed higher than a certain limit because that may create inflation, nor can they be fixed lower than a certain limit because that may create deflation. Similarly, the taxes and public expenditure can be varied only within a certain range. In the same way, interest rate cannot be altered too drastically but has to vary within a certain range.

The important aspect in plan implementation is that there are two sides of implementation, the supply side and the demand side. In the framework under discussion, the magnitudes c_1, c_2 and i_1, i_2 will not be realized if the total outputs corresponding to these magnitudes are not produced. Total outputs x_1 and x_2 can be obtained from consistency analysis. The implementation problem on the supply side is to ensure that the physical magnitudes x_1 and x_2 are produced. On the demand side, the problem is to see that the consumption and investment volumes of sectors 1 and 2 given as target are actually realized. In the present discussion, consumption and investment are only specified for the sectors, not for the classes of consumers and investors.

Given the wage rates, the factors which will affect the production of outputs of sectors 1 and 2 are prices of the outputs, taxes, and interest charges. Hence we have the following relations:

$$x_1 = x_1 (p_1, T_1, R)$$

$$x_2 = x_2 (p_2, T_2, R).$$

Consumption is a function of disposable income and prices. Therefore, we have

$$c_1 = c_1 \ (y-T, p_1, p_2, T_c)$$

$$c_2 = c_2 \ (y-T, p_1, p_2, T_c),$$

where $y = W_1 + W_2 + T_1 + T_2 + S_1 + S_2 + R_1 + R_2$

$$T = T_1 + T_2.$$

Investment depends on many factors; the most important of them listed in Table 6.2 are income, taxes, prices, interest rate, and government investment. We can write them as

$$i_1 = i_1 \ (y, T_1, p_1, R, T_i)$$

$$i_2 = i_2 \ (y, T_2, p_2, R, T_i)$$

We have thus six equations to determine the values of instrument variables $p_1, p_2, T_1, T_2, T_c, T_i$, and R; y is not an independent variable, and neither are R_1 and R_2.

With seven instrument variables and six targets we have one degree of freedom. We can fix the value of one of the instruments at will and solve for the other six. We may, thus, have more than one set of solutions, out of which the one most desirable may be chosen by the responsible politicians.

In the above example, however, the one degree of freedom we have may be used up by the requirement that $T_1 + T_2$ must equal $T_c + T_i$.

In this illustration again we have used one tax only. We could have introduced other taxes, thus adding to the number of instruments and degrees of freedom. Side by side we could have added some more targets such as consumption and investment by income classes. These and other extensions were not undertaken, with a view to keeping the table less crowded and the analysis simpler.

Before ending this section, it is instructive to consider a few limitations on the instrument variables and their lower and upper bounds.

Consider first the prices p_1 and p_2. They must be fixed with a view to prevent inflation or deflation. Hence $p_1 x_1 + p_2 x_2$ must not be above a certain upper limit and not below a certain lower limit. Hence the constraints on p_1 and p_2 may be expressed as

$$L \leqslant p_1 x_1 + p_2 x_2 \leqslant H,$$

where H and L are well-chosen numbers. For example, H may be ten percent higher than the corresponding value of $p_1 x_1 + p_2 x_2$ in the preceding year; part of this rise is to cancel the increases in x_1 and x_2. The lower bound L may not be lower than the value of $p_1 x_1 + p_2 x_2$ in the preceding period. Once the values of p_1 and p_2 are known from the solution, we know the value of $p_1 x_1 + p_2 x_2$. Comparing this with the corresponding value in the preceding period we can determine the approximate percentage increase in the money supply required.

The lower and upper limits on T_1 and T_2 have also to be fixed with reference to the past trends and the present circumstances. The same goes for T_c and T_i, though the range between the lower and higher limits for these variables may be considerably larger since public expenditure is an effective instrument in bringing about a balance in the supply and demand; hence it should be allowed greater leeway.

The margin between upper and lower limits on R may be rather small. Rate of interest usually cannot be changed too much at one stroke since it may be too unsettling.

The above is the simplest possible view of the implementation problem. For greater depth and details, reference may be made to Ragnar Frisch.[3]

III. Derivation of an Optimal Set of Instrument Variables

1. *Introduction*

In the preceding section a set or sets of policies were derived to achieve a set of physical magnitudes arrived at through consistency or optimality planning. Since each such set of policies is feasible and consistent, the responsible politicians may choose the set which they think best. Thus they have to show their preference ordering over sets or combinations of policies. An alternative procedure would be to assign to individual policies weights which have been arrived at through questioning politicians and responsible persons and to formulate an implementation model to find the optimal combination of policies. This procedure can be applied in two ways: two-stage optimization or overall optimization. In two-stage optimization, the physical magnitudes are assumed as before to have already been derived, as illustrated in the preceding section. An optimality implementation model is then formulated to achieve such given magnitudes. In overall optimization, in contrast, physical magnitudes are also considered flexible, and an optimal set of both the targets and instruments are derived simultaneously. We now turn to the formulation of an optimizing implementation model.

2.   *Choice of an Optimal Set of Policies: A Linear Two-Stage Case*

Let us suppose that the plan magnitudes, targets, or the magnitudes derived from them have already been arrived at through consistency or optimality planning. Suppose we have a system of linear equations involving these magnitudes, which we call target variables, and instrument variables, irrelevant variables, and the data as before.

$$\sum_j a_{ij}x_j + \sum_k \beta_{ik}y_k + \sum_l \gamma_{il}z_l = u_i \qquad \begin{aligned} i &= 1, \ldots, I \\ j &= 1, \ldots, J \\ k &= 1, \ldots, K \\ l &- 1, \ldots, L. \end{aligned} \qquad (14)$$

In a well-structured model, $I = J+K$. Now we eliminate x_j's and solve for the y_k's. The reduced system may be written as

$$\sum_l \gamma'_{il}z_l = \gamma_i + u'_i \qquad i = 1, \ldots, I\text{-}J. \qquad (15)$$

Substituting the values of the y_i's which represent the plan magnitudes, we express $y'_i = y_i + u'_i$. Now the optimizing problem can be stated as follows:

Maximize $\sum_l \xi_l z_l$,

subject to $\sum_l \gamma'_{il}z_l = y_i$ $\qquad\qquad i = 1, \ldots I\text{-}J \qquad (16)$

and $\underline{z}_l \leqslant z_l \leqslant \bar{z}_l.$

ζ_l's are the weights assigned to individual policies showing the relative preference of the political authorities. For example, if the authorities prefer raising interest rates to raising tax rates, they will indicate higher weights to interest-rate policy and lower to tax rate. The problem can be stated in a minimizing form, that is, maximize $\sum_l \zeta_l z_l$ in (16) can be replaced by minimize $\sum_l \zeta_l z_l$. In this case, if the authorities prefer raising the interest rate to raising the tax rate, they would choose lower weights to interest rate and higher to tax rate. Most of the policies can be used only within certain range; hence there are upper and lower limits on the values which the instrument variables can assume. In some cases, some other constraints relating two policies may have to be introduced, such as

$$z_h \leqslant z_m.$$

There may be some other constraints relating the instrument variables with target variables.

In model (16), if $L > I - J = K$, not all the policies will be included in the optimal set but only $I-J$. This is obvious since any feasible basis will have $I-J$ dimensions, not more. But if $L \leqslant I-J = K$, then all the policies may appear in the optimal set, though not all the targets may be fulfilled. If the implementation problem is feasible at all, there may be assurance of only L of the targets being fulfilled, unless the remaining targets can be derived from these targets as explained earlier. When $L - I - J = K$ and if a solution exists, then all the targets may be fulfilled using all the policies.

3.   *Flexible Instruments and Targets: A Linear Case*

When targets are all considered flexible and the aim is to find the optimal set of these along with the optimal set of instruments, then the preference function of the problem will contain both sets of variables. In the case of linear preference function weights have to be attached to each of these variables. In this case the model can be stated as

$$\text{Maximize} \quad \sum_l \zeta_l z_l + \sum_k \xi_k y_k,$$

$$\text{subject to} \quad \sum_l \gamma'_{il} z_l + \sum_k \beta'_{ik} y_k = u'_i \qquad\qquad i = 1, \ldots, I\text{-}J \quad (17)$$

$$\underline{z}_l \leqslant z_l \leqslant \bar{z}_l \underline{\xi} \underline{y}_k \leqslant y_k \leqslant \bar{y}_k.$$

In (17) the first set of constraints has been derived by eliminating the irrelevant variables from (14). The model has $L+K$ variables, and there are only K constraints apart from the boundary conditions on the targets and the instruments. Since both the instruments and targets are assumed flexible, the number of variables is greater than number of constraints. In the optimal set, therefore, only K number of variables from the instruments and targets may appear.

The drawback of this approach is that, in assigning weights, it is difficult to compare policies with targets, and hence the preference function may be subject to a greater degree of arbitrariness.

4. *Nonlinear Case*

When the preference function containing the target and instrument variables is nonlinear, and the constraints are linear or nonlinear, the problem becomes one of nonlinear programming. In case the preference function is nonlinear and the constraints are linear, the problem can be expressed as follows:

Maximize $\quad F(z_1, z_2, \ldots, z_L; y_1, y_2, \ldots, y_k)$,

$$\text{subject to} \quad \sum_l \gamma'_{il} z_l + \sum_k \beta'_{ik} y_k = u'_i \tag{18}$$

and the upper and lower bounds on z 's and y 's.

In order to show that, in an optimizing problem of this nature, the number of targets and instruments do not matter, let us form the Lagrange function,

$$\omega = F(z_1, z_2, \ldots, z_L; y_1, y_2, \ldots, y_k) - \lambda_i (\sum_l \gamma_{il} z_l - \sum_k \beta'_{ik} \gamma_k - u'_i). \tag{19}$$

If the values of target variables y's are given, then, substituting these values in (19) and differentiating with respect to z's and equating to zero, we get L equations for finding the L values of z's. Again, if the values of y's are not given but flexible, then ω can be differentiated with respect to y's also and equated to zero. Now we have L+K equations to solve L+K unknowns z's and y's. Thus in a nonlinear implementation model of the optimizing type, the equality of number of instruments and targets is not necessary.

5. *Some Illustrations: A Linear Model*

An interesting example of the optimal derivation of economic policies has been provided by Van Eijk and Sandee,[4] who maximize a linear function of target variables to derive the values of instrument variables. They set up a system of linear equations relating the target variables with instrument variables, and, after eliminating the irrelevant variables, get the reduced form, as shown above,

$$y_i = \sum_{l}^{L} \gamma'_{il} z_l + u'_i \qquad\qquad i = 1, \ldots, I\text{-}J. \qquad \cdot (20)$$

In (20) the coefficients γ'_{il} of z_l give the effect of the lth instrument variable on the lth target. The instrument and target variables and the values of γ'_{il}'s included in the model of the authors are reproduced in Table 6.3.

Table 6.3

Values of Coefficients Relating Targets to Instruments

Instruments ↘ Targets ↓	Autonomous Investment	Government Expenditure	Nominal Wage Rates	Indirect Tax Rates	Wage Tax Rates	Profit Tax Rates
Balance of Payments	−0.787	−0.549	−1.175	+0.580	+0.480	+0.226
Investment	+1.107	+0.118	+0.018	−0.120	−0.100	−0.047
Real Wages	−	−	+0.560	−0.055	−0.070	−
Consumer Prices	−	−	+0.360	+0.055	−	−
Employment	+0.570	+1.070	+1.540	+1.070	−0.880	−0.410
Government Surplus	+0.199	−0.715	−1.484	+0.779	+0.763	+0.888

In Table 6.3, nominal wage rates, real wages, and consumer prices are in fractions, employment in percentages, and the remaining variables in billions of guilders. To take an example, an increase of 0.100 billion in indirect taxes is estimated to improve the balance of payments surplus by 0.058 billion, lower real wages by the fraction of 0.0055, that is, 0.55 percent, and reduce employment by 0.107 percent.

The welfare function is expressed in terms of the target variables. In the Netherlands, the group that decides upon the policy decision consists not only of the members of the cabinet but also of elected representatives, pressure-group leaders, officials, and technical experts in varying combinations. Moreover, the cabinet is advised on economic problems by the Social Economic Council. This Council is composed of representatives of labor, of employers' organizations, and of independent experts.

In the Netherlands, the government and the Social Council have repeatedly indicated as targets of economic policy the following:

(i)   a maximal real national income;
(ii)   a high and stable level of employment;
(iii)   a balance of payments equilibrium;
(iv)   a high level of investment;
(v)   a stable price level to maintain real income of fixed income earners;
(vi)   a reasonable income distribution.

They arrived at the coefficients of the target variables through following discussions with the members of the government and the Social Economic Council regarding the relative weights to be given to the individual targets. After careful consideration, they decided for barter terms such that against a 100-million balance-of-payments surplus (E-M) could be set as the following alternatives:

400 million of government expenditure (X_G);
500 million of investment (i);
2 percent increase in real wages (l_R);
1.33 percent decrease in consumer prices (P_c);
0.5 percent increase in employment (a);
or   200 million of government surplus (S_G).

The welfare function resulting from these marginal rates of substitution is

$$\Omega_1 = 1.0 \, (\text{E-M}) + 0.25 x_G + 0.20i + 5.0 \, l_R - 7.5 \, P_c + 0.20a + 0.50 S_G + \text{constant.}$$

Connected with this function are the limits within which it is valid. The authors decided upon the lower and upper limits of the target variables after discussions with the people concerned. For example, suppose that the improvement *of the balance-of-payments surplus* required to restore the equilibrium in the external economic relations is 300 million. As soon as this level is reached less value will be attached to this variable. Similarly, if employment is already on a very high level, a further increase will certainly not be positively valued. The preference function is therefore only defined for decreasing employment, and so on. The limits of the target variables are not technical but can be surpassed only after changing one of the coefficients of the welfare function.

As Table 6.3 shows, the instruments used were government expenditure, autonomous investment, the nominal wage rates, indirect tax rates, wage tax rates, and profit tax rates. Technical limits are placed on these instruments in agreement with the experience in recent years as to the extent to which they can be applied.

In the model, there are seven targets and six instrument variables, while government expenditure appears as both instrument and target. The solution of the model gives values of the instruments which would maximize the weighted sum of target variables. This model thus falls in the category of those which derive the optimal policies from maximizing a linear function of target variables.

Nonlinear Implementation Model. For an illustration of a nonlinear model we can profitably outline an approach developed by Theil[5] and his associates.

Let there be only one instrument z, say, government expenditure, and let there be one target variable y, the gross national product. Let the GNP be a linear function of government expenditure,

$$y = \gamma z + u. \qquad (21)$$

The decision maker is supposed to have certain desired values in mind for GNP and government expenditure; call these μ and η respectively. For example, μ may represent a 5.5 percent increase of GNP and η a 4 percent shift of government expenditure. In general, it may be found that the desires cannot be fully realized, since there are constraints such as those typified by (21). The next step then is to formulate a quadratic form in the deviations between desires and the corresponding actual values of targets and instrument variables. This is done by expressing the weighted sum of the squares of the deviations.

$$h(z-\eta)^2 + k(y-\mu)^2. \qquad (22)$$

The above expression is to be minimized, since we want to reach as close to our desires as possible. But, if we wish to express our preference function (22) in the maximizing form, the expression (22) can be multiplied by -1, and then our implementation model will be as follows:

Maximize $\quad \omega\,(y,z) = -h\,(z-\eta)^2\, -k(y-\mu),^2$ $\qquad\qquad$ (23)

subject to $\qquad\qquad$ $y = \gamma z + u$
$\qquad$ and any other constraints on y and z.

In this model both the target variable y and the instrument variable z are flexible, and the objective is to find that value of the instrument variable z which will result in y and z's being as close to μ and η as possible.

The system (23) can be solved through substitution and making the derivative with respect to z vanish; we get

$$z^o - \eta = \frac{k\ \gamma}{h + k\gamma^2}\ (\mu - \gamma\eta - u), \qquad\qquad (24)$$

where z^o is the solution value of the model, that is, the optimal value of z. This has been written in such a way that on the left hand it shows the difference between the optimal value of z^o and the desired value η, while the parenthesis on the right hand shows the difference between the desired value μ and the value the GNP would attain if z took on the desired value η. The expression in parentheses, therefore, is a measure for the inconsistency of the policymaker's desires. If he desires a value η for the instrument variable, he would not get, in general, the desired value μ for the target, but $\gamma\eta + u$. If he wants to achieve μ for the target, he should fix the value of the instrument variable equal to z^o. Therefore, though η is considered the best value of the instrument in isolation, z^o is optimal when we take into account the effect of the instrument on the target variable.

It would appear that we would get optimal values of both the target and the instrument variables if we optimize the system (22) and (23) with respect to both the instrument and target variables. Forming the Lagrange function and making the partial derivative with respect to y and z vanish, we get

$$z^o = \frac{h\eta -\ ku - \mu k}{h} \qquad\qquad (25)$$

$$y^o = \frac{\gamma(h\eta - ku - \mu k) + hu}{h}. \tag{25 cont'd}$$

Although z^o and y^o may both differ from their desired values η and μ, it seems that these would be optimal in a more complete sense than optimizing with respect to instrument variable alone, as was done by Professor Theil. The difference between the optimal values and the desired values are

$$z^o - \eta = \frac{-ku - \mu k}{h}$$

$$\tag{26}$$

$$y^o - \mu = \frac{\gamma(h\eta - ku - \mu k) + hu - h\mu}{h}.$$

In this optimization, though the planners might have failed to achieve the desired values of either of the variables exactly, they might have attained the best overall position, considering their preference for both the target and the instrument variables.

IV. Dynamic Implementation Models

1. *Introduction*

If the effectiveness of instruments started soon after their introduction and lasted only until the end of a year or other unit period, there would not be any need of a dynamic model for plan implementation, for then such instruments could be introduced in each year so as to achieve the plan magnitudes of that year. Thus we would require only a static implementation model for each year to find the appropriate values of the instrument variables. There may be some instruments which produce their effects rather immediately and whose effectiveness wears off by the end of the year. Some taxes and some monetary policies may fall into this category. However, there may be some instruments whose effectiveness starts with a lag and spills over in the following year or years. For example, interest-rate policy, some indirect taxes, public investment, and so forth, may take longer to produce results, and these may be spread over a longer period than a year. It is, therefore, necessary that a dynamic approach to plan implementation involving such instrument variables is adopted. Since very limited information regarding the lag and spread of instruments is available, we explain the dynamic aspect of the policy of implementation by two simple examples.

2. *Macro-Dynamic Policy Formulation*

Let us suppose that the target of the plan is to achieve rate of growth of private consumption per annum equal to ψ over the plan period. As noted, ψ would tend to be a compromise among planners and politicians and is one which reflects in some sense their preferences between present and future consumption. Suppose the implementation problem is to find the tax rate for each year of the plan which leads to the realization of the planned rate of growth of consumption.

The planned level of consumption in plan year t is

$$c_t^p = \underline{c}\ (1+\psi)^t, \tag{27}$$

where $\underline{c}$ is some given base consumption level.

The realized level of consumption in year t is a function of disposable income in that year. Supposing this function to be linear, it is

$$c_t^r = c_0 + c'(y_t - T_t), \tag{28}$$

where c_0 is autonomous consumption, c' the marginal propensity to consume, T_t the total tax, and y_t total income.

The income identity is

$$y_t = c_t + i_t + g_t$$
$$= c_t + i_t + T_t. \tag{29}$$

Here c_t is private consumption, and i_t investment in year t. Government expenditure g_t is assumed to be equal to total tax T_t.

In order that the consumption plan is realized,

$$c_t^p = c_t^r. \tag{30}$$

It follows, for an income y_t in year t, that the planned consumption will be realized if

$$T_t = \frac{-\underline{c}(1+\psi)^t + c_o}{c'} + y_t. \tag{31}$$

Further, the value of i_t in (29) must be such that the required expansion in income takes place so that

$$i_t = b(y_{t+1} - y_t), \tag{32}$$

where b is constant capital output ratio.

Substituting (31), (32) and (27) in (29), we get

$$y_{t+1} = y_t + \frac{c}{b}(1+\psi)^t(\frac{1}{c'} - 1) - \frac{c_o}{bc'}, \tag{33}$$

By iteration or by direct solution, we can obtain the values of y_t, $t = 1, 2 \ldots$. Putting this value in (31), we can derive T_t, $t = 1, 2, \ldots$. Taking the ratio $\frac{T_t}{y_t}$, we get the tax rate which will ensure the planned rate of growth of consumption. The solution of (33) is

$$y_t = y_o + \frac{(1+\psi)^t - 1}{\psi} \cdot \frac{c}{b} \; (\frac{1}{c'} - 1) - \frac{tc_o}{bc'}. \tag{34}$$

Putting (34) in (31), we get T_t, and the rate of tax in year t of the plan T_t is

$$\tau_t = \frac{T_t}{y_t}. \tag{35}$$

In a dynamic setup, it is thus seen that the derivation of the value of the instrument variable even in the simplest possible structure as the above becomes involved. It may be verified that equation (34) checks out. Using (34) we have

$$i_t = b(y_{t+1} - y_t) = \underline{c}(\frac{1}{c'} - 1) \; (1+\psi)^t - \frac{c_o}{c'} \tag{36}$$

$$c_t = \underline{c}(1+\psi)^t \qquad \text{given as target} \tag{37}$$

$$T_t = \frac{1}{c'} \; [-\underline{c}(1+\psi)^t + c_o] + y_t. \tag{38}$$

Summing (36), (37), and (38), we get

$$i_t + c_i + T_t = y_t.$$

This satisfies identity (29).

3. *Another Example*

We now give another example where an instrument applied in a plan year affects the target variable not only in that year but in a subsequent year or years. This is the same as saying that the value of a target variable in a period is affected not only by the policies effective in that period but also by the policies in the preceding periods. As before, to keep the matter simple, let us discuss a case where there is one target and one instrument variable. Let us suppose, as in Professor Theil's example, they are GNP and public expenditure, respectively. It will be supposed now that GNP in the current year depends both on the public expenditure in the current year and in the preceding year, so that

$$y_t = u_t + \gamma_0 z_t + \gamma_1 z_{t-1}. \tag{39}$$

Here y_t represents GNP in year t, and z_t the public expenditure in year t. γ_0 and γ_1 are coefficients, and u_t is autonomous GNP in year t, even when $z_t = z_{t-1} = 0$.

Let us assume for further simplicity that we have a plan of two years only, say, years 1 and 2, and that our target, as before, is to maximize the negative of the weighted sum of squares of the deviations of the target and instrument variables from their desired values in the two years. Hence our policy model is as follows:

Maximize

$$\omega(y_1, y_2, z_1, z_2) = -h[(y_1 - \mu_1)^2 + (y_2 - \mu_2)^2] \tag{40}$$
$$-k[(z_1 - \eta_1)^2 + (z_2 - \eta_2)^2],$$

subject to

$$y_1 = u_1 + \gamma_0 z_1 + \gamma_1 z_0 \tag{41}$$
$$y_2 = u_2 + \gamma_0 z_2 + \gamma_1 z_1$$

and whatever other restrictions may be on the variables.

As in the preceding section, μ_1 and μ_2 are the desired (fixed) values of target variables y in years 1 and 2, and η_1 and η_2 are desired fixed values of the instrument variable z in years 1 and 2. Substituting for y_1 and y_2 in (40) and making the partial derivatives with respect to z_1 and z_2 vanish (z_o being a given constant), we find the optimum values z_1^o and z_2^o of the instrument variables. The difference between the optimum values and the desired values of the instruments is given by

$$z_1^o - \eta_1 = \frac{(\gamma_o^2 + \frac{h}{k})\,\gamma_o d_1 + \gamma_1 \frac{h}{k}\,d_2}{A} \tag{42}$$

$$z_2^o - \eta_2 = \frac{-\gamma_o^2 \gamma_1 d_1 + (\gamma_o{}^2 + \frac{h}{k})\,\gamma_o d^2}{A}\ ,$$

where

$$A = (\gamma_o{}^2 + \frac{h}{k})^2 + \gamma_1{}^2\,\frac{h}{k}$$

$$d_1 = \mu_1 - (u_1 + \gamma_o \eta_1 + \gamma_1 \eta_o)$$

$$d_2 = \mu_2 - (u_2 + \gamma_o \eta_2 + \gamma_1 \eta_1).$$

Here d_1 and d_2 are the differences between the desired values of the target variables and their values which will be attained when the instrument variables take on desired values. It is noted that the desired values of the target will be achieved only when the instruments in the two years take on their optimum values z_1^o and z_2^o instead of η_1 and η_2. When there are no inconsistencies between the desired target values and the target values which can be achieved at the desired instrument values, $d_1 = d_2 = 0$. But, when there are inconsistencies, they determine the discrepancies between the optimum values of the instruments and their desired values. It is interesting to note that the absence of the target inconsistency in one year does not result in the vanishing of discrepancy in the instrument variables in that year. That is, when $d_1 = 0$, $z_1^o - \eta_1 \neq 0$, and similarly for the second year. This is because there is interdependence between the two years. The inconsistency in the target variable in the second year is partly caused by the value which the instrument variable takes on in the first year. This shows the interaction between periods in a dynamic policy model when the effectiveness of measures taken in a year spills over in the following year or years.

4.   *Concluding Remarks*

The above is a simple demonstration of the problem of plan implementation and the logical procedure to follow in handling it. The assortment of policy measures and instruments available and applicable in various countries differ greatly in the extent and duration of their effectiveness. The monetary, fiscal, banking, and financial institutions, moreover, vary greatly in their setups, operations, and influence on the economy. Also, the degree to which these institutions are directly or indirectly controlled by the state or their planning agencies differs from country to country and even from time to time in the same country. Related, and in some respects basic, to these considerations is the fact of the size and role of the private sector in the country's economy. In a predominantly private enterprise economy, the measures and methods of plan implementation are by necessity very different from the directives and regulations practiced in the predominantly controlled economies. In mixed economies various combinations of these two sets of policies and measures are available and practicable.

The given constellation of plan magnitudes, therefore, may well have to be linked variably to types of instruments suited and appropriate to the country under consideration. Though the essential logic of implementation models may be common, the structural models may differ widely from one country to another.

NOTES

1. For a survey of the various instruments used to achieve various targets see Table 5-2 in E. S. Kirschen and L. Morissens, "The Objectives and Instruments of Economic Policy," in Bert G. Hickman (ed.), *Quantitative Planning and Economic Policy* (Washington, D. C.: The Brookings Institute, 1965).

2. J. Timbergen, *On the Theory of Economic Policy* (Amsterdam: North Holland, 1952); and *Economic Policy: Principles and Design* (Amsterdam: North Holland, 1967).

3. Ragnar Frisch, "General Theory of the Kernel Model," memorandum, University of Oslo, Institute of Economics, February 7, 1958.

4. C. J. van Eijk and J. Sandee, "Quantitative Determination of an

Optimum Policy," *Econometrica* 27 (January 1959).

    5. Henri Theil, "Linear Decision Rules for Macrodynamic Policy Problems," in Hickman (ed.), *Quantitative Planning.*